Mission to Yenan

Mission to Yenan

*American Liaison with
the Chinese Communists
1944-1947*

Carolle J. Carter

THE UNIVERSITY PRESS OF KENTUCKY

Publication of this volume was made possible in part
by a grant from the National Endowment for the Humanities.

Published by The University Press of Kentucky

Scholarly publisher for the Commonwealth,
serving Bellarmine College, Berea College, Centre
College of Kentucky, Eastern Kentucky University,
The Filson Club Historical Society, Georgetown College,
Kentucky Historical Society, Kentucky State University,
Morehead State University, Murray State University,
Northern Kentucky University, Transylvania University,
University of Kentucky, University of Louisville,
and Western Kentucky University.

Editorial and Sales Offices: The University Press of Kentucky
663 South Limestone Street, Lexington, Kentucky 40508-4008

97 98 99 00 01   5 4 3 2 1

Library of Congress Cataloging-in-Publication Data

Carter, Carolle J., 1934–
  Mission to Yenan : American liaison with the Chinese communists,
1944–1947 / Carolle J. Carter
    p.   cm.
  Includes bibliographical referendes (p.   ) and index.
  ISBN 0-8131-2015-2 (cloth : alk. paper)
  1. United States—Foreign relations—China. 2. China—Foreign
relations—United States. 3. United States—Foreign relations—1933–
1945. 4. United States—Foreign relations—1945–1953. 5. Government
missions, American—China—Yenan shih—History—20th Century.
I. Title
E183.8.C6C37   1997
327.73051'09'044—dc21   96-53110

To Jess
for his patient encouragement
and good-natured support

Contents

Foreword

Since the 1940s, the Dixie Mission has been ignored at some times and engulfed in controversy at others. During the 1950s, American politicians eager to exploit the loss of China as a campaign issue persistently argued that the Mission and its participants had been the dupes—or worse—of the Chinese Communists. However absurd, these charges proved professionally fatal for many of the career diplomats affiliated with Dixie. During the 1970s and 1980s—the time of President Richard Nixon's "opening to China"—a new generation of scholars rediscovered the Dixie Mission. Many of them came to regard it as a tragic lost chance in China. Reading the optimistic reports sent by the Mission's military and diplomatic observers in 1944-1945, we can readily see why.

This is the first book-length study to evaluate the origins, organization, personalities, and impact of the Dixie Mission from its inception in 1944 through its conclusion in 1947. Dixie was hardly a static enterprise. Its purpose and impact changed along with its membership and fluctuations in Sino-American military and diplomatic relations.

Carolle Carter has used a wide array of documentary primary sources to supplement her interviews with Dixie veterans—many of whom tell their stories here for the first time. Her work affords us new insights into the Dixie Mission. Carter strips away many clichés and shows that the American observers in Yenan were neither the naive dupes of right-wing folklore nor the ignored harbingers of a new Golden Age in Chinese-American cooperation. They were, in fact, a diverse and dedicated group of soldiers, diplomats, and technicians trying hard to serve their country, win a war, and learn about momentous developments in the interior of the world's most populous country. This book gives them the history they deserve. All those interested in the history of Chinese-American relations during the Second World War will appreciate Carolle Carter's contribution.

Michael Schaller
University of Arizona, Tucson

Acknowledgments

The documentary sources that I used to write this book include published primary sources and archival materials located in the National Archives, Washington, D.C., and Suitland, Md., or at the Hoover Institution on War, Revolution, and Peace at Stanford University. I began my research many years ago, however. I was fortunate to have been able to speak personally with most of the direct participants in the Dixie Mission and with those who interacted with it either as civilians or as military personnel. These men and women were invaluable, not only because they were directly involved but also because they could explain the rationale behind particular reports, the undocumented restlessness that prompted trips behind the Japanese lines, and the genesis of decisions made in remote field posts. Their perspectives and astuteness, even their disagreements with one another, have enriched this account.

I conversed extensively with all of Dixie's commanding officers. As a result, I gained insights into the organization of the group, its daily duties, its relations with the Chinese Communists, and the bonds between the men. When I spoke to them in their retirement, David Barrett talked wistfully about China and the Chinese people, but Ivan Yeaton was as intractable as ever regarding the Dixie Mission and American policy toward China. Clifford Young and Wilbur J. Peterkin were especially gracious about making their personal diaries, photographs, and letters available to me for this work.

Former Foreign Service officers John S. Service, Raymond Ludden, and John K. Emmerson gave generously of their time, as did S. Herbert Hitch, Arnold Dadian, John Colling, Jack Klein, Charles Dole, Alfred Harding, Louis Jones, Anton Remenih, and Paul Domke. Not only did Melvin A. Casberg describe his trip behind the Japanese lines and his relations with the famous doctor Ma Haide, but he taught me a great deal about the psychological aspect of small, remote military outposts. Syndicated columnist Joseph Alsop and Israel Epstein, the editor of *China Today,* showed me the journalist's point of view, and Mrs. Sufei

Ma Haide, "Doc Ma's" widow, shared her impressions of the Dixie Mission and her recollections of life with her famous husband in Yenan.

Several military and G-2 men helped me too. General Alfred C. Wedemeyer, commanding general of the China Theater during most of Dixie's existence, General Thomas Van Natta, G-2 for the Theater, as well as Alfred Burden, Kenneth Lau, Carlton Swift, General Frank Taylor, Major General Ernest Easterbrook, and one-time downed flier George Varoff, all made significant contributions to this book.

In the course of writing, I visited several people formerly with the Office of Strategic Services who had not been directly associated with the Dixie Mission but who were able to illuminate the Dixie experience. They included John Coughlin, Gustav Krause, Elizabeth MacDonald McIntosh, Wilfred Smith, and Lieutenant General William R. Peers.

The government of the People's Republic of China and the China Association for International Friendly Contact (CAIFC) have shown considerable interest in my work, for which I am especially grateful. In 1991, the CAIFC made it possible for my husband and me to visit Yenan and the remains of the Dixie compound and airstrip as well as other historic sites. Everyone was most hospitable. I especially thank Sun Zhen Gao, research fellow at the Center for Peace and Development Studies, CAIFC; Ma Beiqiang, secretary-general, CAIFC; Zhang Wei, vice-director of the Yenan Foreign Affairs Office; and Zhang Zhong Qiang, assistant section chief of the Yenan Foreign Affairs Office. All of these people went out of their way to make our visit enjoyable and productive. Special thanks go to John Taylor of the Military Branch of the National Archives and Charles Palm, Deputy Director of the Hoover Institution Archives. Others who assisted, encouraged, prodded, and offered constructive, thoughtful feedback included Rhea C. Blue, formerly of OSS and the Department of State; Charles B. Burdick, retired dean of the School of Social Science, San Jose State University; Michael Schaller, University of Arizona; Jess Kitchens; Claude Buss, formerly of Stanford University; Russell D. Buhite, of the University of Tennessee; E. Bruce Reynolds of San Jose State University; F. MacCracken Fisher, who served in the Office of War Information during World War II and with the U.S. Information Agency afterward; Romayne Ponleithner; and Louis Beaudet, for interpreting World War II radio terminology.

I received grants to do research at the Army War College, Carlisle, Pennsylvania, and the Eisenhower Institute at the Smithsonian Institution, Washington, D.C. The latter not only gave me a chance to look at the many records located in the Washington metropolitan area but also gave me opportunities to talk with Forrest Pogue about General George C. Marshall and his unfortunate mission of reconciliation.

Many friends supported me also, as did Menlo College, in Atherton, Calif., by giving me a chance to escape from teaching duties long enough to put it all together. I believe the result is a sound analysis of an extremely important deviation from traditional American policy toward China. I regret that all of the principals did not live to read and critique the finished product. I hope that as more information becomes available, future historians will be able to build on it.

Because this is a work of history, I have chosen to retain the historical romanization of the Chinese names and places. The appendix will help those who wish to convert to the modern spelling.

Introduction

Most Americans are unaware that for part of World War II the United States maintained a detached military unit in Yenan, Shensi Province, China, as a liaison with the Chinese Communists. This group, the U.S. Army Observer Group (USAOG), known as the Dixie Mission, was created in late 1943 and early 1944, when mainly American forces were spearheading the war in China against Japan. As Jonathan Spence has noted, China's greatest contribution lay in holding down large numbers of Japanese troops, although development of the B-29 and plans to bomb Japan from bases on the Chinese mainland were also important.

The war changed the traditional patterns of Western exploitation. Extraterritoriality was abolished by mutual agreement in January 1943. In December of that year, Chiang Kai-shek, the leader of Nationalist China, joined Prime Minister Winston Churchill of Great Britain and President Franklin Delano Roosevelt at the Cairo Conference, where the leaders agreed that Manchukuo and Formosa would be returned to Chinese Nationalist control at the end of the war. In early June 1944, B-29s began bombing raids from some of the airfields that Major General Claire L. Chennault of the Fourteenth Air Force had built with tens of thousands of Chinese laborers. The need to rescue the men who might crash these planes, together with journalists' reports of atrocities perpetrated by the Chinese Nationalist Army against the people, added weight to suggestions that direct contact with the Chinese Communists would further the war effort.[1] Indeed, as Steven L. Levine has written, top Chinese Communists in both Chungking and Yenan carefully cultivated American connections and promised effective cooperation in the war against Japan in return for aid. Although they opposed foreign intervention in China's internal affairs, they tried to persuade the United States to put pressure on Chiang Kai-shek.[2]

The Communists had been in Yenan since 1936, under the leadership of Mao Tse-tung. In addition to the journalists, prior to January 1944, some American Foreign Service officers and military men had spoken to General Joseph W. Stilwell, the American commanding general of the China-Burma-India Theater (CBI), about possible affiliation with the Communists. The recommendation reflected the advisers' knowledge that the Chinese Communist armies had been actively pursuing the war against the Japanese, sometimes in a united front with Chiang Kai-shek's Kuomintang, or Nationalist Chinese government, but more often on their own. Those who favored this action also suspected that the future of China might lie in Mao's hands, not in those of Chiang and his followers.

Chinese interest in Marxism had begun during World War I. At its Second Congress, in May 1922, the infant Chinese Communist Party joined the Comintern in calling for a meeting of the extremist elements of Sun Yat-sen's Kuomintang and revolutionary socialists "to discuss creating a united front for struggle against landlords of the feudal type and against all relics of feudalism." The new party was weak and numbered only 432 members, so it sought an alliance with the Kuomintang, and such a coalition existed from 1924 to 1927. During these years, the Kuomintang was remodeled structurally along the lines of the Russian Communist Party. Communists were accepted into it, and Mao Tse-tung and five other Communists were elected as reserve members. Sun's Three Principles of antifeudalism, antiimperialism, and democracy served as the group's philosophical rallying point, although at that time "democracy" was the least important principle. A revolutionary army was created, complete with Soviet arms and advisers, and a new military academy was established at Whampoa, with Chiang Kai-shek at its head. Vassili K. Bluecher (alias Galen), a Soviet general from the Siberian civil war, served as chief of staff, and French-educated Chou En-lai was deputy political commissar.

On May 31, 1924, the Kuomintang and Moscow signed an agreement that reestablished diplomatic relations and provided for joint administration of the Chinese Eastern Railway. The Soviets recognized China's sovereignty over Outer Mongolia and renounced special rights and privileges previously obtained through "unequal treaties." Many warlords would not accept either the Sino-Soviet rapprochement or Kuomintang domination, however. Heavy fighting soon broke out between the warlord-dominated north and the revolutionary south. In May 1925, the Kuomintang Central Committee at Canton adopted a resolution that severed connections with Peking and proposed cooperation with Moscow. The Kuomintang could not implement this resolution, however, because of the power struggle that followed Sun's death from cancer in May. Neither could it capitalize on the wave of antiforeignism that swept China after British police in Shanghai massacred twelve Chinese students.

The following March, Chiang Kai-shek suddenly charged the Communists with plotting to undermine his authority. He declared martial law, arrested a number of Communists and labor organizers, and seized a gunboat. He quickly consolidated his political control and made himself commander in chief of the National Revolutionary Army. In the meantime, the Nationalist government, dominated by the Kuomintang Left, had moved from Canton to Wuhan. They recognized the genuine potential for social revolution that existed at this time, especially among workers engaged in China's antiquated agricultural system. Strikes were held in the industrial city of Hankow and demands made for higher wages and better working conditions.

While many Kuomintang supporters were prepared for a "bourgeois nationalist" revolution, such moderates neither anticipated nor desired a peasant "liberation." They certainly did not want the kind of trade dislocation and labor unrest that was underway in Hankow. A split in Nationalist leadership resulted between Chiang and his conservative supporters on the one hand and the more socialist Left on the other hand. It widened in April 1927, when Chiang ordered a general attack on the Shanghai labor unions and workers' organizations. Three hundred Communists, labor leaders, and "radicals" were massacred. The Kuomintang Central Executive Committee then passed a resolution charging Chiang Kai-shek, now head of the Kuomintang's right wing, with twelve "crimes," expelling him from the Party, and stripping him of his offices. Chiang then organized his own government at Nanking. Soon, the Kuomintang left wing, reflecting resistance to the sweeping revolution for which Moscow was calling, declared that the Chinese Communists were no longer members of the Kuomintang. There followed a purge. By October 1928, Chiang's government headquartered in Nanking had defeated enough opponents to call itself the Nationalist government of China. The Organic Law, passed that same month, provided for Kuomintang "tutelage." Chiang ruled in strongman style while continuing to pay lip service to Sun Yat-sen's Three Principles.

By 1934, Nanking controlled about one-half of the traditional eighteen provinces of China. The Communists kept a hard core of fighting men ready to take advantage of any political shifts in their direction, although their membership had dropped from 58,000 to 10,000 immediately after the bloodbath of 1927. Persistent turmoil, unbearable taxation, and the government's policy of making the army live off the land wore down the peasants, who sometimes retaliated by becoming bandits or by forming secret protective societies that fought against soldiers and bandits.

Meanwhile, in April 1928, troops under Chu Teh joined a small band of Mao Tse-tung's followers in the western Kiangsi Mountains, and the Chinese Red Army was born. Chu Teh served as commander in chief, and Mao was political commissar. Over the next few years these two successfully withstood four campaigns to suppress bandits that were launched by Chiang Kai-shek. The number of followers increased.

Chiang's fifth campaign to suppress bandits began in October 1933. After hanging on for a year, some 90,000 Red troops, divided into five army corps, broke out of the Kiangsi-Fukien base area where they had been trapped. Marching by different routes and accompanied by a mass of peasants with carrying poles, they trudged through province after province, fighting both national and provincial forces. As they moved, they left their dead behind, but they also left hard-core cadres charged with the task of carrying on the work of the revolution in each locale. One year and 6,000 miles later, they reached their destination of Paoan, in southwestern Shensi Province.

For years, Chiang Kai-shek's troops continued to clash intermittently with his assorted opponents. The climax came in December 1936, when dissident Nationalists arrested Chiang at a spa in Sian and circulated their list of eight demands. These included reorganization of the national government into a coalition, the immediate cessation of the civil war, and concentrated resistance to the Japanese. The most radical insurgents wanted to kill Chiang because he had helped wreck the Kuomintang-Communist partnership in 1927 and had brought death to many Communists. The eight-point program fit the Comintern's 1935 directive, however, and so the Chinese Communists supported it and the united front. After a week of negotiations with Chou En-lai, Chiang accepted the conditions and agreed to redirect Kuomintang fighting energies toward the Japanese rather than the Communists. Chiang was released on Christmas Day and returned to Nanking. During the same month the Red army occupied Yenan, which was south of Paoan but still within Shensi Province.

In their first coalition, both Nationalists and Communists included antiimperialism in their propaganda. In the second coalition China's ultimate political future seemed to depend in large measure on which party could best exploit this theme. The Communists recognized that their ability to survive many outside pressures and challenges had strengthened their position. Furthermore, they now had their own army, and the enemy was Japan, not Chinese warlords. As a result, anti-imperialism–that is, nationalism–could be given free play. The Communists envisioned a mass uprising of the Chinese people in a national war of resistance against Japan. Finally, communism was linked officially to a national strategy of resistance, and so the Communists were at least temporarily protected from police persecution.

In the years that followed, the great power struggle in China was waged chiefly between Japan and the USSR, both of which regarded China as more of a prize than a combatant. Japan occupied Manchuria in 1931. Faced with the rise of Nazi Germany, Russia made a tactical retreat on its eastern front. It liquidated its Manchurian position by selling the Chinese Eastern Railway to Japan in 1935 and at the same time signed a mutual assistance pact with the Mongolian People's Republic in March 1936.

The 1937-1938 phase of the Sino-Japanese war is often called the "special undeclared war." It followed the surrender of Shanghai, when the national government moved to Chungking. In the fall of 1938, the Japanese tried to negotiate a peace settlement that would bring China within Japan's Greater East Asia Co-Prosperity Sphere. Not unexpectedly, Chiang refused, because the paternalistic East Asia bloc could not accommodate Chinese independence or politicians like Chiang. Another reason the Generalissimo failed to agree was that he considered Japan and the United States to be on a collision course. This belief spawned the conviction that the United States would go to bat for China and would ensure victory, a prospect that both sapped the Nationalists' war effort and further corrupted their relationship with the Communists. Yet Chiang's stand against the Japanese proved to be his finest hour. The years to come were marred by political and economic decay.[3]

When hostilities broke out in 1937, the United States offered its good offices informally. When the offer failed to elicit a response from Japan, the Americans publicly condemned world lawlessness. Shipments to Japan of certain critical war supplies were restricted in January 1940. New restrictions were implemented after the Japanese expanded into Indochina.[4]

After the Japanese attacked Pearl Harbor, China formally declared war on Japan, Germany, and Italy. The Soviets promptly reduced military aid to China. They reasoned that since China had become an ally of the United States, it was "safe" to cut back assistance. In keeping with Marxist theory that major wars stimulate revolutionary trends, they planned to watch China's social structure to see the effects of the "imperialist war."

The American goal was to win the war, but the United States, concerned with "political legitimacy," was unwilling to deal with any groups in China apart from the Nationalists. American strategy sought to strengthen China and to keep China in the war to inflict damage on the Japanese.[5] In January 1942, the China-Burma-India Theater of War was created, with Chiang Kai-shek as commander in chief of the China Theater. Infantry Lieutenant General Joseph W. Stilwell served as Chiang's chief of staff and U.S. commander of the CBI. This arrangement essentially forced Stilwell to serve two masters: Chiang, who had very different ideas about how to wage the war, and Chennault, a fervent advocate of airpower.

Chennault, who had resigned his army commission in 1937 because of deafness, went to China as an adviser to the Chinese air force. In 1941, during the period of American neutrality, he organized the American Volunteer Group, the "Flying Tigers," for service against the Japanese. When the United States declared war on Japan, he was given command of the U.S. Army Air Corps China Air Task Force. Chennault was totally committed to the notion of air superiority. He never hesitated to bypass Stilwell as necessary to win acceptance for his own theories. In particular, he attracted the attention of Chiang Kai-shek.

While these developments were unfolding in early 1942, the emerging Office of Strategic Services (OSS) became interested in expanding its role in China and in establishing contact with the Communists in Yenan. Its efforts in this direction began in 1942 when Washington decided to send two OSS men discreetly to the remote, theocratic nation of Tibet. The men selected were Ilia Tolstoy, grandson of the great Russian novelist, and Brooke Dolan, a skilled adventurer and Far Eastern explorer. Their purpose was to assure the ten-year-old Dalai Lama of American friendship and to explore the possibility of constructing a road from India to China through the Tibetan mountains. This was to be a military route that could be used to transport goods into China to support the war effort against the Japanese.

Because the terrain was rough, it took Tolstoy and Dolan three months to travel from New Delhi to Lhasa, the capital of Tibet. There they exchanged gifts with the Dalai Lama, who received them as formal ambassadors from President Roosevelt.[6] He asked whether the United States could supply him with a radio transmitter that would allow him to communicate with the far reaches of his country. OSS could have provided one easily, but State Department concerns over possible Chinese reaction led them to decline the request.[7]

In their report, Dolan and Tolstoy noted that they considered Tibet a supporter of the Allies and sympathetic to America's wartime goals although fearful of possible subsequent Chinese aggression. A document alleging that Generalissimo Chiang Kai-shek had issued orders for Chinghai and Szechuan troops to invade Tibet reinforced Tibet's apprehension. Also, rumors circulated in Tibet that the Chinese government had asked the government of India for permission to move 13,000 Chinese troops stationed in India into Tibet from Bengal. Allegedly, India had denied the request.

Tolstoy and Dolan left Lhasa in March 1943. After five months on the road, they arrived in Chungking. The photographic record they made of their journey appeared in the August 1946 issue of *National Geographic Magazine*. In their report to OSS, they stated that they had not broached the subject of a trans-Tibet road, because the Tibetan government regarded motor vehicles as modern and "un-Tibetan." Such a road would face no major obstacles, however, and could be built in about two years. Tolstoy and Dolan also reported their observations regarding existing Tibetan airfields and the problems that aircraft such as the DC-3 could anticipate when using them. The modernization of Tibetan air transportation, like road building, would require advanced technology.[8] Even so, Tolstoy did not think the idea of creating some kind of supply line from India to China through Tibet should be abandoned. Pack animals and possibly Tibetan traders could be used. Tolstoy estimated that even if a primitive route were used, up to 1,000 tons could be sent the first year. While supplies on this order of magnitude might not be terribly significant in the Chinese war effort, they could certainly assist OSS operations in China.[9]

OSS director General William J. Donovan liked Tolstoy's suggestion. In a letter to the State Department's James Dunn, Donovan noted that the "intelligence by-product of such a route was not to be ignored" and that Tolstoy's proposal offered an alternative to flying the Hump if that supply route were threatened.[10]   ·

At about the time that Tolstoy and Dolan were pushing toward Tibet, more than one of the Foreign Service officers stationed in China was expressing reservations about Chiang Kai-shek and favored putting pressure on him to allow the Americans a greater role in managing the war in China. John Davies, a young Foreign Service officer detailed to Stilwell, wrote a memo to Clarence E. Gauss, the American ambassador to China, that was passed to General George C. Marshall, U.S. Army chief of staff, and to the White House. In it, Davies recalled that Stilwell had gone to China in 1942 to help Chiang Kai-shek's armies resist the Japanese but that he had encountered fundamental policy differences as to how the war should be waged. Though exhausted militarily, Chiang wanted to appear strong at the peace table, particularly because a post-war showdown with the Chinese Communists seemed inevitable. Chiang really wanted the United States to fight the war against Japan so that he could save his strength for the battle with the Communists.[11] For his part, Davies wrote, Stilwell wanted to capitalize on China's position on Japan's flank and to carry the war to Formosa, to northeast China, and finally to Japan, building a land link across northern Burma so that his efforts could be synchronized with those of Admiral Chester Nimitz and General Douglas MacArthur.[12]

Because he commanded a military force in China, could issue orders in the Generalissimo's name, and controlled lend-lease distributions, Stilwell was important in Chinese politics. This prominence was ironic, since Stilwell did not approve of Chinese politics or China's way of running its army. He regarded the Generalissimo as a man who manipulated a delicate and shifting balance of power, using a "gangster" secret police headed by an old-time thug named General Tai Li. Chiang was not officially a dictator, a fact that made Stilwell's position even more difficult. There seemed to be no single final authority with whom he could deal. Nor did he regard the Chinese army as a "real" modern fighting force in the usual Western sense. Rather, it was an agglomerate of feudalistic military forces held together by personal loyalties, endowments, grants-in-aid, threats, and tolerance. Like his political authority, the Generalissimo's military control fluctuated. He could count on only a few divisions to obey orders faithfully. He often had to negotiate with representatives of the various commanders prior to issuing orders. The Chinese army was organized badly, burdened by politics, poorly equipped, and barely trained. Except in the Communist divisions and the small body of troops at Ramgarh, army morale was low. In addition, as previously noted, the apathetic, venal troops lived off the land, in line with Chinese army tradition. Not even officers whose homes the Japanese had occupied expressed enthusiasm for going into the field and fighting. Things were so bad that by March 1943 Chinese commanders in areas bordering Japanese-occupied territories had settled down with their families, gone into trade, and made enormous profits in contraband traffic across the "fighting lines." Although the Japanese were also corrupt in these matters, the Japanese, unlike the Chinese, fought when their commanding officers ordered them to do so.

Foreign Service men like John Davies did not believe that China could be transformed into a fighting machine by sending in lend-lease arms and pushing the Generalissimo to issue attack orders. Davies wanted the United States to treat any arrangement with Chiang as a deal. The flow of lend-lease munitions should be cut off, in other words, if the Chinese did not fulfill their part of the contract.[13] The United States could thus use its strong bargaining position to take control on major issues.[14] This strategy contravened the desires of Chinese pressure groups in the United States. Known collectively as the China Lobby, they had considerable voice in the American press, which eulogized the Chinese army extravagantly and favored supplying lend-lease equipment to China without restrictions. Stilwell was tough-minded and opinionated. Davies believed that his conflicts with the Chinese stemmed from the general's unwillingness to compromise or to conceal his thoughts.[15] Davies also worried that the United States' association with the British in the South East Asia Command (SEAC) would taint its credibility with the colonial and native peoples in that part of the world and would paint America as a "whiteocracy" out to reimpose Western imperialism.[16] "Our major role in Asia lies in China," he wrote. "If, in the future, dynamic nationalism in Asia, possibly with Russian support, and a decadent imperial system come into conflict, a strong, independent, and democratic China can serve with us as a stabilizing force."[17]

Davies speculated Chiang Kai-shek was uncooperative because he was gearing up for a future, calamitous civil war against the Chinese Communists. Since Chiang counted on American help, however, Davies believed that he could be persuaded to collaborate for the sake of achieving internal unity. If Chiang remained unresponsive, Davies thought the United States should support elements in China more sympathetic with U.S. goals.[18]

Personally, Davies regarded the Generalissimo as a man whose limited intelligence, Japanese military education, and former close association with German military advisers prevented him from appreciating genuine democracy. Using Tai Li's ruthless secret police, Chiang adroitly manipulated the various residual warlords, dissident groups in the Kuomintang army, provincial cliques, Communists, minor parties, and sometimes even the puppets set up by the Japanese. Liberals and intellectuals inclined to challenge his power lacked organization. In 1943, Chiang faced the worst crisis yet in his career, brought on by his lack of a popular base, the growth of divergent forces due to prolonged economic strain, and the specter of the Soviets entering the war and moving into Manchuria and North China.

Davies maintained that the United States should not commit itself unalterably to Chiang Kai-shek. A provisional arrangement would make it easier to avoid backing a possible alliance of the Kuomintang and the degenerate puppets against a democratic union of the Russians and their sympathizers. While the war continued, America needed to adjust to political realignments in China, to be tougher with Chiang, and to work for a coalition government.[19]

Davies reported to Gauss his observations on all of these developments and personalities. He noted that only the Generalissimo himself shared the popular American misconception that Chiang was China. Stilwell had to deal with the fact that Japan's attack had caught China in midpassage between semifeudalism and modern statehood. America should not abandon military objectives that involved China, nor should America lose interest in seeing China become a strong and independent nation after the war. The United States needed to remain flexible and realistic while recognizing that Chiang was vulnerable to firm, coordinated American pressure. In other words, Davies advised driving a stern bargain by looking angrier and shouting more loudly than Chiang did.[20]

All parties would be better able to concentrate on the common objective of achieving victory over Japan, Davies thought, if information could be procured from sources other than the Nationalists. In January 1944 Davies wrote that no American had visited the Chinese Communist areas since 1938 and that information about them was conflicting, having been obtained secondhand. He noted that the region the Communists controlled was important because it contained a base of military operations in and near Japan's largest military concentration and its second largest military base. As a result, the region was a potential source of abundant intelligence about the Japanese. Davies described the Chinese Communists as the most cohesive, best disciplined, and most aggressively anti-Japanese regime in China. The Communists also posed the single greatest challenge to Chiang Kai-shek's control of the areas that the Soviets could be expected to enter, should they join the war against Japan. Presumably, the Chinese Communists could become the foundation for a rapprochement between a "new" China and the Soviet Union. Davies recommended dispatching military and political personnel to act as a liaison with the Communists in Yenan. The Communists, he enthusiastically added, would welcome such a development—or so they had repeatedly said.[21]

At this time, the American president, Franklin Delano Roosevelt, was becoming more distant with Chiang and was beginning to deal with him more firmly. China's relations with the United States were shifting with the decay of the Kuomintang-Communist coalition, which had not gone unobserved. As early as October 1943, Ambassador Gauss in Chungking concluded, "If civil war is prevented and if the Kuomintang is forced by . . . circumstances to give way to demands for the broadening of the government with resultant liberalizing influences, China may be saved both from communism and from the perhaps worse evil of the Chinese brand of fascism." In his article "China and East Asia in America's Global Strategy," Luo Rongqu cites Gauss's comments as reflecting the wishful thinking about the China problem that was typical of Americans.[22]

The Communists disputed Chiang's leadership and refused to honor their promise to surrender territorial and military controls to the national government until the Kuomintang gave up its one-party dictatorship. They knew the war was against the Japanese, but like the Kuomintang, they saw that it presented an opportunity to increase their own strength. They organized a vast political network, carried on guerrilla activities behind Japanese lines, and consolidated their bases in "Free China." Their political authority, especially in North China, had begun to expand visibly right after war broke out, and they were helped by Nationalist guerrillas, who regularly defected. Chiang was quoted in 1941 as saying privately: "The Japanese are a disease of the skin. The Communists are a disease of the heart."[23]

Influenced by Harry Hopkins, his close adviser, who had read Davies's memos on the subject, Roosevelt put pressure on Chiang to let observers go to Yenan, and he sent Vice President Henry A. Wallace to add persuasive power. The purpose of the observers, from FDR's point of view, was to control the Chinese Communists as well as the Kuomintang.[24]

Even after hearing tough words from Wallace, Chiang stalled. He did not allow the first detachment to fly into Yenan until July 1944. The number of men attached to the unit fluctuated, starting at seventeen and reaching its maximum of about forty-five just before the atom bomb was dropped, when an invasion of Japan seemed likely. The unit was designated the U.S. Army Observer Group from July 22, 1944, to April 20, 1946, when it was turned over to the Peking headquarters. On June 24, 1946, it was redesignated the Yenan Liaison Group and was placed under the administrative and operational control of the Army Reorganization Section, Peking executive headquarters. The last American personnel left Yenan in March 1947. Despite the transitions and the name changes, throughout its entire existence the operation continued to be known by as the Dixie Mission, its code name. No one knows for sure how the name originated. It may have started because the Communist Chinese, labeled rebels, occupied a position that seemed to the Americans like that of the Confederates in the American Civil War.

The men who served with the Mission came from various branches of the service and were selected for their expertise. They exerted more influence than was usual in traditional military units. The group had four commanding officers plus two men who "filled in," one after its founder had been reassigned and one who was the "last man out."

The first commanding officer and the man most closely associated in people's minds with the Dixie Mission was Colonel David D. Barrett. In the spring of 1944, Barrett was stationed in Kweilin, Kwangsi Province, as Army Military Intelligence (G-2) in the headquarters of the U.S. Army Z Force, an organization preparing to serve with the Chinese national government army much as the Y Force cooperated in fighting the Japanese in Burma. Barrett had been in China on military duty since 1924. He spoke fluent Chinese and greatly admired the Chinese culture and people. Considered a "China hand," he learned on March 25, 1944, that the Dixie Mission was about to be created and that he would probably be a part of it. Barrett served as Dixie's commanding officer until December 1944, when he was reassigned.[25] His liberal political thinking inclined him to further friendly relations with the Chinese Communists.

Colonel Morris I. De Pass was named to succeed Barrett. The Communists believed that De Pass was closely tied to Tai Li, the head of Chiang Kai-shek's secret police. They wanted him removed, and so in February 1945, De Pass was reassigned to a base in South China. Major Wilbur J. Peterkin (he was later made a lieutenant colonel) took over command of the Mission on March 4.[26] Peterkin had midwestern American origins and was politically conservative. He had taught journalism, mathematics, and high school band and served in the Army Reserve until he was called for active duty in 1941. He instructed at Fort Benning, Georgia, until he was sent to China near Kweilin in September 1943 to instruct young Chinese army officers in tactics and the use of American equipment. Peterkin did so using three interpreters, since no one Chinese dialect was understood by all the Chinese in South China.[27] When Kweilin fell to the Japanese, he arranged an assignment for himself in G-2 Plans and Training in Chungking, where Barrett was organizing the Yenan Observer Group. Barrett had met Peterkin and asked that he be assigned to Dixie as his executive officer.[28] Peterkin served with the Mission until July 1945, when he was rotated back to the United States and discharged.[29]

Colonel Ivan D. Yeaton succeeded Peterkin. A very senior colonel, he was serving in Moscow as American military attaché at the time Hitler invaded Russia in June 1941. When Harry Hopkins traveled there, Yeaton predicted that Stalin would be able to hold out for only ninety days. He therefore recommended that the United States not commit itself to aiding the Russian war effort extensively. Yeaton's incorrect prediction led him to be recalled to Washington, where he served at the Pentagon until the CBI was split and General Alfred C. Wedemeyer replaced Stilwell as commander of the China Theater. Wedemeyer requested that Yeaton be sent to his headquarters as a specialist in communism. Yeaton arrived in Chungking in June and took over command of the Dixie Mission in July. He remained until he was sent to Shanghai the following April.[30] His executive officer, a Chinese-American named Captain Clifford F. Young (he was later made a major), replaced him as Mission head. Unlike the dedicated anti-Communist Yeaton, Major Young adopted an objective, more easygoing yet patriotic stance with his hosts. Young served with Dixie from November 1945, till November 1946, and when he left, Major James Butler took over. Colonel John Sells, who ultimately closed down the Mission, succeeded Butler.[31]

Throughout its existence, the Dixie Mission performed valuable services. Its duties and membership changed over the years, especially after Wedemeyer assumed command of the China Theater. In the beginning, it was responsible for exploring means of cooperating more closely with the Communists. Increasingly this focus gave way to an emphasis on intelligence gathering as cooperation with the Chinese Communists went out of political favor. As part of its ongoing responsibilities, the group gathered weather information, assisted in the rescue of downed American fliers, and did what it could to obtain intelligence about Japanese military and political achievements and setbacks along the broken line of the war front. At various times, members of the Mission, escorted by Chinese Communist military forces, traveled behind the Japanese lines and filed reports about the military situation, social conditions, and the state of medical care. They also analyzed the Communists' delicate political position in relation to the Nationalists. Although the OSS often seemed uncertain as to its proper goal, it maintained an active presence in the Dixie Mission.

As civil war between the Nationalists and the Communists intensified, the Dixie Mission helped transport Communists from Nationalist-controlled areas to Yenan. The Mission also dealt with the repercussions of John Birch's assassination when Birch posthumously became the idol of ultrarightist political thinkers in America. Finally, the Mission relayed information from the Communists to the rest of the world. As late as February 1947, personnel sent to Yenan to mediate between the Nationalists and the Communists, as well individuals who reported on their activities, bunked with the Mission.[32] We know from Barrett that they occasionally acted like good guests. One brought Barrett a bottle of whiskey, which the visitor accidentally broke before the commanding officer could enjoy its contents. The airman apologized, saying he would bring another on a future trip. Out of his earshot the salty Barrett commented, "If I'd had a pistol I'd have shot the SOB."[33]

The Dixie Mission served as a hostel for the many journalists and sightseers who traveled to Yenan between 1944 and 1946. Some observers came to see whether a rapprochement was possible between Mao's followers and the Kuomintang. Visitors in this category notably included Patrick J. Hurley, who tried unsuccessfully to reconcile the two sides first as FDR's personal representative, then later as American ambassador to China. Chief of staff General George C. Marshall also made a fruitless attempt to accomplish the same goal in 1946. The first histories written about the group would tie the decline in relations between the United States and the Communist Chinese first to the visit of presidential envoy Patrick J. Hurley and then to the failure of the Marshall Mission.[34]

Shortly after the war ended, many firsthand observers who had advocated warmer relations, including the sharing of information and matériel with the Chinese Communists, were called before Congress, where they were accused of being soft on Communism. This development marked the end of the Dixie cycle. The Mission, controversial before its inception and during its lifetime, continued to be discussed for many years after its disbanding.

Past inquiries into the effectiveness of the Dixie Mission have overlooked the possible influence of the different political and military styles on the Mission's day-to-day operations and on its relations with the Chinese Communists. In fact, the diverse personalities of the leaders and those who served under them helped shape the Mission and its relations with the Communists almost as much as did the progressively tougher policies that Washington issued via Chungking. The men and their subordinates have recollected events in different ways and hold their differing views on the potential or actual importance of the Mission in relation to the war effort and the uncertain peace that followed V-J Day. Their memories and observations are vital if we are to understand fully the significance of the Dixie Mission as a critical episode in World War II.

This book considers the reasons for Dixie's creation, its performance of its assigned tasks, and its accomplishments in light of the uproar that resulted because the Mission existed. The appraisal reflects several different perspectives: that of fifty years ago, that of the immediate postwar period, and that of the 1990s. Communists as well as Americans have contributed to my account. The Nationalists, who always steadfastly opposed the Mission, remain perhaps the only constant element in the story. As Steven M. Goldstein has observed, at the time of the Dixie Mission the Chinese Communist leaders' interest in rapprochement with the United States was neither a ploy to mislead Washington nor a request for unconditional ties with the Roosevelt administration. Rather, it was sincere outreach that envisioned Soviet-American cooperation on a global scale.[35]

Fifty years after its creation, the Yenan Observer Group continues to merit attention. For one thing, in recent years the Chinese have recalled the Mission with almost as much nostalgia as was expressed by the majority of the participants during my interviews. In 1978 and 1991 the government of the People's Republic invited the Dixie alumni and their families for return visits and gave them red carpet treatment. During the summer of 1991, the government of the People's Republic of China and its China Association for International Friendly Contact invited me to visit Yenan, the Dixie compound and airstrip, the restored Chinese Communist compound, museums, and other historical sites. It seemed to me at the time—a scant two years after Tiananmen Square and in the face of recurring disputes with the United States over human rights—that the Chinese were trying to draw attention to the cooperative spirit of Sino-American relations during World War II. In their eyes, the Dixie Mission showed that they were willing to work harmoniously with an official American group. The Chinese estimate of the Mission's importance, which contrasts sharply with American views, has emerged alongside Mao's resurrection as a folk hero.

1

The Origins of the Dixie Mission

By May 1943, many young Americans in the CBI were anxious to obtain accurate information about developments in the Communist-held areas of China. During the early part of that year, John Davies discussed the subject with General Stilwell, who seemed interested but whose many other problems prevented him from giving the matter his full attention. Davies did not let the matter drop, however. On June 24, 1943, he prepared a lengthy memorandum to Stilwell, with a copy to the State Department, setting forth reasons why the United States should send an observer mission to Yenan.[1]

Davies was to write many subsequent reports urging such action. The following January he sent a detailed memo noting that no American observer had visited the Chinese Communist areas since Marine Captain Evans Carlson went there in 1938. Carlson, a "Lincolnesque" man who spent months campaigning with the Eighth Route Army, later founded a Marine Corps unit called Carlson's Raiders and introduced the Communist slogan "gung ho" into the English language.[2]

Davies believed that a serious gap in American sources of information existed because contact was lacking. Everything learned about the activities in Communist China was secondhand information. At the moment, he wrote, the Communists were receptive to the idea of having Americans observe them, but if the United States failed to act soon, they might change their minds.

At that time there was some question about how to set up an observation operation outside the regular diplomatic or army channels, using some group that could be disavowed by the government if necessary. Davies thought that the political and military observers could be justified to Chiang on grounds that, as our common war against Japan increased in intensity, a mission to the Communists could collect information on the enemy as well as assist in and prepare for certain limited military operations in the area. It could seek accurate estimates of the strength of Communist armies, report on Russian operations in North China and Manchuria if Russia attacked Japan, and assess the possibility that North China or Manchuria might become a separate Chinese state or Russian satellite. Davies regarded the last as a possibility because Chiang's blockade of the Communists and their consequent isolation were forcing the Communists to depend on Russia.

Davies believed an American observer mission would break the isolation while at the same time curbing Chiang Kai-shek's desire to destroy the Communists through civil war. Because Davies did not believe that Chiang would cooperate, he thought the request to send observers to the Communists should come directly from the president of the United States, who could overcome any initial refusal by exercising his considerable bargaining power.[3]

Davies also understood America's eagerness to minimize Soviet influence in China. As John W. Garver has noted in *Chinese-Soviet Relations, 1937-1945,* the United States rather than the Soviet Union was dominant in China in 1944-1945. Chiang recognized that Stalin had aided China in the pre–1941 period chiefly to enhance Soviet security vis-à-vis Japan. Stalin's attitude toward the Chinese Communists was fundamentally conditioned by Soviet-American relations, and Mao's Soviet policy was closely linked with his American policy. The preeminence of American power in the parts of China that were not occupied by Japan encouraged Mao to maintain good relations with the United States, so that he was receptive to the Observer Group.[4]

Davies discussed his proposal at great length with a number of people, including Captain Joseph E. Spencer and Lieutenant Charles Stelle, both of OSS, who urged that he speak of it to OSS director General William Donovan. Spencer noted that a new bomber group was interested because it needed assistance in air crew rescue, in acquiring weather reports for current operations, and in collecting the ground data from North China and southern Manchuria that were needed for successful air operations.[5]

In October 1943, President Roosevelt directed General Donovan, who seemed to have unlimited interest in expanding his intelligence operations, to do what he could to obtain more intelligence from China, from the Communist areas and from others.[6] Donovan traveled to the CBI Theater in December of that year and told General Tai Li that he would personally lead a mission into North China. General Tai Li, who carried the title of Chinese chief of the Sino-American Special Technical Cooperation Organization, was responsible only to the Generalissimo, and he approved the mission as proposed.

Donovan did not clear his plan with Forward Echelon or with theater headquarters, New Delhi. When he returned to the United States, he found that he needed to go to Great Britain. He therefore selected Lieutenant Colonel Ilia Tolstoy to lead the mission in his stead and asked OSS China to clear the replacement with Tai Li. Colonel John Coughlin, the top OSS man in China, sent General Tai Li a memorandum to which he received no reply. OSS in Washington then advised its representative in New Delhi of the proposed mission and requested air priority for Tolstoy and his special equipment. Theater headquarters, New Delhi, granted a high air priority for Colonel Tolstoy "plus 2,000 pounds of operational equipment for [an] important OSS mission."[7]

Davies's recommendations for establishing an observer group reached Harry Hopkins, the president's closest adviser, who forwarded them to FDR. Hopkins concurred with Davies that FDR was the only person who could persuade Chiang Kai-shek to play ball. Hopkins reminded FDR that he had met Davies, who had accompanied Stilwell to the Cairo Conference. He also warned the president that it would be essential for the Army and State Departments to choose carefully the people who would serve in the Mission.[8]

On February 9, after consulting with chief of staff General George C. Marshall and others, FDR sent a message to Chiang Kai-shek. In it he stated that although the principal concentration of the Japanese army was in North China, only meager news was available from the region and from Manchuria. The president therefore found it highly advisable to dispatch an American observer mission immediately to the north of Shensi and Shansi Provinces and to other parts of North China as necessary to increase the flow of information and to survey the possibility of future operations. He asked for the Generalissimo's support and cooperation in this undertaking and ended by expressing confidence that he would receive it, because, after all, the enterprise was designed to hasten the defeat of the common enemy and to recover China's lost territories.[9]

The Generalissimo replied on February 22 that he would do all he could to facilitate sending an American observer mission to North China and Manchuria. To this end he had issued instructions to his Ministry of War to contact Stilwell's headquarters to map out a prospective itinerary. The mission would be permitted in all areas over which the national government had political and military authority.

The following day, General Thomas G. Hearn, Stilwell's chief of staff in Chungking, spoke to the War Department. The Generalissimo had explained to him at great length, he said, that the authorized area would exclude parts of China that were controlled by the Communists. General Marshall believed, however, that if Americans could enter the Communist-controlled areas, much worthwhile information could be obtained. At his urging, FDR sent Chiang the following message:

> Thank you for the steps you have initiated as stated in your message of February 22 to facilitate our plan for sending American observers into North China to gain more accurate information regarding large Japanese concentrations there and in Manchuria. The area of North and Northeast China should be a particularly fruitful source of important military intelligence of the Japanese. We shall therefore plan the dispatch of the observer mission in the near future.[10]

Meanwhile, Acting Secretary of State Edward R. Stettinius, Jr., had informed Secretary of War Henry L. Stimson that the steady deterioration in relations between the Kuomintang and the "so-called Chinese Communists" worried the State Department because it interfered with the war, might in time lead to civil war, and might complicate relations between China and the Soviet Union in the future. Stettinius said Ambassador Gauss and others had reported that as many as 500,000 Nationalist troops were blockading Communist troops that would otherwise see active duty. To ease relations between the two factions, the State Department was considering dispatching a small group of observers to the Communist areas of North China. Gauss recommended that the group include John Service, who like Davies was a second secretary of the U.S. embassy in Chungking detailed to Stilwell. He considered Service a competent political observer and reporter.[11]

In his reply, Stimson brought Stettinius up to date regarding FDR's requests to Chiang. The War Department was informing General Stilwell, Stimson said, that State and War were in agreement on the group's composition. Stimson asked Stilwell to discuss the entire matter with Ambassador Gauss and then to submit his recommendations.[12]

Roosevelt again asked Chiang to approve a mission on March 22, adding that its presence might be able to provide the Generalissimo with useful information about the Sinkiang border troubles. To underscore the president's message and apply some additional pressure, Stilwell delayed the departure of Chinese air cadets bound for training in the United States.[13]

On April 4 Stilwell told Stettinius that he and Gauss regarded an

American military/political detachment in Yenan as essential to the flow of intelligence about the enemy. Once in place, such a unit would be invaluable. Its men could assist military air operations by organizing evasion and rescue squads in guerrilla and occupied areas and could study the possibility of using Communist guerrillas in ground operations. Politically, they could provide inside information on relations between the Communists and the central government and could report also on relations between the Chinese Communists and the Russians.[14]

Although Chiang resisted dispatching an official American mission to Yenan at this time, he did allow Chinese and foreign press correspondents to visit the area. On March 16, 1944, the writers, whose spokesman was Brooks Atkinson of the *New York Times,* formally asked Chiang for permission to go there. The request was granted after considerable delay. The Chinese minister of war justified allowing the press to visit Yenan while refusing to allow American observers to do so by arguing that the visits differed in purpose. The reporters were civilians, he explained, and their views would not represent official policy, but a military mission in Yenan might suggest that the United States was on the verge of cooperating with the Communists.

The journalists went to Yenan in mid-May 1944. Their reactions could not have pleased Chiang. Most of them were favorably impressed by the Communists' enthusiasm, simple lifestyle, and sense of purpose. In greater or lesser measure, the press also praised the Communists' dogged resistance to the Japanese.[15]

That same month Chiang also learned that Vice President Henry A. Wallace would soon be traveling to China on special assignment for FDR. The trip would serve two purposes: it would remove Wallace from the United States while the Democratic Party wrestled with the selection of its vice presidential nominee for the 1944 elections, and it would show Chiang that FDR took America's commitment to China seriously. Not having been informed otherwise, the American embassy in Chungking assumed that Wallace would want to discuss the deteriorating situation in China, American difficulties in gaining Chiang's cooperation, the existing tension between China and the Soviet Union, the ongoing Kuomintang blockade of the Chinese Communists, and Chiang's refusal of Roosevelt's February request to send observers to Yenan.

Wallace and Stilwell were not destined to meet during this visit. The vice president spent most of his time in China talking with the Generalissimo and Chennault.[16] John Service, not knowing whether Wallace would consult with Stilwell or would want to be briefed, prepared a summary paper analyzing the roots of the Chinese problem.

He finished it on June 20, the day Wallace arrived in Chungking. Almost half of the paper described the Kuomintang's shortcomings. The rest mentioned positive political factors in China and proposed an American policy that combined aid with political pressure designed to force Chiang to broaden the base of his government.

This proposal for active political intervention with Chiang's government departed from America's traditional hands-off diplomacy but represented a less direct form of intervention than a proposal to place Chiang's armies under American command would have been. Although Service made his case in active rather than passive terms, he did not believe that his paper differed substantially from the State Department's long-range policy except that he urged bringing long-range policies into the short term. The State Department commended the paper, which had wide circulation, and it provided background information for an article that appeared in *Collier's* in 1945.[17]

Roosevelt had first suggested in early March that Wallace visit Chiang Kai-shek to straighten things out. The vice president did not take the idea seriously at first, but once he became convinced that he could accomplish something, he agreed to go. Because he also wanted to put Moscow and India on his itinerary, he asked the State Department to assign men to accompany him who knew the Chinese language and who were familiar with recent Chinese affairs and personalities. They chose John Carter Vincent, chief of the Division of Chinese Affairs, who had recently served in Chungking; John N. Hazard, a Russian-speaking member of the Soviet Supply Section of the Foreign Economic Administration; and Owen D. Lattimore, a scholar serving in the Office of War Information (OWI).[18]

Wallace flew to Tashkent in mid-June to confer with W. Averill Harriman, the American ambassador to the Soviet Union. According to Harriman, Stalin agreed with Roosevelt that Chiang was the only man who could hold China together, but Stalin was not optimistic about the possibility of reconciling the Chiang and Mao factions in China.[19] Following this conversation, Wallace proceeded to Chungking where, unbeknownst to him, for cosmetic reasons Chiang had ordered all beggars to be rounded up, roped together, and sent out of the city before June 20, when Wallace was due to arrive.[20] On the twenty-first, Wallace met with Chiang and T. V. Soong, who acted as interpreter. Ambassador Gauss was not invited to attend any of these meetings.

Roosevelt assumed that the Kuomintang and Chinese Communists were basically friends, Wallace told Chiang, because they were both Chinese. If the Chinese could not come together on their own, they might call in a friend. The British did not regard China as a great power, Wallace went on, and the Russians were cool toward the Chinese, but President Roosevelt wanted China to be a great power in fact as well as in theory. Wallace was emphatic: no question that might result in conflict between Russia and China should be left pending. Chiang then proposed Roosevelt as a possible middleman or arbiter between China and the Russians. The American president had indicated that he might be willing to play such a role.

Later, Wallace hastened to dispel any misunderstanding as to whether the United States would help smooth China's relations with Russia.[21] He said American policy toward Sino-Soviet relations represented a commitment to help China fight Japan but not necessarily to support Chiang Kai-shek in all circumstances. The United States wanted to see a program in China that would benefit the Chinese people generally, without regard to the political complexion of the group affected.[22]

The next day, Wallace spoke of the poor showing that Chinese troops were making in central China. Chiang's not unexpected excuse was that after seven years of war China had sought aid from abroad but that Roosevelt had let him down by withdrawing from the projected amphibious campaign against Burma. He remarked that American officers lacked faith in China but that he continued to have confidence in his army, although he questioned Stilwell's judgment. The Chinese Communists were subject to the Comintern's orders, Chiang continued, and caused the Chinese people to have low morale. They wanted to break down resistance to Japan in order to strengthen their own position. Stalin had called them "margarine Communists," but he was wrong: the Chinese Reds were more Communist than the Russians. The Kuomintang wanted the Chinese Communists to back them, to uphold and obey the government, to support the war effort by incorporating their forces within the Chinese army, and to integrate the areas that they controlled with the rest of China under the national government. If the Chinese Communists would meet these requirements, the desired observers' mission would be permitted to go to North China under national government auspices and to train "converted" Communist troops. The observers would, however, have no direct contact with the top Chinese Communists. In fact, Chiang said, the best contribution that America could make to a settlement would be to display aloofness to the Reds. His final comment on the matter of the observers was "Please do not press."[23]

In spite of Chiang's request, the next morning Wallace and Vincent did press, possibly because Wallace had received a radiogram from

Roosevelt stressing the need for military intelligence from North China, particularly in connection with B-29 operations.[24] Bowing to this pressure the Generalissimo suddenly relented. He consented to the dispatch of observers under the auspices of the National Council but without regard to the progress of relations between the Kuomintang and the Chinese Communists.[25]

In July 1942 Lauchlin Currie urged Roosevelt to remove Stilwell, Gauss, and T. V. Soong. Currie was a Harvard economist and administrative assistant to the president who had gone to China for six weeks in 1941 and again in 1942 as a special envoy. At the time that he made his recommendation, he also suggested to Marshall that Stilwell should be transferred to another theater. Marshall rebuffed this idea when it became apparent that Currie spoke without the president's authority. That fall Wendell Willkie, who had unsuccessfully campaigned against FDR in 1940, went to China while barnstorming through Africa, the Middle East, and Russia. He ignored Ambassador Gauss, and Davies thought Madame Chiang found him easy to manipulate.

Through Willkie and Wallace, Chiang had tried to persuade Washington to remove both Gauss and Stilwell.[26] With Wallace, the Generalissimo attempted to short-circuit the ambassador and the theater commander. Chiang complained that there were too many channels through the State Department. While Chennault was most cooperative, Chiang said, Stilwell lacked any understanding of political matters. Chiang urged Wallace to recommend that Roosevelt send a personal representative to handle both political and military affairs.

When the vice president arrived in Kunming on June 26, he cabled the president a summary of his thoughts about the talks with Chiang Kai-shek. He described Chiang as bewildered regarding the economic situation and said that though the Generalissimo expressed confidence in his armies, military developments distressed him. Wallace thought the situation in China warranted such anxiety.[27] He agreed with Chiang that FDR should appoint a personal representative to act as liaison; after all, it seemed highly likely that eastern China, including the American air bases, might be lost to the Japanese in three or four weeks. This eventuality would nullify the American military effort in China and would hasten the disintegration of the Chungking regime. The president must take both military and political actions to preclude a political vacuum "which might be filled in ways the President will understand." On the other hand, the right man might be able to bring about a semblance of a united front.[28]

Later Wallace explained that in making his recommendation he had envisioned not a coalition with the Chinese Communists, which he thought unlikely anyway, but rather a coalition recruited from within the area controlled by Chungking. It would consist of Western-trained men, whose vision would extend beyond the traditional landlord-dominated rural society of China and the considerable group of generals and other officers who were neither subservient to the landlords nor afraid of the peasantry.[29] The situation called for an American general in whom military and political authority could be united. It could not be Stilwell, Wallace said, for he was immersed in the Burma campaign and did not enjoy Chiang's confidence. The new appointee must be either Stilwell's deputy in China, who would have authority to deal directly with the White House on political questions, or someone outside Stilwell's present command.[30]

Wallace's first choice to supplant Stilwell—and, in effect, Gauss—was Major General Claire L. Chennault, head of the Fourteenth Air Force. According to a story printed in the *New York Times* on October 11, 1951, Wallace told the press that "his first choice to replace General Stilwell . . . had been Major General Claire L. Chennault, head of the American air force which was giving the Chinese Nationalist troops the only protection they had against the mounting Communist [*sic*] military power." Wallace claimed that John Carter Vincent supported this choice, but that Joseph Alsop, Chennault's right-hand man, opposed it. Wallace then proposed Lieutenant General Albert C. Wedemeyer as Stilwell's replacement,[31] possibly because he realized that the War Department would also oppose Chennault.[32]

Wallace's visit had considerable effect on United States policy toward China. Not only were military leaders shuffled around and/or changed on his recommendation, but the vice president's trip probably shook things loose and allowed the Dixie Mission to come into existence. The fact that Chiang gave in and allowed observers into Communist territory right after his meeting with Wallace makes this conclusion unavoidable.

In the meantime, Ambassador Gauss continued to try to resolve the impasse between the Kuomintang and the Chinese Communists. On July 4, George Atcheson, the embassy counselor, proposed that Chiang Kai-shek call all factions, including the Chinese Communists, into a high military council and make an appeal for their cooperation in the interest of saving the rest of the country. Reviving the united front in this way would be statesmanlike, he said. Sun Fo received the idea well, and the State Department liked it enough to urge the embassy to pursue it. Two subsequent conversations with T. V. Soong were only mildly encouraging, however, and on July 14 Gauss transmitted a message to Chiang from FDR. It mentioned Chiang's conversations with Wallace and recommended that a working association with the Communists be created to pave the way for better relations between China and the Soviet Union.[33]

On June 4, 1944, Captain Joseph E. Spencer, OSS Chungking, wrote a memo to Dr. William Langer, head of the Research and Analysis branch (R&A), and Burton Fahs, also of OSS, which said regarding the establishment of an observer unit: "Everyone agrees it ought to be done, but also everyone is agreed that it cannot be done openly by any regular American diplomatic or army agency." Spencer then suggested that the mission be code named Palisades, after his hometown in California.[34] His memorandum showed not only that the OSS was determined to be involved in the project but also that there was no communication within the organization, since the Donovan/Tolstoy mission had already been planned. Before he left Washington, Tolstoy had been told to check in at theater headquarters, New Delhi, to advise staff there of his proposed mission and to coordinate his mission with Forward Echelon, Chungking. Evidently he had failed to do either of these things, because staff members at Forward Echelon later complained that he had arrived in China without consulting them.[35]

A month after writing his memo, Spencer informed Langer and Fahs that there had been developments regarding the "Palisades situation." The Chinese government had sanctioned a mission to be directed by Army Military Intelligence (G-2). Several agencies would take part in it, and so OSS would not need to act on its own.[36] Tolstoy would accompany this mission if Forward Echelon asked him to do so. Colonel Coughlin, speaking for OSS, assured the War Department that OSS would take the necessary steps to ensure that in the future all of the organization's planned operations in CBI Theater would be coordinated thoroughly with Forward Echelon to avoid misunderstandings.[37]

The outfit destined to go to Yenan officially was labeled the U.S. Army Observer Group because Chiang Kai-shek objected to the term "mission." Davies and his colleagues, however, had jokingly called the Chinese Communist-controlled area Dixie, recalling rebel territory in the American Civil War. Chiang's objections notwithstanding, the unit immediately became known among Americans as the Dixie Mission. Colonel David D. Barrett headed the Observer Group when it finally came into existence. Davies considered Barrett a good choice because he read and spoke the Chinese language and had an unusual ability to establish rapport with Chinese people.[38] Barrett had been attaché for language study and, from 1924 to 1928, military attaché in the U.S.

legation in Peking. From 1931 to 1934 he served with the Fifteenth Infantry in Tientsin. Then, in August 1936, he returned to Peking as assistant military attaché in the American embassy under then colonel Joseph W. Stilwell. Promoted to military attaché in 1942, Barrett asked to be relieved in fall 1943 so that he could return to active duty.[39] Barrett had written a textbook on the Chinese language that some considered unsophisticated, but Nancy Stilwell Easterbrook, General Stilwell's daughter, found him a good person who truly loved the Chinese people. He lived with Chinese women when in China and had taken advantage of the educational program and other experiences offered by the army to better himself.[40]

On March 25, 1944, Barrett was ordered to proceed to CBI headquarters for "temporary duty." On the twenty-ninth he learned from John Service that he would probably be accompanying the Dixie Mission, because Stilwell wanted the Mission to be headed by an officer who could speak Chinese and whom the Chinese Communists would respect. When he arrived in Chungking, he assumed that the Mission was set to go as soon as he and John Service could complete final arrangements, but on May 1 he was told to return to Kweilin, to resume duty with Z Force, and to forget about Dixie.

In early July Barrett was again ordered to Chungking.[41] He arrived on July 4, the day on which, the War Department noted, Chiang

Col. David D. Barrett, first commanding officer of Dixie, in August 1944. Courtesy of Col. Wilbur J. Peterkin.

Kai-shek had agreed to allow the observers full freedom of movement, direct radio communication, and relief from the usually obligatory use of Chinese liaison officers and interpreters. Chiang had also authorized the inclusion of ground, air, and service personnel as well as regular intelligence personnel in the Dixie Mission. The Generalissimo continued to object to calling the group a "Mission," however, and so it was designated a section instead. Chiang also declared that he could promise cooperation only in areas under his direct control; the Americans would have to fend for themselves with the Communists.

The news was dispatched promptly to the Chinese Communist representative in Chungking. He replied the same day, welcoming the American observers and promising unqualified cooperation, direct communications, and freedom of travel and operations. David Barrett was placed in command, and the Twentieth Bomber Command and Fourteenth Air Force were asked to send representatives to Chungking for consultation regarding their participation.[42] Barrett assumed that Stilwell had chosen him to command the group because of his language ability. He also thought Stilwell wanted the unit to be as representative as possible without including anyone whom the Chinese Communists would not respect.[43]

The day before the Dixie Mission was scheduled to leave, Barrett went to Colonel Joseph Dickey, head of G-2, in CBI headquarters, and said that he had received no instructions regarding the group's activities. Dickey then gave him a typed list of topics on which the Mission was to collect information and a description of objectives relating to weather reporting and the rescue of downed fliers. The orders bore no signature or authentication of any kind and read more like a set of general instructions for guidance than like orders of the sort usually issued to an army unit. They were the only orders Barrett ever received.

HEADQUARTERS, U. S. ARMY FORCES, CHINA,
BURMA, INDIA
21 July 1944
MEMORANDUM TO COLONEL DAVID D. BARRETT, GS.C.

In connection with the despatch of an Observer Section to areas under the control of the Chinese Communists, information is particularly desired on the following subjects:

Enemy Order of Battle
Enemy Air Order of Battle
Puppet Order of Battle
Strength, composition, disposition, equipment, training, and
    combat efficiency of the Communist forces

Utilization and expansion of Communist intelligence agencies
   in enemy and occupied territory
Complete list of Communist officials (who's who)
Enemy air fields and air defense in North China
Target intelligence
Bomb damage
Weather
Economic intelligence
Operation of the Communist forces
Enemy operations
Evaluation of present contribution of Communists to war effort
Present extent of areas under Communist control (with maps)
Most effective means of assisting Communists to increase the
   value of their war effort
Naval intelligence
Order of Battle of Communist forces
Evaluation of potential contribution of Communists to war
   effort[44]

At 8:05 A.M. on July 22, 1944, an Army Air Force C-47 cargo
plane carrying the first contingent of the Observer Section left Chiu
Lung Po Air Field. Fifteen minutes before the plane arrived at Sian, at
9:45, the men were ordered to put on parachutes. The pilot, Captain
Jack E. Champion, said that if the Japanese knew about the trip and
wanted to intercept it, they would probably do so at that point. The
plane circled Sian for twenty minutes so that three fighters could take
off to escort it to Yenan. Accompanied by the fighters, the plane continued an uneventful flight to Yenan, where it landed at 11:30 A.M. on
a makeshift runway built before the war by the Standard Oil Company.
Captain Champion made a perfect landing, but as he pulled off the
runway to park and clear the strip for the fighters to land, his left wheel
fell through the surface into an old grave that had not previously been
visible. The impact knocked the left propeller and nose section off. The
propeller, rolling like a wheel, sliced into the cockpit, damaging the
fuselage and barely missing the pilot and crew chief. Captain Champion sustained a slight bruise on the arm, but no one else was injured.[45]
   Barrett unhooked his seat belt, jumped out the door, and ran to
the front of the plane. Champion was standing beside the gaping hole
that the propeller had cut in the fuselage. He had been leaning forward
to shut off the engines just as the propeller had slashed into the side of
the plane, or he might have been killed.
   A large crowd had assembled to greet the plane. It had been vis-

The "Wounded Duck," the C-47 that brought the first detachment of Dixie to Yenan in July 1944. Courtesy of Col. Wilbur J. Peterkin.

ible from the air, and as it approached some people had given signals to aid the landing, since the field lacked a control tower.[46] A guard of honor had been drawn up, but because of the confusion caused by the accident, for several minutes no one moved to greet the men leaving the plane. Soon, however, General Yeh Chien-ying, chief of staff of the Eighteenth Group Army; General Peng Te-huai, vice commander of the Eighteenth Group Army; Chou En-lai, a member of the Politburo of the Chinese Communist Party; and other officials cordially welcomed the Americans. After reviewing the guard of honor, the Americans got into trucks for the ride to the official government guest house and an informal reception. During this gathering, General Chu Teh, commanding general of the Eighteenth Group Army, appeared and warmly greeted all members of the section. Both the Americans and the Chinese snapped many photographs. All of the dignitaries expressed great concern over the plane accident, which everyone agreed was not the pilot's fault. Chou En-lai made a short, very graceful speech to Captain Champion, beginning, "A hero has perished," by which he meant that an airplane had been destroyed. He regretted the accident but expressed his relief that no one had been hurt. Later, General Chu Teh wrote Barrett a formal letter expressing his remorse over the accident, apologizing for the faulty preparation of the airfield, and asking that his respects and good wishes be conveyed to General Stilwell.

The reception was followed by a luncheon, after which the Chinese showed the Americans to comfortable quarters near the guest house. Barrett felt that the Communists were doing everything possible to make them feel welcome. At 3 P.M. he and John Service, the Foreign Service officer assigned to the Mission, met with Chou En-lai and General Yeh Chien-ying. Barrett outlined the purpose of their assignment but did not cover every point of his instructions. Chou and Yeh told him they had been informed that the section's objectives were air-ground aid and the collection of enemy intelligence. They said they had not heard of any other tasks. Barrett explained that the Mission's responsibilities included investigating the arms and equipment needs of the Chinese Communist forces, but that he could make no commitments about supplying matériel.

Later that day, Barrett wrote General Chu a letter confirming in general terms their earlier discussion about the mission's purpose. Chu replied that although the Eighteenth Group Army and the New Fourth Army wanted to help Dixie procure the information they needed, they were well informed on some but not all subjects. Some matters would need to be investigated and studied cooperatively. Chu concluded that in the interest of advancing the cause of victory over the common enemy, Japanese fascism, he had directed General Yeh Chien-ying to discuss concrete problems and other matters with the Americans.[47]

The first plane, which earned the nickname "Wounded Duck," had carried nine members of the Dixie Mission. A second plane, scheduled to arrive almost immediately thereafter, was delayed by the acci-

Members of the Dixie Mission, August 1944. Left to right: Ludden, Jones, Stelle (hidden), Gress, Domke, Nakamura, Cromley (hidden), Barrett, Dole, Service (hidden), Peterkin, Remenih, Hitch, Whittlesey, Colling, Dolan. Courtesy of Col. Wilbur J. Peterkin.

dent. Because Forward Echelon did not enjoy good relations with the Fourteenth Air Force, few planes were placed at its disposal.[48] As a result, the second group of nine men did not arrive until August 7. The number of men detailed to Yenan was then eighteen.[49] The personnel roster included the following men: John S. Service and Raymond P. Ludden, both second secretaries of the American embassy attached to the staff of the commanding general for CBI; Major Melvin A. Casberg, Medical Corps; Major Ray Cromley, Captain Charles G. Stelle, Lieutenant Colonel Reginald E. Foss, Major Charles R. Dole, First Lieutenant Louis M. Jones, U.S. Army Air Corps; Captain John C. Colling, First Lieutenant Henry C. Whittlesey, Major Wilbur J. Peterkin, Captain Brooke Dolan, Infantry; Captain Paul C. Domke, Staff Sergeant Anton H. Remenih, Sergeant Walter Gress, Signal Corps; Lieutenant Herbert Hitch, U.S. Navy; and Technician Fourth Class George I. Nakamura, Detached Enlisted Men's List.[50]

Not all of these men really belonged to the units or the branches of service that were listed after their names. Cromley and Stelle were from the Air and Ground Forces Resources Technical Staff, known humorously as AGFRTS. Remenih, Gress, and Colling, who carried "a big bag of R and D toys," were from OSS. They shared OSS confidence that Dixie looked promising for long-range plans. The OSS view of the Mission's possibilities clearly differed from the short-range, official view.[51]

The men attached to Dixie each received seven dollars a day while they were in Yenan.[52] Most of them had personal backgrounds and skills that made them appropriate for their assignments. For example, John Service had been born in Chengtu, the capital of Szechwan, into a missionary family. His parents eventually moved back to the United States, where he received most of his secondary and college education. After one year of graduate school, he decided to enter the Foreign Service. In 1933 he went to China as a clerk in the American consulate, Kunming, and in 1935 he was commissioned as a Foreign Service officer and sent to Peking as a language attaché. He served with Gauss in Shanghai and Chungking and became third secretary in the embassy.[53] In late summer 1943, he was detailed to Stilwell after John Davies asked that four additional Foreign Service officers join him under Stilwell's command to supervise political, economic, and psychological intelligence and warfare operations. Davies wanted Service to be the first of the four officers to go to Yenan because he was fluent in Chinese, the ablest political reporter among the China specialists, and a prodigious worker.[54]

Raymond Ludden had been a Foreign Service officer since 1931. The Japanese interned him after Pearl Harbor, but he was released and volunteered to return directly to China. He served in Chungking and Kunming before flying to Yenan on the August 7 plane.[55] Ludden and Davies had spent time in Mukden. Davies knew that Ludden understood guerrilla operations in harsh country. Davies also thought Ludden had an adventurous streak, a good trait in a man who was to go into the field and behind the Japanese lines with the Communists. Davies had confidence in Ludden's ability to make realistic appraisals of the Communists' organization, operations, and potential.

Davies and John Emmerson, both of whom joined Dixie after it was established, also represented the State Department. Davies went to Yenan on the same plane as Emmerson, in October 1944, but he stayed only sixteen days, while Emmerson remained until December 17. Emmerson, appointed Foreign Service officer in 1935, was a Japanese language specialist. He had spent some time with an OWI propaganda team in the northern Burma combat zone and had investigated propaganda use and the collection of intelligence from Japanese prisoners of war in Burma, India, and China.

Major Melvin A. Casberg, a surgeon born in India who had grown up in St. Louis, served as the unit's first medic. In Dixie he performed intelligence as well as medical duties. He spent four months far behind the Japanese lines, hiking with the Chinese Communists by night and hiding during the day. He helped treat wounded Communists in makeshift cave hospitals. In Yenan he interacted professionally with their doctors, Doc Ma Haide, and the Russian physicians attached to the Eighth Route Army.

Major Ray Cromley, of OSS, was Dixie's Japanese order-of-battle man. He had been with the *Wall Street Journal* before the war and had a Japanese wife and two children who were still in Japan. Cromley always looked forward to the dances that the Communists regularly held, which he regarded as giving him a great chance to learn to dance.[56]

Another OSS man, former professor Captain Charles Stelle, had been born and educated in Peking. Stelle first headed the China section of OSS Research and Analysis in Washington. Later, seeking more action, he transferred to Chungking in early 1944 as an intelligence officer. Twenty-five-year-old Captain John Colling was the son of an American officer who had served twenty years at Tientsin. He left a demolitions post with Detachment 101 in Burma for Dixie, supposedly to train Communist operatives for sabotage.[57] First Lieutenant Louis M. Jones, a law school graduate, was also a demolition expert who had been trained to collect intelligence as well.[58]

Major Wilbur J. Peterkin had been a high school principal in Sumner, Washington, and was a member of the Army Reserve. In 1941, when he "saw the war coming," he volunteered for the Fifteenth Infantry. He spent two years in China, initially in Kweilin as a small arms instructor, before becoming part of the Dixie Mission.[59] He was to succeed Barrett as the Mission's commanding officer.

Technical Sergeant Fourth Class George Itsuo Nakamura, the first but not the only Nisei member of the Mission, was in India when Dr. Alfred Burden, an expert on Japanese intelligence serving in theater headquarters, offered him the Dixie assignment. His job was to translate documents and interrogate Japanese prisoners captured by the Eighth Route Army.[60] Lieutenant Colonel Reginald Foss of the Twentieth Bomber Command, the oldest of the original group to go to Yenan, was originally given air intelligence duties, but he stayed with Dixie only until August 28.

Captain Paul C. Domke, the group's signal officer, had taught in a missionary college and spoke fluent Mandarin. In March 1944, Barrett appointed him supply officer and instructed him to gather the things needed for the trip to Yenan.[61] Staff Sergeant Anton H. Remenih, also a signal officer, had been with the *Chicago Tribune* and had amateur radio experience as well. He had been sent to Kunming to help set up the first base station there. Looking back after the war on his service with Dixie, he said that his radio equipment in Yenan had been no more sophisticated than his amateur radio back home.[62]

Colonel Richard Ellsworth, commander of the Tenth Weather Squadron, chose Air Corps Major Charles E. Dole to be part of Dixie. Twentieth Bomber Command wanted information from Yenan about weather. Dole's job was to train some Chinese there and in the far reaches of China to gather data. Dole had helped set up the theater weather center, which he commanded at the time of his selection. He stayed in Yenan till mid-November 1944, when he was called back to his previous post.

Lieutenant Simon Herbert Hitch was the only U.S. Navy man attached to the unit. Born in Seoul, Korea, he was one of the few sent to Yenan who was not a China hand.[63] He had served as assistant naval attaché in Chungking before taking the Dixie assignment, although later it was alleged that he had represented Admiral Milton E. Miles's Sino-American Cooperative Organization (SACO).[64]

First Lieutenant Henry C. Whittlesey went to Dixie as a representative of Air Ground Aid Service (AGAS), which was charged with assisting in the escape of American military personnel held prisoner by the Japanese. He was fated to be the only member of the Dixie Mission to die in the line of duty (see chapter 2).[65]

Early August 1944 found the Dixie Mission installed in a rough compound in Yenan and performing its assigned tasks. It differed from most liaison groups in China. Others had been created to improve the combat efficiency of the Nationalist Chinese army. In those units, Americans acted as advisers to Chinese commanders and conducted a series of schools within each Chinese army for both officers and enlisted men. They held classes and training for four or five months in subjects such as weapons and their maintenance and ran signal schools to upgrade the Chinese soldier's combat performance. When the advisers deemed the unit combat ready, the American teams accompanied it and assisted in operational and logistical matters. The first of these teams were sent out by headquarters, Y Force, and joined their Chinese units in late August and early September 1943. By July 1945, sixteen armies and over fifty divisions had American personnel attached.[66]

Dixie, on the other hand, was comprised of men from various branches of the service, a pattern that continued as the original men left and new ones took their places. The name of the unit changed over time, too, as mentioned before. From July 22, 1944, to April 11, 1946, it was known as the Yenan Observer Group, and from April 13, 1946, until the last man left in 1947, it was the Yenan Liaison Group. As long as it existed, the Mission followed the guidelines that Colonel Dickey had laid down to describe its purpose. Unlike the American teams that worked with the Nationalists, Dixie did not provide training, although there were many demonstrations and field exercises. When the Americans accompanied the Chinese Communists into battle, they did so to observe.

The U.S. Army Observer Group functioned as a unit to gather intelligence about both the Japanese and the Chinese Communists and to provide whatever support it could in the rescue and return of downed American fliers. The careful selection of its personnel illustrates Stilwell's awareness of the need to place men in Yenan whom the Chinese Communists would respect. At least many of its members spoke Chinese.[67] Still, it was a motley unit, and the Chinese Communists soon noticed that it lacked firm military discipline, which they interpreted as a reflection of Washington's attitude toward them.[68] They did not demonstrate hostility, as they had in spring 1944, when American troops and airmen began constructing airfields for B-29 Super Fortresses at Chengtu.[69] Zhang Baijia has written that the Chinese Communists regarded the arrival of the American military observers as a new starting point in diplomacy. To show his high esteem for the members of the Dixie Mission, Mao revised the August 15, 1944, *Liberation Daily* editorial, which commented on the observers' arrival, and inserted "our friends" into the original title, "Welcome American Military Observers." In the editorial Mao noted that the arrival of the Mission was the most exciting event since the start of the war against Japan.[70]

In time, of course, it became all too clear that the United States was not going to recognize the Chinese Communists' contributions to the war effort by giving them a place at the conference table and that assistance to the Communists' enemies was going to continue and increase. Still, the Communists showed only minimal animosity and remained unfailingly polite.

2

Life in Yenan

The city of Yenan, famed for its ancient pagoda located high atop Chaling Hill, lies in extremely isolated and ruggedly mountainous country. In July 1941, its airfield was only a clearing on the plain. Pilots and passengers on incoming planes surveyed both the pagoda and the famous Yenan caves. Pilots used the pagoda to sight their landings. The caves provided warm lodging and also contained many shops.

Most people would not consider the climate of the area ideal. Summers were hot and humid. Snow fell abundantly in the winter. When spring rains melted the snows, the loess soil turned into a sea of mud. The town peacefully hugged the foot of the mountains, its sleepiness a sharp contrast with the bustle in South China's cities. Streets were narrow, and buildings were often constructed of mud because wood was scarce. When heavy rains came, people clustered along the bank of the swollen river. Men waded out to grab firewood. The powerful current sometimes knocked them down and dragged them several hundred yards before they could scramble back up the bank.

Yenan had a noisy, interesting marketplace and several bookstores where a shopper could buy various publications, including, of course, the writings of Mao Tse-tung. The Communists regularly put out a newspaper using outdated presses they had installed in the Caves of the Ten Thousand Buddhas on Cool Mountain just outside town. Not far away, a rug factory made beautiful rugs by hand and sometimes produced special orders. An art academy, famous for its woodcuts and written up in the April 9, 1945, issue of *Life*, functioned in what had once been a Catholic church.

Still, Yenan was a backward place where people lived and worked as they had for centuries. Any stranger who drove a motorized vehicle into town attracted large crowds. People peered in the car windows

Downtown Yenan in August 1944. The Yenan pagoda can be seen in the background, with the caves visible below it. Courtesy of Jack Klein.

with well-meaning curiosity. The mule and horse remained the common forms of transportation. Automobiles and trucks were an unusual sight.[1]

The Dixie compound lay about half a mile from Yenan. By American standards, living accommodations were primitive. The men lived in what they called caves, which were actually tunnels about fifteen feet long, cut into the hillside and lined with stone. Each was one room, with a door and a window in front set in wooden frames with white paper pasted over the frames in place of glass. Gray bricks with sand between them covered the floor.[2] In front of each door was a windbreak that was pulled down when the strong north winds blew.[3]

Each cave contained a rough table, one or two plain wooden chairs, a stand for an enameled washbasin, a rack for towels, and, for each occupant, a trestle bed made by setting planks on sawhorses. Tallow candles or kerosene lamps provided lighting. The caves had neither running water nor indoor plumbing. Latrines were located a considerable distance away.[4] Charcoal braziers provided heat, but the carbon monoxide they produced made the cave dwellers sick. Dr. Casberg continually warned the men not to close their doors when the braziers were burning. He rescued Barrett, Service, and Davies at various times when they had been overcome by fumes.[5]

The caves became damp when it rained. The men's shoes and other leather goods molded. In dry weather, flies buzzed in and out, sometimes after having been in the open toilets. The men fought moths, gnats, and centipedes with aerosol sprayers. Some contact with these pests could be avoided by keeping the doors to the caves shut, even on the most humid nights. If the doors were not closed, large rats sometimes ran in.[6]

Every morning, Chinese orderlies filled a large earthenware receptacle outside each cave door with hot water, which the men transferred to their washbasins. Drinking water was sometimes stored in captured Japanese saki bottles. Orderlies from the Eighth Route Army attended the Americans and cleaned their quarters. The Americans, careful to avoid the demeaning terminology with which Westerners traditionally addressed Asians, referred to them as *chao tai yuan,* literally "entertain-the-guests officers."[7]

When Colonel Ivan Yeaton headed the Mission, he lived in a two-room house with mud walls. He had a sitting room and a bedroom. There was no bath or latrine, but that didn't bother Yeaton, who did not bathe during the winter anyway. The weather tower was near the colonel's house. The weathermen screamed their readings, so that Yeaton never needed an alarm clock.

The bathhouse contained two large hot water drums that were fired from the outside. The men filled buckets with hot water and took them into a smaller room where a charcoal stove was always burning. They would pour the hot water into small cans with shower heads, hoist these cans to the ceiling, and tilt them to take a shower. The water was heated at 2:30 P.M.. By 5:00 it had cooled, and so the men usually showered in the afternoon. Army regulations required bathing at least once a week, and during the winter most men just showered on Fridays. Yeaton did not enforce the bathing regulation when he was in charge, although he was a stickler for Saturday morning inspections. Once, shortly before the Mission was scheduled to pull out, General Chu Teh was asked to come for the Saturday inspection. He was impressed with the orderliness of the post, which his people expected to take over after the Americans had gone.[8]

The men attached to Dixie drew seven dollars a day in lieu of rations, though at first the Communists took care of all messes except the morning coffee break. Barrett offered to pay something for this service, but Chou En-lai said the Communists felt that it was their obligation to feed and house the Mission. The food was mainly simple Chinese cuisine. The men ate with chopsticks, and soon even the novices became very skilled with these tools. Watermelon—a common, popular fruit—and hot tea were served at the end of every dinner. Watermelon was also offered with tea and cigarettes whenever the men of Dixie toured a factory, an arsenal, or a school. One or more of the

Communist leaders frequently visited the Americans after being invited to "take rice." Once, when General Chu was eating dinner with the Mission, he asked whether the food was Chinese or Western. Barrett replied that he thought it more Chinese than Western and that he liked it. Chu replied that he found it neither Chinese nor Western, which meant that it did not please him.

The Americans often attended dinner parties as guests of the Chinese. Whether the food was good or not, the wine was always terrible. Barrett thought that a local imitation of shaohsing, a famous Chekiang wine similar to dry sherry, was the best they had to drink. Mostly, they had pai-kan (white-dry), a colorless spirit distilled from millet that was the traditional wine of China. American soldiers in Chungking called pai-kan "alarm juice" or "white lightning." They usually drank it warm from small cups. It was very strong. Another sort of wine that the men in Yenan tried was "tiger-bone." It was supposedly made by soaking real tiger bones in pai-kan to give the drinker the strength, courage, and fierceness of the beast. Beef bones, sometimes not the freshest, were used to make the drink, since tigers were rare in the border area. According to Barrett, tiger bone could lift your scalp.[9] The *real* scalp lifting occurred every Friday, when the barber came.

Although the Communists were warm and gracious when they entertained, members of the Mission who were socially sophisticated considered them unpolished.[10] The first major party, held to welcome the group, was given in a large hall. No food or drink was served at that time. The proceedings were confined to speeches and singing by a chorus of boys and girls. During their stay in Yenan, the men of Dixie saw many plays. Most were entertaining, laced with propaganda, and well acted. In fact, the high caliber of acting impressed even Brooks Atkinson, for many years the *New York Times* drama critic and the paper's correspondent in China during the war. The Chinese Communists operated a drama school near Yenan, which probably influenced the quality of these performances. Students who trained there learned the traditional Chinese drama, which provides for the singing of many lines.[11]

Politics sometimes intruded into social matters. In June 1945, General Yeh gave a farewell luncheon for several of the men who were leaving the Mission. After a few drinks of white lightning, Yeh began criticizing the Mission for fighting Japanese fascism while continuing to support Chinese fascism. No open exchange took place, but the incident suggests that relations had begun to deteriorate less than a year after the Mission's creation.[12] Essentially, however, the Communists did not alarm the Americans, in their rough and rumpled clothes, with their earnest talk. Simplicity was their chief charm. Their dedication to hard work and a simple life, and their energy, vitality, and sincerity, made them a refreshing contrast to the corrupted Kuomintang.[13]

Dances were another common form of entertainment. They were held either in a part of the compound that was an orchard or in a meeting hall. At first, an old phonograph provided music, since neither the Communists nor the men from the Mission had musical instruments. Later, the Chinese put together a makeshift orchestra consisting of a harmonica, broken-down violins, Chinese flutes, and some banjolike instruments. They played old American songs, waltzes, and Chinese tunes. The Chinese would do folk dances to entertain the Americans, who would reciprocate by demonstrating the dances currently popular in the States, such as the conga. Sometimes the Chinese also did a congalike dance, the "rice-sprout" dance, which involved bowing and weaving. General Chu Teh rarely missed a dance, and Mao Tse-tung and other Communist leaders always attended. Mao, dressed in a white shirt and dark trousers without a jacket, danced with the girls who asked him and mixed with the other guests. A national government major and a colonel, nominally on liaison duty, were always invited to the entertainments and were treated with great courtesy.

No troop or soldier dance band from the United Service Organizations (USO) ever visited the Yenan Observer Group. Other people did, however. Sometimes they seemed to come in droves. Once, some visiting dignitaries from Chungking brought a gas-powered movie projector and a film that played again and again to a packed house. Eventually, the Office of War Information gave the Chinese a projector. The Dixie Mission borrowed it to show films to visitors brought in on the weekly plane. Ultimately, the Chinese also acquired a new phonograph and records and received such things as liquor, tobacco, and American-style food from the same source.

Many of the Chinese Communist leaders attended the films regularly, although Mao and his wife came only rarely. In spring 1946, however, Madame Mao began attending more frequently, which Young regarded as a sign that the Communists still held the group in high regard even though relations with the United States were deteriorating rapidly. When the Americans knew the Chinese were coming, they made an effort to show musicals rather than complicated stories that would be hard to translate as they flashed on the screen. Sometimes before the show General Yeh would talk politics, especially American politics, through a translator. Everyone, both Chinese and American, watched each film many times, to fill otherwise empty evenings.[14]

In July 1945, John Colling, an OSS man attached to Dixie, made a motion picture entitled *Mission to Yenan,* about daily life in the group and the demonstrations that OSS was giving the Communists. He sent the completed film to OSS headquarters in Chungking at about the time that Commanding General Alfred C. Wedemeyer ordered a directive distributed throughout the theater, including to OSS. Among other things, the new policy instructed the people in Yenan to distance themselves from the Chinese Communists, not provide them with arms, ammunition, or supplies, and to make no commitments to them.[15] Because of this order, Colonel Richard P. Heppner, head of OSS Chungking, decided to submit the script of Colling's movie to Patrick J. Hurley, the American ambassador to China. Heppner worried that although the script was not objectionable from a factual point of view and did not go into large political issues or compare the Nationalists and the Communists, some parts of it were fairly enthusiastic about the project underway in Yenan.[16] Although the Ambassador was anxious to show the film, he had insisted on seeing the text first.[17] In the fifty years since the film's production, clips from it have been used in several documentaries dealing with twentieth-century China.

On evenings when there was no movie or party, the men stationed in Yenan gathered around the radio to hear the war news. They quickly learned that news about China was seldom mentioned. Usually, one man with earphones listened to the 11:00 A.M. broadcast from Honolulu, typed it out, and posted it on the bulletin board. Sometimes more printed information was available from enemy sources than from the Allies. The Tokyo newspaper *Asahi* reached Yenan about ten days after publication, which Barrett considered pretty good and an example of the Chinese Communists' efficiency. He believed they combed the *Asahi* for military information.[18]

In sum, with duties to perform, local places of interest and importance to explore, and dances and other forms of entertainment in which they could participate, the men of the U.S. Army Observer Group had no problem keeping busy. When they had the time or inclination for "back home" exercise, they played Ping-Pong or volleyball, sometimes against the Chinese, and, once, softball against the Japanese prisoners of war, as traditional security hardly existed in Yenan.[19]

Pheasant hunting was an especially popular pastime. The mountains seemed to have unlimited birds but no game wardens. Sometimes hunting and exploring were combined, as when Brooke Dolan and his friend Major David R. Gascoyne said they were going on a "road surveying" trip to Chien-Lu on the Tibet border. They were actually going to hunt wild goat.

The crews that flew planes to Yenan always wanted to go after pheasants. Often they and the men of Dixie hunted together with the Communist leaders, like General Chu Teh, who was especially fond of the sport. They would drive trucks into the mountains as far as they could, then switch to horses, accompanied by Chu's soldiers. The Chinese gently helped them on and off the animals, held onto the reins when they headed downhill so that the riders did not fall off, and carried their rifles until the hunters wanted to take a shot. On expeditions like these, the Americans always let Chu take the first shot.

The most important, most anticipated event in Yenan was the arrival of an airplane, especially the courier plane that flew in from Shanghai approximately every two weeks. When the men heard the drone of engines overhead, they all headed out to the airfield. Morale sagged anytime the expected plane failed to appear.

When a plane left for Yenan, notice was to be wired ahead in time for the radio beam at Yenan airfield to be turned on to guide it in. It was not uncommon, however, for planes to arrive unannounced or for the wire to arrive only shortly before the plane. Occasionally the news of a scheduled flight arrived two or three hours after the plane had come and gone. These irregularities sometimes meant that needed supplies were not delivered. According to Young, Yeaton moaned when the Thanksgiving turkey had not arrived by December 10 and the men had to eat canned turkey and Spam on the holiday.

The group needed items from the outside world to make life bearable, and some things were of course essential to complete the assigned tasks. They needed spare parts for bicycles and fuel for vehicles, for example, although the unit had relatively little mechanized transportation—two quarter-ton jeeps, four three-quarter-ton weapons carriers, and a few bicycles. In winter, the men used alcohol as antifreeze or drained the truck radiators every night to prevent them from freezing and cracking. It was a serious matter when an engine block cracked or a piece of equipment broke down or wore out, because the Mission's isolation made it difficult to get replacements. Sometimes it was even a challenge to get the men new clothes and the charcoal and sadirons needed to press them.[20]

Lieutenant Colonel Wilbur J. Peterkin, Barrett's successor, wanted planes to be sent up more frequently. He also complained that new arrivals had to be put up in the Chinese guest houses two miles away because living quarters were so crowded. According to Peterkin, conditions were so tight that all working space was preempted for sleeping quarters, with the result that the men worked and slept in the same room. Even the commanding officer had to bunk with two other offic-

Building the airstrip in Yenan in the fall of 1944. Courtesy of Jack Klein.

ers. Such circumstances made concentration difficult and conferences hard to arrange. At one point, three men were sharing one typewriter, while a fourth was writing his reports in longhand. The lack of privacy and space also led Peterkin to request a safe, so that he could secure papers and money.[21]

In spite of its crude beginnings, the Mission gradually began to resemble a small army post. Jointly the Americans and Chinese put in a new airstrip long enough and strong enough to accommodate C-46s, B-25s, B-24s, and B-29s if they took off lightly loaded.[22] The men also erected a kitchen and mess hall and replaced the trestle beds with bunk beds with rope "springs." Of course, construction materials had to be flown in for the new buildings and the airstrip. The completed structures housed weather equipment and personnel, a power plant, radio sets, an encrypting room, an order-of-battle workroom, and a darkroom.[23] There the men developed the many pictures they took on their travels or when they roamed Yenan, as they did freely. Mr. Wu, who was in charge of the Chinese Communist photographic unit, also used the Dixie darkroom, sometimes for himself and sometimes for the Americans. He was not paid money for his work but was given gifts of film and other hard-to-get photographic supplies.

The Dixie Mission was not run like an ordinary military post. For instance, there was no morning report, as in most units. While the men reported to Dixie's commanding officer, they also reported to the units from which they had been sent to Yenan.[24] The lack of strict regimentation originated with Barrett. Nevertheless, the men considered him astute. They particularly respected his command of many Chinese dialects, an accomplishment in which he took great pride. He had long experience in China, as did many of those who served in this unit, especially the original participants. Several were old China hands, missionary children, or both.[25]

Inevitably, however, there were personnel problems. Some were relatively minor and easy to solve. On one occasion, for example, Walter Gress made a pass at a Chinese girl during a dance. The Chinese were prim about relations between their women and the American servicemen. Chou En-lai told Barrett that they frowned upon flirtatious behavior except between two people who were really in love. Barrett immediately warned Gress that he would be relieved of his duty with the group if such an incident occurred again. There is no evidence that it did.[26]

Other problems had to do with the inner workings of the group. Peterkin grumbled that a G-2 officer should be sent to Yenan to train new men, since Dixie was, after all, a G-2 mission. He was also worried because there were only two sergeants who knew order of battle (three were needed).

Sometimes the men drank too much. The commanding officer found this problem especially difficult to handle when the drinker was an officer because of the close contact between officers and enlisted men. Peterkin considered Stelle, for example, a "brilliant, lazy drunk." Captain James Eaton from Air Ground Aid Service was irritating in a different way because he harbored the "empire-building" ideas that Peterkin associated with AGAS. Peterkin did not care much for Army Airways Communication System (AACS) either and considered its members malcontents, troublemakers, and goldbricks. Major Clifford Young was unhappy with Corporal William Eng, his mess sergeant, who seemed unable to learn how to keep the mess accounts straight.

Some incipient feuding took place among the men too.[27] In some cases, inevitably, it was exacerbated by an individual's idiosyncrasies. Ray Cromley, for example, had a penchant for sleeping all day and working all night. Cromley had worked in Japan as a reporter for the *Wall Street Journal* when the war broke out. He was captured by the Japanese and spent some time in solitary confinement, where he was allowed only one cup of water per day, to use as he wished. According to Charles Dole, one of the Mission members, the experience continued to affect Cromley's bathing habits. In Yenan Cromley allegedly washed from a cup using his fingers. Cromley regularly received jars of cream deodorant from home, which he kept lined up on his window ledge.

Another, less innocent idiosyncrasy was Brooke Dolan's habit of playing with his loaded .45 in the cave. One time it went off. The bullet ricocheted around the cave and terrified Charles Dole, his roommate. Dolan, who was smart but unstable, committed suicide after the war.[28]

Several of the men experienced depression in the lonely circumstances of Yenan. In April 1946, when there were only three men left, Corporal Eng became so melancholy that his commanding officer considered sending him away. Eng's mood was exacerbated by the lack of rations, gasoline, and movies; the mission was closing down at the time.[29] Still, there were relatively few incidents involving serious gloom or bizarre behavior—remarkably few, given that normal people often act strangely in settings as unusual as Yenan. Furthermore, many of those sent to Dixie were young single men, who tend to be less stable than older married soldiers.[30]

Before he became commanding officer, Peterkin and several others made a four-month trip to Fouping, behind the Japanese lines. Barrett directed Peterkin to examine the organization, arms, and equipment of the Chinese Communists as well as their physical condition, food and clothing, morale, and intelligence potential. He was to note the type, number, and condition of their weapons and determine how many had been salvaged from Kuomintang throwaways, how many had been captured from the enemy or from friendly troops, and how many had been manufactured by the Communists themselves. Peterkin was also asked to determine the extent to which the Chinese Communists were fighting the Japanese, if at all, and to make a general estimate of their particular capabilities and weaknesses. He was expected to observe firsthand the relations between the Chinese Communist Army and the people, as well as to scrutinize their training facilities and make a determination regarding their army's ability to support itself by its own production. Barrett hoped that Peterkin and the men with him would be able to bring back newspapers and periodicals.

The trip to Fouping was almost 1,000 miles each way. The men, riding mules with wooden saddles, were escorted by 1,200-1,500 Communist Chinese troops. One detachment accompanied them for a while before being replaced by another. Villagers along the way served the troops hot water and gruel. Colonel Peterkin carried documents identifying himself as an officer on a special mission for the government of

Peterkin says farewell to Barrett on leaving for Fouping, October 6, 1944. Courtesy of Col. Wilbur J. Peterkin.

the United States and asking all military and civilian authorities along the route to extend him every possible courtesy.

The observers moved at night when the Japanese were nearby, which was mainly in the mountains. As they traveled they met puppet prisoners traveling unguarded. They visited hospitals where medical personnel used red lead, garlic, and opium to cure opium addiction and where patients had to go two miles from the hospital to receive x-rays. They inspected airfields and saw a military academy and a school for training teachers. The Chinese staged demonstrations and drills for their benefit and feted and fed them at each stop. John Colling once showed their hosts how to use locally made mines. They observed the Min Ping, or People's Militia, planting land mines, saw peasants buying food and fleeing from the Japanese, and noticed that the Japanese had laid waste to several of the villages they passed. Children followed the Americans everywhere. One day they met a traveling opera company, its gear packed in boxes precariously balanced on mules. The women with the opera company also rode mules, some carrying one or more of the dozen Pekingese lapdogs that appeared to be part of the entourage.

At most places where the observers spent the night, doors were taken down and were placed across sawhorses, with air mattresses laid

Fording the river, October 1944, with Li Hsiao-t'ang and another guide leading. Members of Dixie are, left to right: Dolan, Gress, Ludden, Whittlesey, and Domke. Courtesy of Col. Wilbur J. Peterkin.

on top to create makeshift beds for the travelers. Sometimes the Chinese presented them with gifts such as small squares of native silk. Occasionally, they ate in village restaurants, sitting on stools only six inches high and eating from foot-high tables.[31]

On this trip and others, the Americans saw caves and tunnels that the Chinese had rigged for defense. They hid one entrance beneath the mud of a pigpen, located another behind a false rock in front of a manger, and concealed a third under the false side of a low clay bed. The Americans crawled through tunnels filled with mantraps designed to make it easy to shoot the head of a Japanese soldier coming through. Little recesses had been dug into the side walls and filled with oil that could be lighted. These tunnels were lighted in such a way as to conceal the marksmen stationed there while illuminating the mantraps. One trap was an eight-foot plank placed across a hole thirty feet deep. If the Japanese came, the plank would be pulled away. Sometimes the Communists rolled a millstone across a tunnel or blocked it with heavy timbers to keep out the Japanese. An entire village could disappear into these tunnels in twenty minutes. A village of 200 families might access two miles of winding tunnel by perhaps fifteen entrances. The tunnels,

Building caves for U.S. personnel in Fouping, November 1944. Courtesy of Col. Wilbur J. Peterkin.

like wells, were first constructed from the bases of newly driven shafts. As soon as one had been extended in either direction to the next site, say 150 meters away, a section was constructed that bypassed the shaft and joined the two extensions. The original hole was then filled. Though they were constructed without bracing, the tunnels rarely collapsed, because they were dug in clay soil. There was no ventilation or sanitation provisions in the tunnels. The Japanese tried to find these tunnels when they entered a deserted village. When they did, they dropped tear gas bombs and grenades into them.[32]

Peterkin stayed in Fouping, the behind-the-lines headquarters of the Chinese Communist guerrillas, until December 28, 1944. He and his men toured Communist arsenals, drug factories, and medical schools. They inspected the Keken-Hankow Railroad, where the Japanese had erected blockhouses about every one-third mile, each manned by an armed watchman who scanned the countryside. Once, ten Japanese from a blockhouse attempted to intercept the Americans, who used fast footwork to get away. They were lucky to have escaped, since a reward had been posted for Peterkin: $5,000 dead or alive.

For this and other trips, the Americans dressed in Chinese clothes made of padded cotton. Goatskin overcoats worn with the hair on the inside protected them when the strong winds blew. Most of the peasants in Shensi Province lived in unfurnished caves that were cool in summer and warm in winter. The family slept on a *k'ang,* a mud or brick platform through which a flue ran back and forth, supplying heat. A stove with a large semicircular iron pot built into it was connected to the k'ang. The family used the pot for cooking. Their diet was limited to rice and millet, small quantities of Chinese cabbage and occasionally other vegetables, and a little meat. People commonly ate garlic raw, by the clove.

Party members usually sent their children to a community center for child care and sometimes saw them only once or twice a month. Each family had a spinning wheel, and each person had a bowl, a set of chopsticks, and four or five jars for food storage. There were no closets or chairs. In winter the Chinese wore all of their clothes all the time— three or four padded suits, one on top of the other. In the north, men and women dressed the same. Most cut their hair in a short bob and wore a dull blue cotton cap, pants, and a jacket. It was so hard to tell a man from a woman that more than once the GIs attending the dances in the pear orchard cut in on two girls dancing only to find themselves dancing with a man. Women eschewed cosmetics in the north, but in the south a lipstick could bring as much as fifteen dollars in gold coin. Women in the south wore dresses. Much of the clothing worn by men, women, and children was knitted. Throughout China a peasant usually sewed himself into his knitted underwear in the early winter and did not take it off until spring.

The group from Dixie stayed in Fouping over Christmas. Although their hosts opposed all religion for Marxian reasons, they put hospitality first and held a big feast honoring the holiday. They presented Peterkin with gifts of smoked roast chicken, knit caps and scarves, brandy, a Japanese officer's overcoat, and the Chinese conception of an American cake.[33]

Actually, the Communists scrupulously observed days that they knew the Americans regarded as important. On Christmas Eve the Chinese never failed to send formal good wishes. On Christmas Eve, 1945, the Mission invited some of the most important of the Chinese to dinner and a movie. An exchange of gifts took place, although as usual they had to be selected from the limited number of items available. For Chinese New Year, 1946, Colonel Yeaton received a lamb and a chicken. Theater headquarters tried not to overlook these men stationed far away. General Wedemeyer sent, via courier plane, a Christmas tree with ornaments and the makings of a special meal and provided each man with a quart of Scotch.[34] Very stern, always polite, and quite kind, the Communists laughed and joked, but the Americans thought that they took themselves and their Spartan life very seriously.

They were "a people apart from the average Chinese in that they have a mission." There were no visible class differences between shopkeepers, workers, and peasants. One never saw the heavy black cane that members of the upper ruling class carried in their travels elsewhere in China.[35]

Peterkin's group left Fouping and returned to Yenan by a more direct route, though it was still a 600-mile journey that was not completed until January 23. Most of the men walked, as it was too cold to ride the mules.[36] The travelers brought back a pile of gifts and artifacts. One was a 7.9mm rifle, a locally made copy of a Mauser, called in South China the "Generalissimo." It had been made from rails taken from the Ping Han Railroad turned on a lathe powered by four or five men in a "squirrel cage" who ran for one minute before being replaced. A total of sixteen men had been involved in the gun's manufacture.

Another weapon they brought back was the "guerrilla," a one-shot pistol manufactured like the 7.9mm rifle. Because it often misfired, it was primarily a badge of office for local guerrilla leaders. There were also "potato mashers," small hand grenades specially designed for use by women and children.[37]

Once back in Yenan, Peterkin wrote a number of reports detailing his observations. He noted that the Chinese Communists gathered intelligence from a variety of sources. They relied mainly on civilians, many of whom were behind Japanese lines and were paid a little money to serve as informants. Peterkin was impressed that the Communists could operate, within twenty-five miles of the Japanese lines, a munitions plant that turned out rifles and pistols made from railroad steel using hand-powered lathes. He was also impressed by the contrast between his observations in the field and his knowledge of the Kuomintang. While the Chinese Communists paid their soldiers little, a man could work in his spare time, and the sum of his incomes, though not lavish, afforded him enough to survive. Communist uniforms were in good condition, and morale was high—a different situation from that in the Kuomintang, where morale was low and where officers, often men who had used political pull to get their commissions, were frequently of poor quality. The Nationalist government was so graft-ridden that in areas it controlled, lend-lease items were the goods most commonly available for sale.[38]

Men were loath to serve in the Nationalist Army and had to be roped together and dragged to the recruiting centers. Sometimes they were locked in jails so that they would not run away. No one from the Dixie Mission ever reported seeing men resist military duty in the Communist parts of China, nor were officers there ever seen to strike en-

listed men, as officers commonly did elsewhere in the country. Sometimes, however, Barrett had reason to suspect that the Communists did
not have things altogether under control. Once he and Chou En-lai
went through a village that appeared so unusually clean that Barrett felt
prompted to remark that it reminded him of Potemkin's habit of putting the Russian countryside in order whenever Catherine the Great
was passing through.

As his men were traveling to Fouping, Barrett made a trip to Suiteh,
approximately eighty miles northeast of Yenan, to see the Second Battalion of the Japanese Resistance Military-Political University. The road
from Yenan to Suiteh was very bad. It followed a fair-sized river almost
all the way, and there were no bridges. Rivers without bridges were not
uncommon, because in many parts of China there was no forest cover,
and most precipitation ran immediately into nearby streams. A dry
streambed could become a raging torrent virtually overnight. Bridges
therefore had to be built high, with strong abutments and long ap-
proaches, or they would not survive. At the time of Barrett's journey,
the river along the way to Suiteh was about three feet deep in mid-
stream, and its waters concealed many rocks capable of overturning a
jeep. For this reason Barrett insisted on driving himself, although he

Barrett and Ludden stuck in the Yen River, September 1944. Courtesy of Col.
Wilbur J. Peterkin.

had a Chinese chauffeur. Sometimes his jeep frightened mules that were pulling wagons or carrying peasants. The trip took almost two days because of the road conditions. The men stopped overnight in a village, and Barrett slept on a k'ang.

Before touring the university, Barrett examined the city of Suiteh. In the meantime the citizens examined him. People crowded as close as the Communist guide would permit while the two men walked through town. Barrett noticed that most of the articles for sale were homemade and utilitarian. The university disappointed him. He had expected to find a military school but instead found a sort of recreational and rest center for party workers, officers, and enlisted men. The place had no special buildings. The Communists had taken over a small village on the outskirts of the city and had driven out the inhabitants so as to use their houses for barracks and classrooms. The people at the school put on a demonstration of troops performing calisthenics and close-order drill and staged a sham battle. There seemed to be little classroom study. Back in Yenan, General Yeh Chien-ying asked Barrett what he thought of the university. Barrett replied that it had a major problem: it was a military school that did not teach military training.[39]

At no time during their stay in Yenan did a member of the Dixie Mission see police or similar law enforcement personnel of the sort that outsiders usually associate with repressive societies. They knew, however, that there was a concentration camp not far from their quarters where the Communists confined persons considered suspect. The Americans learned about this place from a tall, young Yugoslav who showed up in camp one day wearing a Communist uniform. He told them that his name was Dimitri Yellacich and that before Pearl Harbor he had been working for a Ford automobile dealer in Peking. Afterward he had left the city and traveled, mostly on foot, through Hopei and Shansi Provinces to Yenan, where the Communists had kept him until the day before he saw the Americans. He spoke good English and mixed freely with the group but never discussed his experiences living with the Communists. He had apparently arrived in Yenan in good physical condition, not abused, and had gone to work promptly for the Communists as a motor mechanic. He maintained their two trucks (one was so old that it had a little wood-burning stove that generated heat and steam to start it) and their two equally old passenger cars. Until the Americans got a mechanic of their own, Yellacich also took care of their jeep. Barrett liked Yellacich and recommended that his background be checked out so that he could be commissioned in the American army, but nothing came of the suggestion. Peterkin took him along when he and a couple of American engineers investigated the oil fields forty or fifty miles from Yenan.

Yellacich worried about the validity of his passport, since his country, which had been conquered by Germany, had in a sense ceased to exist. He asked Peterkin to go to the Russian embassy when he was in Chungking to see whether it would update his passport. Peterkin did, explaining things and giving the passport to the Russian ambassador, who said it would have to go to Moscow because he could not do anything personally. Peterkin went back to the embassy three or four weeks later and subsequently made repeated attempts to complete the transaction, but he never got back Yellacich's passport or received a satisfactory explanation of why it had not been returned.[40]

During his sixteen-day visit to the Dixie Mission, John Davies made a point of eliciting Yellacich's views about the Communists. Davies noted in his diary that the man was a Yugoslav with a Russian mother and that he looked Eurasian because of his Mongoloid eyes and indeterminate complexion. He wore a North China teamster's gray felt cap with a long flap for the back of the neck, a peaked visor flap, and two ear flaps, all turned up and tied on top. His jacket was very old and worn, with leather patches on the elbow, but Davies thought it must once have been very sporty. His trousers were wadded cotton. Davies regarded Yellacich as having one foot in each of two cultures.

Yellacich told Davies that although the Chinese Communists wore no insignia, there was a difference between officers and men and that the officers lived and ate better. The Red soldiers were not beaten, as they were in other Chinese armies, however, and the army was considerate of the people—too much so, he thought. In policy disputes between the army and the people, the people were always judged right. Yellacich told Davies that the Japanese kept the railroads from being sabotaged by holding the villages responsible for their security. When sabotage nevertheless occurred, nearby villages were subjected to fierce punitive action. Yellacich was very impressed with the fighting ability of the Eighth Route Army and the Shantung guerrillas. He thought that, given enough ammunition, the northern Communist armies and militia could tie up Japanese communications.[41]

In the 1950s, Alfred Harding, who had joined Dixie in January 1945, saw Yellacich in Hong Kong. The man said he was on his way back to Yugoslavia and was helping the Chinese dig an oil well. He claimed to have acquired rope and composition C from Barrett for the purpose, but Harding never verified this report.[42]

Many "outsiders" were interested in the work of the American detachment in Yenan. As a result, the Mission had so many visitors that Peterkin complained. Some of the guests were newspapermen or writers, like Harrison Forman and Theodore White. Visiting newsmen had

the run of the compound and could photograph freely and travel behind the Japanese lines. They were expected to observe protocol, such
as not letting politics intrude on social occasions. When Associated Press
correspondent John Roderick used a New Year's Day dinner as an opportunity to interrogate General Chu Teh about Chiang Kai-shek's
Three Point proposal, Colonel Yeaton became bored, then angry. Most
of the journalists stayed ten days to two weeks, the usual length of time
between planes, but Roderick arrived in Yenan on December 3, 1945,
for a "short visit" and stayed until April, much to the displeasure of
Yeaton and Clifford Young, his executive officer.

Journalist Anna Louis Strong also irritated Yeaton because she
expected to be catered to. The afternoon of her arrival, Mr. Yang, the
secretary-general of the Chinese Communist Party, went to her cave
and talked with her at length. After they had finished talking, she instructed him and Major Young to move the furniture around, giving
the impression that although she subscribed to Communist ideology,
in her opinion the Chinese were still coolies. Young noticed that in the
twenty days she was there, Strong took only one shower.

Women writers like Anna Louise Strong were the only non-Chi-
nese Communist women in the area except for the girlfriends of junketeers. The Communists treated them all politely, even Freda Utley, who
represented *Reader's Digest* and who had written critically about them.
Another woman, Mrs. Campbell, flew up from Chungking sitting next
to General Chou En-lai. Not knowing who he was, she commented:
"These Communists are a bunch of nit-wits."[43]

The junketeers, military people or politicians, went to Yenan to
see the sights, to hunt pheasant, or, like General Randall of the 312th
Spider Wing, to impress their girlfriends. Regardless of their background,
Peterkin usually found visits from these individuals a nuisance. People
of little or no military significance disturbed his routine. Guests had to
be shown the town and points of interest and usually wanted to do the
shops. After a while, Peterkin began providing very thorough inspection tours. The less interested the visitor was in military matters, the
more detailed the tour.

The Chinese did not restrict the movements of these visitors or
the above-mentioned journalists, although the terrain somewhat limited them and mules were the main form of transport. Harrison Forman,
from the *Times* of London, made quite an impression. The man weighed
about 300 pounds and virtually ruined the animal.

Occasionally, the men assigned to the Mission were as annoying
to the commander as the junketeers. One was Winston Churchill Guest,
an American in AGAS who was related to the British prime minister.

Guest was very anxious to go behind the Japanese lines, but Peterkin did not allow him to do so. He was six feet six inches tall and therefore easy to spot, and his naturally officious manner made him less than competent in dealing with the Chinese Communists.[44]

One man who was not part of the Mission but who frequently mixed with it was Dr. Michael Lindsay, later Lord Lindsay of Birker. Lindsay was the son of the master of Balliol College, Oxford, and an economist by trade. Before Pearl Harbor he had been teaching in Yenching University, where he lived with his Chinese wife. On the side he also taught guerrillas how to blow up railroads. After Pearl Harbor he and his wife went to Chin-Cha-Chi, where he became the Chinese Communists' principal radio technical adviser.[45] While not representing himself as a Communist, Lindsay openly expressed great sympathy for the Communist program.[46]

Another interesting man who interacted with the Dixie Mission was Ma Haide. "Doc Ma" had been born George Hatem in North Carolina. In the 1930s he attended medical school at Chapel Hill until he got into trouble and went to Europe. There he met Edgar Snow, whom he accompanied to China. He met and married a beautiful Chinese woman, and though he had never completed his formal medical studies, he began practicing medicine. While the Dixie Mission was at Yenan, Doc Ma was accepted into the Communist Party. He often acted as Dixie's interpreter, for even though many members of the group spoke fluent Chinese, the Communists always had an interpreter present.[47] Ma was actually an American, but the Chinese accepted him as one of their own.

Ma hobnobbed with the journalists and Foreign Service dignitaries who flew in and out of Yenan and provided them and the other Americans with some interesting insights into Communist thinking. He told John Davies and Theodore White, for instance, that the Communists feared the British. They worried, he said, that the British might use Chiang Kai-shek to divide South China into the old spheres of influence. The Communists wanted to move slowly and make every attempt to compromise in order to avert the possible splitting of China in two, according to Doc Ma. He was assigned to White and Davies during their stay and returned home only on weekends. Davies suspected that the close contact with American language and breeziness, cigarettes, field jackets, and GI boots made Doc Ma homesick.[48]

After the war, Doc Ma remained in China to become one of China's leading medical authorities and a folk hero. The accomplishments of his postwar career included the creation of a program that is credited by the Chinese with having conquered leprosy and venereal disease in China.[49]

Doc Ma did not present himself to Dixie as a healer. Rather he served as a sympathetic, informal liaison between the Mission and the Chinese. In the beginning, the unit's official medic was Melvin Casberg, who had met Barrett in May 1944, when the latter had been hospitalized in Chungking for hepatitis. The two men became friends. Barrett asked Casberg if he would be interested in joining the group he expected to be taking to Yenan. Casberg thought it might be interesting duty and agreed to go. Once the Mission had been established, Barrett told Casberg that he could do as he pleased once he had taken care of the Mission's medical needs. Casberg quickly discovered that the Chinese doctors in Yenan were fairly good, so he turned his medical practice over to Doc Ma, whom he had helped care for Mao's wife when she had bronchitis. Casberg gave Doc Ma an army medical kit, which Ma later placed in a museum.

Casberg then approached Barrett for a broader assignment. Barrett gave him permission to investigate medical practice among the Chinese in the vicinity. The commanding officer told him to check out their facilities and determine whether they could use American equipment if it could be brought in.

First, Casberg explored the area close to Yenan, going to medical schools, meeting with nursing personnel, and trying to gauge the level of local professional skill. Afterward, he went to Barrett and said that he

Some of the Dixie Mission members go to visit the cave hospital in Yenan. Courtesy of Jack Klein.

could not learn anything about how the Chinese evaluated their patients or how the troops were handled by sitting in a chair in Yenan. To do so he needed to go into combat with the Communist troops. Barrett liked the idea and told him that while he was at it he should find out whatever he could about morale and other matters of interest. Casberg then headed out, accompanied by an interpreter and a muleteer. When they reached Japanese territory, the party picked up an additional two or three people who knew the terrain. Once some Mongolians joined them. The Mongolians rode small ponies with level saddles. Sometimes, if they were riding in front, they would turn their bodies around by flipping their legs into the air. The advent of the Mongolians worried Casberg because he knew that the Japanese had put a price on his head.

Over a two-month period Casberg covered hundreds of miles. He sometimes felt psychologically isolated and lonely. He helped evacuate and care for the wounded and gave the Chinese advice on how to nurse their sick.[50] He briefly ran across journalists Maurice Votaw, Israel Epstein, and Harrison Forman, who had left a couple of days before him to go behind Japanese lines.

When Casberg returned to Yenan, he wrote a detailed report that Barrett sent to CBI headquarters. Besides Casberg's professional medical observations, it included an account of a Communist attack that he had witnessed on a Japanese-held village.[51] Casberg also shared his opinions about what he had seen with Doc Ma and Yeh Chien-ying, commander of the Eighth Route Army. He amused them by saying he thought the medical system he had seen in the course of his travels was not sufficiently Communistic. Casberg said that the level of medical care he had seen varied greatly, because some doctors had trained at the Union Medical College, while others had not and were therefore mediocre. When a man who was a professor in a medical college moved, he would take his equipment with him, so that a hospital was sometimes left completely without equipment.

Casberg had noticed that the Chinese Communists always evacuated their wounded, even men who would clearly not live. He wanted them to move some of the doctors with better training near the front so that they could recommend treatment, instead of having to rely solely on medics who carried a little opium but little else in the way of medical supplies. He also suggested the establishment of additional special relief hospitals, to enable the few specialized doctors to serve a large area. Casberg had observed that where such facilities had been created, the doctors had taken over a few caves. A small field hospital might use twelve or so caves close to a combat zone, so that the wounded could be transported to them in less than three or four days. The doors could easily be removed, and in times of danger the doors were lifted out and laid flat, so that patients could be placed on them for transport into the mountains to hide. The nurses then took guns and planted land mines, stringing horse hair across the path to make a trip. The nurses also set up cannons and hid in trenches from which they could control the road.[52]

Captain Julius Pomeranze replaced Casberg as doctor after Casberg left the Mission. Peterkin, then the commanding officer, was pleased with the new medic, because he quickly began to improve mess and sanitary conditions, got along well with the Chinese, and showed real interest in his profession. Peterkin wrote Dickey that Pomeranze planned to do some work in the local hospitals, which he thought would foster goodwill. Furthermore, the Americans sometimes had to use the local hospitals, and some of the men were afraid of getting sick and having to go there for treatment. That was the situation when Nomura had an emergency appendectomy in March 1945. Peterkin concluded that the men of the Mission felt better with GI doctors.[53]

During their stay, the Americans helped the Chinese through more than one medical crisis. In January 1946, for example, an epidemic of spinal meningitis broke out. The local medical authorities had their hands full. Dixie had no resident medic at that time, because Casberg and his successors had been sent elsewhere. Clifford Young, acting commanding officer in Yeaton's absence, administered sulfadiazine and wired Shanghai to send up 1 million units of penicillin. He also put all the Americans on the base under quarantine because there had been eighteen cases of the disease among the Chinese and two deaths. Young's appeal for American medicine to help the Communists was not considered unusual. Red Cross medical supplies were frequently flown up on American planes.[54]

Casberg and Doc Ma were not the only foreign doctors in Yenan. Also present were Hans Mueller, a Russian named Dr. Andre Yakovlevich Orloff, and Dr. Fry, an Austrian Jew who had fled Tientsin in 1942 to work for the Communists. These men had no medicines, but Fry was very inventive and grew penicillin cultures, which he used on badly infected wounds even though they were not pure. Fry believed in acupuncture, both as a preventive and as a remedy, and he claimed to have cured malaria with it. Fry was anxious to acquire Casberg's medical knowledge, although Casberg did not share Fry's faith in the needles. Casberg made Fry happy by giving him a military trench coat and some hiking boots to replace his homespun sandals, but what pleased the European doctors most was copies of articles from Casberg's medical journals.[55]

Orloff was a surgeon who had been called into the Russian army in 1938. He had served at Lake Nomanhan and in the Finnish War and was granted three years' leave of absence in 1942 and flown to Yenan.[56] He did not mix with the Dixie Mission men, but Casberg saw him at the hospital. Once Casberg asked him how he liked being out in the boondocks, to which Orloff replied that being in Yenan was better than being in Finland.[57]

The Russian news agency TASS had two representatives in Yenan. They were known by their Chinese names, Kuo Li and Sheng Ping. Kuo Li's real name was Proshenko. Sheng Ping was the pseudonym of Peter Vladimirov. They were about twenty-six and forty years of age, respectively, in 1944. About two years earlier, they had replaced other correspondents who had been assigned to Yenan. Although they said they dispatched news only through Chungking, they employed Chinese translators and appeared to collect a large amount of material that they probably smuggled out. Michael Lindsay, who served as a radio adviser to the Chinese Communists and who visited the Russians' quarters, claimed that they had no radio equipment except a receiver.

Whether Orloff, Vladimirov, or Proshenko had special liaison responsibilities to Mao seemed unimportant to John Service and others in Dixie. Service did not believe that Orloff and the other Russians were important individuals, because none of them spoke Chinese, had the earmarks of "China experts," or appeared to be on close terms with the major Chinese Communist leaders. Service later said that everyone knew Vladimirov was a Soviet watchdog, but there were things the Communists were doing that he did not learn about for many years. The Communists raised opium north of Yenan, for instance, to trade with the Japanese-occupied cities for medicines and other items that the Communists needed. Service himself did not hear about this commerce until 1993. While Dixie was present, the Russians were not accorded the "face," or status, shown to Okano Susumu, the Japanese Communist who was in Yenan during much of this period, and they were rarely seen except at large social occasions, when they were only part of the crowd. Except for a number of White Russian refugees from cities like Tientsin, most of whom were treated with suspicion as probable Japanese spies, no other Russians appeared in the Yenan area on a regular basis.[58]

Once, while Clifford Young commanded the Mission, he found himself unable to cross the swollen river to return to the American compound. As a result he had an impromptu evening get-together with the Russians, with tidbits to eat and a samovar and cognac. When Young sipped his drink, the Russians laughed and told him through an interpreter that what he was doing was not Sovietsky, which they explained meant drinking a whole glass at once. "Well," said Young, "in order to maintain the honor of the U.S. government, I'll drink Sovietsky," and he did. Wine followed, which was also drunk Sovietsky from a tumbler, and more cognac. Then it started to rain, and Young and Mr. Yang headed to Yang's cave. Young felt he had proven that Americans were not sissies.

On January 7, 1946, two Russian planes flew into Yenan. The Chinese gave the Americans no explanation. The Americans assumed that the pilots stayed in the Chinese Communists' guest house. The airmen, bedecked with beautiful medals, flatly refused to let the Dixie people photograph either them or their planes, which sat next to a C-47 that had come to take Yeaton to Chungking to see Marshall. As the Russians were getting ready to leave, however, Yeaton ordered Young to go inside the C-47 and take pictures of the Russian planes through a window.

Once, a Nationalist aviator tired of the civil war flew his bomber to Yenan, landed on the airfield, and defected. The Communists pushed and dragged his aircraft by hand into one of the valleys in an attempt to conceal it, but a few days later a sortie of fighters came, circled the field several times, and strafed the plane. The next day a bomber appeared, flew over Yenan several times, and on its last run dropped a string of bombs in an unsuccessful effort to destroy the aircraft. Neither the Chinese Communists nor the Americans had the proper weaponry to respond to such an aerial attack. Eventually, the Chinese dismantled the defector's plane to salvage its parts.

Not every Nationalist visit was unfriendly. In December 1945, a C-47 bearing Kuomintang markings brought three letter cases. The pilots stayed overnight in the Chinese Communist guest house. At night they visited the American camp to watch the movie. The next day a Nationalist plane from Sian arrived, which Mao and Chou En-lai greeted. The following month, a Kuomintang P-40 buzzed Yenan. As it passed over the compound, it dropped leaflets signed by Chiang Kai-shek announcing peace terms. The pamphlets landed just outside the compound, in the empty space by the river. People swarmed to get copies.[59]

While many aspects of the Dixie Mission are open to debate, all the participants agree that one of its greatest tragedies occurred when the Japanese killed Captain Henry C. Whittlesey, of AGAS. Whittlesey's job was to set up a sort of chain for evacuating downed fliers. Accompanied by a Communist photographer, he went to an area close to the Japanese lines. The two men entered a village the Communists had told them was clear of the enemy. When they entered the town, however, it turned out that Japanese snipers were still there. They killed both

Whittlesey and the photographer. The Chinese Communists tried in vain to retrieve their bodies and lost many men in the attempt. The Chinese were extremely distressed, not only because of their own loss and their high regard for Whittlesey, but also because they had lost face, since Whittlesey had entered the village after they had assured him there were no Japanese in it. Whittlesey might have avoided death if he had followed Casberg's advice, which was never to sleep or rest in villages. The saddened men of the Dixie Mission honored their comrade by naming their new mess hall Whittlesey Hall.[60]

Apart from the loss of Whittlesey and the discomfort that followed the deterioration of American relations with the Chinese Communists, the Dixie Mission experienced few unpleasant ordeals. Considering that it was a wartime detachment located in a remote spot, service in the Yenan Observer Group was not only relatively safe but also interesting duty. When Clifford Young went to Peking in May 1946, however, he learned that Peking headquarters had been misinformed about what went on in Yenan despite the American unit stationed there. The army's map of China showed twenty Communist planes sitting on the Yenan airfield when in fact there were none. Nonexistent aircraft were also shown on other airfields. Army people in Peking did not even know Young was stationed in Yenan, which amazed him, and when they were informed of his presence, many of them seemed not to care.

Whittlesey Hall, Dixie's recreation and mess hall. Courtesy of Col. Wilbur J. Peterkin.

Young wrote his wife that Peking was filled with fat-bellied colonels, and he preferred to be in Yenan, where he was important, rather than in Peking with luxuries and comforts.[61] Those who participated in Dixie appear to have understood that the Chinese Communists and their leaders were destined to play important roles. The Americans were influenced by their encounter with the Chinese more than they could have predicted and sometimes in ways they would not have chosen.

3

The Observer Group in Operation

Long after the final shots of World War II, when all the treaties had been signed and the cold war was underway, a variety of opinions continued to exist about Dixie. There was some question as to whether the Dixie Mission had earned its keep or whether the Communists were doing anything thanks to Dixie that they had not already been doing when Dixie arrived.

In *Chinese-Soviet Relations, 1937-1945*, John Garver observes that just as Stalin's attitude toward the Chinese Communists was fundamentally conditioned by Soviet-American relations, so Mao's Soviet policy was embroiled with his American policy. By 1944-1945, it was clear that Mao could not realize his goal of crushing Chiang, his rival, without agreeing to peaceful cooperation with the Kuomintang. At the same time, Mao needed to drive a wedge between Chungking and Washington and to win support for Yenan. Alternatively, according to Garver, Mao could attempt to detach the Soviet Union from the United States, secure Soviet support, and move with Soviet backing against a Kuomintang regime sponsored by the United States. The success of the first strategy depended to a considerable degree on Mao's ability to manipulate Soviet fears of the United States. Because American power was preeminent in parts of China not held by the Japanese, Mao initially pursued the American option. As noted in Chapter 1, this was his reason for courting the Observer Group.[1]

The Communists had seen the Dixie Mission as the first step in winning international recognition that they controlled sizable territory and had a right to participate in the planning of China's political future. Only three months after the Mission was established, however, Stilwell was removed as CBI commander, the theater was split, and General Alfred C. Wedemeyer was made commanding general of the China

Theater. At that time, theater interest in the Communist-controlled areas appeared to diminish, and the Dixie Mission's importance in the war effort changed. The men stationed in Yenan did not alter their conduct noticeably because of these developments, however, since they were busy with a variety of tasks and obligations.

One of the primary reasons for establishing the group had been to gather information about the Japanese. To that end, the Japanese prisoners of war held by the Communists in Yenan were particularly valuable. The Americans first saw them in a large hall, seated at tables in groups of ten. There were about 150 of them, and they wore Communist uniforms. The Chinese called them not "prisoners" but "members of the Japanese People's Liberation League" or "students of the Japanese Workers and Farmers School." Barrett wrote in his memoirs that he only saw one or two Japanese in the entire Yenan area apart from these prisoners.[2]

In his September 28 report, Ray Cromley reported that he had interrogated sixty-seven Japanese prisoners as well as Okano Susumu and Sawada, two prominent Japanese Communists. He spoke to the former about plans to send Japanese Communists as agents to Manchuria and Japan. They discussed the amount of time required to train men, the length of time an agent needed to travel to Manchuria and Japan, suitable operating locations, types of information that could be acquired, and methods of communication. Cromley talked with Sawada about the practicality of sending an agent, possibly Sawada himself, to Japan, and the chances of establishing a direct line of communication with the Japanese underground.[3]

The Communists succeeded in converting the Japanese prisoners of war to Marxian theory by changing a policy. In 1938 General Chu Tch had ordered good treatment for Japanese prisoners of war. They were not to be tortured or killed in the process of trying to win their sympathies. This departure from the usual Chinese treatment of captives began to pay off in 1940 when Nosaka Sanzo, also known as Okano Susumu, the head of the Communist Party in Japan, escaped to Yenan, where he was destined to remain incognito for three years.

When captured Japanese soldiers were introduced to communism by prisoners who had already converted, the ideology became more acceptable. The tactic of using prisoners to effect conversions began to produce results. The incarcerated Japanese soldiers were brought to Yenan after capture in various parts of the Communist-held regions. Those who were recalcitrant, who hesitated to cooperate, were kept for "education" in the "rest house," a place that the Americans were told about but were not shown.[4] After the Mission had been established for ten months, Captain Julius Pomeranze, the American doctor who had replaced Casberg, had an opportunity to interrogate a prisoner of war who had graduated from the Imperial University in Tokyo. This man had served an eighteen-month internship in a Tokyo hospital before being inducted into the army as a medical officer. He had left Japan in 1937, was captured in 1939, and at the time of the conversation was in charge of the school in Yenan where the Japanese prisoners of war were indoctrinated. He and Dr. Pomeranze discussed medical subjects, and Pomeranze learned that the tuberculosis rate in Japan was extremely high. The Japanese army rejected men infected with tuberculosis, but the physical examination was not thorough, and chest X-rays were performed only in rare cases. At least 10 percent of the Japanese prisoners in Yenan had active cases of TB.[5]

Although more than one American had contact with the Japanese prisoners of war, John K. Emmerson was the man best trained to talk with them. Like Service, Davies, and Ludden, Emmerson was with the State Department and had been detailed to Stilwell. He had spent time with an OWI propaganda team in the North Burma combat zone. He had investigated the collection of intelligence from the Japanese and the use of Japanese prisoners in Burma, India, and China for propaganda. He flew to Dixie on October 22, 1944, on the same plane that carried John Davies, Theodore H. White of *Time,* and Koji Ariyoshi, a Nisei OWI man whose transfer to Dixie had been arranged by Emmerson.

A few days after they arrived, Emmerson and Ariyoshi rode two shaggy horses to the Workers and Peasants School, which was located down the valley, below the pagoda, in caves dug into the side of the mountain. On the way, each man was thrown by his horse, and on the return ride they first lost their horses and then became lost themselves.

Emmerson and Ariyoshi remained enthusiastic about the school despite these difficulties. They reported that most of the captured Japanese soldiers were peasant boys, allegedly the most difficult to convert yet in this case apparently the most enthusiastic proponents of a new Japan. The boys spoke openly about the bad conditions in their homeland, saying that there was much unrest and not enough to eat. The Japanese people kept waging the war, according to these youngsters, because they saw no alternative. They thought America intended to eradicate Japan by killing all the males between fifteen and fifty.[6]

All the prisoner students used assumed names, except for one civilian who was a long-standing party member. They were anxious to show off their school. Most had little education and low rank. Eighty-five percent of them were privates, and only five had gone beyond middle school; two were lieutenants, and none was an officer of higher rank.

Koji Ariyoshi. Courtesy of
Col. Wilbur J. Peterkin.

Seventy percent had been captured in battle, but the rest were deserters or stragglers. The Chinese discovered a number of "spies" in the school while it existed, meaning soldiers who had been sent by the Japanese Army to infiltrate and disrupt the antiwar movement. The Communists informed the Americans that after good treatment and indoctrination, these agents usually confessed to being spies and worked hard for the group, although one had held out for two years.

The stated purpose of the school was "to educate the students politically, and develop strength, ability and unity to stop the war." Instruction included a course in "political common sense," which was an elementary exposition of economics and politics from a Marxist viewpoint using the writings of Mao, Okano, and others. One day some Americans unexpectedly walked in when Okano was lecturing. Looking flustered, he quickly switched his subject from Marxist-Leninism to "democratic principles."[7]

Emmerson polled the "students" and found them predictably unanimous in condemning Japan for the China Incident and the war against the United States. They believed that Japan was going to lose the war. Most wanted to go back to Japan if it was defeated but not if it was victorious. They had concluded, they said, that Communist thinking could not be wholly wrong, given what they had heard from other Japanese in Yenan and the fact that the Eighth Route Army did not kill or torture prisoners but treated them well. In Emmerson's opinion, their answers reflected the conditioning they had received at Yenan. He assumed that their thinking was most influenced by their growing awareness that Japan was going to lose the war.[8]

Usually, Emmerson took Ariyoshi to meet the prisoners. They talked to the men separately or in groups, asking about their ideas and about the war, why and how they had surrendered, and how they saw Japan's future. This activity was part of the psychological warfare that OWI was waging against Japan, which also involved writing leaflets in Japanese to be dropped behind Japanese lines by American planes. The Chinese Communists were writing propaganda too, and they exchanged leaflets with the Americans. Except that the Communists' contained a strong Marxist slant, the pamphlets of the two groups carried similar antiwar messages.

Okano greatly impressed Davies as well as those Americans of Japanese descent who were attached to Dixie. Davies found the former Japanese delegate to the Comintern to be a highly intelligent and attractive person with a good command of English.[9] On the other hand, Okano did not impress Barrett, who thought it likely that Okano felt the same way about him.[10] Since Emmerson spent the most time with Okano, either at the latter's house or at the school, Emmerson probably knew him best. They always talked in Japanese, although Okano spoke to the other members of the Mission in English.

In 1944, Okano was fifty-two years old, kindly, and soft-spoken, with clear, penetrating eyes. His wife had remained in Moscow when he went to China, and so in Yenan he lived with a lively Chinese girl who was fluent in Japanese. They had a modest, newly built stone house surrounded by a large vegetable garden. His study-library was up a steep hill behind his house, in a cave overlooking a small ravine. The library shelves were stacked with Japanese books, magazines, and newspapers, some of which were less than two months old. His "Japanese Research Group" lived in caves adjoining the library.

Okano gave Emmerson masses of material, many of the publications of the Japanese Communist Party, and posters. Long after the war, Emmerson learned that Okano had spent three years beginning in 1936 in New York and Los Angeles. He had come to the United States because the Communist Party was illegal in Japan and could not publish its propaganda there. By accident he and his cohorts discovered and gained access to a complete set of Japanese type in New York City. They sent what they printed in New York to Los Angeles, where Okano and others placed it in envelopes that were then given to sympathetic Japanese sailors on Japanese ships sailing from Los Angeles. When the ships reached Japan, the sailors put Japanese postage on the envelopes and mailed them to avoid the censors who opened mail coming in from abroad. Okano never mentioned this background information to Emmerson when the two men conversed. After the war, he returned to Japan, led the opposition to the Japanese Communist Party, and became chairman of its Central Committee. He served in the part of the government known as the House of Counselors until he was eighty-five.

Okano's Anti-War League first appeared in Yenan in May 1940. It was originally a branch of the Anti-War League founded by Koji Watusu, a man who had fled Japan for Shanghai in 1936. He founded the first Japanese People's Anti-War League in Kweilin with 150 members. League headquarters were soon moved to Chungking, and for a brief time Okano was welcomed and praised by the central government. He set up the Peasants and Workers School and formed the Japanese People's Emancipation League (JPEL) in January 1944. Although Ambassador Gauss disparaged his activities, they impressed many journalists.

Ariyoshi and Emmerson held long conversations with Okano at his house that were interrupted only by the serving of meals and the continuous refilling of teacups. Sometimes their host talked about his experiences in the underground, especially his travels under assumed names using false passports. He had been born in Yamaguchi prefecture, was the youngest of six children, and was orphaned at fourteen. His eldest brother paid for his education at the Kobe Commercial School and at Tokyo's Keio University. By the time he reached the university, he had become aware of the inequalities of wealth. He titled his thesis "Revolutionary Trade Unionism." Immediately after he graduated, Okano went to work for the Yuai Kai (Friendship Society), a labor-oriented study group. In 1919 he enrolled in the London School of Economics, and in 1920 he joined the British Communist Party as a founding member. He was deported for his left-wing activities, and after a long journey that included time in Moscow, he returned to Tokyo. He immediately took a leading role in the Japanese Communist Party. For years he dodged the police but not always successfully, and he served several prison terms. In 1930, he was paroled so that he could have an eye operation. While he was out, the Comintern ordered him to Moscow to serve as its Japanese representative. He skillfully arranged to depart from Japan and reached Moscow in March 1931. He stayed in Russia nine years, visited Japan illegally many times, and, as previously noted, spent three years in the United States. In 1940, he traveled from Moscow to Yenan, accompanied by Chou En-lai and an Indonesian Communist, on orders of Dimitrov, the secretary-general of the Comintern.

Emmerson believed that his most informative conversations with

Okano were about the future of the Japanese Communist Party and postwar Japan. At the time, Okano was the most authoritative spokesman Emerson had found to talk to. The Party's goals in 1944 were those set forth in its 1932 Theses, which the Comintern had approved. They attacked the emperor system, the landlord system, and monopolistic capitalism and spoke of the struggle to create a Soviet republic of workers and peasants. They condemned the imperialistic war that had begun in Manchuria; argued for freeing Japan's colonies of Korea, Taiwan, and Manchuria; appealed for the support of the USSR and the Chinese Revolution; and called for abolition of the Diet.

In Yenan, Okano produced a platform that differed from the 1932 Theses in some important ways. He opposed a hereditary House of Peers and advocated a Diet that would have full government power, would be free from the threat of arbitrary dissolution by other constitutional organs, and would have a cabinet responsible to it. He thought the Diet should have the power to purchase property from absentee landlords but not to confiscate it. He said nothing about supporting the Soviet Union but wholeheartedly endorsed the pronouncements of Mao. He favored permitting the emperor system if the people wanted it.[11] Later, at a party celebrating the defeat of Japan, Okano told Arnold Dadian of the Dixie Mission that the Allies would be foolish to dethrone the emperor because he could easily be used to help govern Japan during the occupation.[12]

Okano's program reminded John Emmerson of the American Bill of Rights and some of the freedoms that Americans had acquired in the course of the nineteenth and twentieth centuries: freedom of speech, universal suffrage, and freedom for trade unions to organize. But Okano did not omit communism and advocated "voluntary collective farming," government control of monopoly capital with confiscation of excess profits, and inclusion of Communists in the government. He believed that the revolution in Japan would take place in three stages and that the last one, socialism, would not come to pass in his lifetime. He did not believe that the Communists would take over Japan. Rather, he looked forward to the legalization of the Party, the release of his comrades from prison, and an energetic Party life that might bring about the acceptance of communism by more people.[13]

Okano was one of three prominent Japanese revolutionaries engaged in propaganda and intelligence activities in China at this time. Wataru Kaji, one of the others, was a liberal writer and organizer of the Anti-War League who was employed by the central government. Kazuo Ayama, another one, had operated a printing establishment in Chungking with facilities for Japanese typography that were used by the central government, OWI, and the British. In late 1944, Emmerson believed that he was employed by the British and Tai Li.[14]

Besides interviewing the Japanese prisoners and Okano, Emmerson spoke extensively about them to members of the Chinese Communist Party. When he talked with K'ang Sheng, the man responsible for getting Japanese informational materials for the Americans, Huang Hua went along as interpreter. The acquisition work was not easy. In 1944 five people lost their lives doing it. K'ang thought an international organization of Japanese should be formed to go to the United States and train prisoners of war being held there.[15]

In his report of November 7, 1944, Emmerson concluded that the Eighth Route Army had proven that Japanese prisoners of war could be converted and used effectively for propaganda operations on the front lines. He believed these personnel, with their invaluable specialized knowledge and proficiency in the language, could help American army officers establish order among the Japanese population following an invasion of Japan. Furthermore, the Japanese People's Emancipation League, whose existence was known to the Japanese Army and whose influence was respected and feared, could be used to disseminate democratic ideas and encourage the organization of cells within Japan to spread defeatism and thereby reduce resistance at the time of invasion. Emmerson also noted that preparations were being made in Yenan to send agents directly to Japan, presumably to work with fifth columnists. He advocated setting up a radio transmitter in a Chinese Communist base area such as Shantung Province to permit broadcasts to Japan, Korea, and Manchuria.[16]

Emmerson's November 1944 report mentioned the approximately 2,500 Japanese troops who had been captured by the Chinese Communists since July 1937. Most were returned to their own lines, but retribution at the hands of their officers was frequently so cruel that during 1944 many prisoners stayed with the Chinese. Some 300 of them participated in propaganda efforts that year, both at Yenan and in outposts in the Communist-controlled regions.[17]

Propaganda workers followed a routine that helped them capture prisoners. Operating at night, they went straight to the blockhouses, which were usually guarded by unreliable puppet soldiers, and shouted at the occupants through megaphones. Comfort kits were distributed to the soldiers in the blockhouses, and the telephone lines were tapped so that the Communists could talk directly to the troops inside. The nature of blockhouse duty made some of their work easier. The abusive Japanese officers forbade the men from leaving their posts except in groups. Living conditions were bad for all the men except the officers. The soldiers looted and pillaged periodically, and they feared retaliation for burning villages to the ground and killing innocent people in the process. Retaliation usually came in the form of guerrilla attacks, a method very effective in North China where the people were well armed and hostile to the enemy and were not reluctant to encircle and attack the isolated blockhouses.

Each Chinese propaganda barrage often lasted six or seven hours and was especially convincing because it was delivered by a Japanese whose accent was unmistakable. Soldiers did not always defect, but the Japanese People's Emancipation League always worked hard and tenaciously. If their "gentle" methods did not work, they used more persuasive means. One night the Eighth Route Army failed to persuade a blockhouse full of Japanese to surrender. The following night, the Eighth Route Army blew up the blockhouse.

The Chinese knew that Japanese soldiers frequently chose to commit suicide rather than surrender. Most of the Chinese believed that the enemy soldier killed himself in order to avoid capture, not from his love of the emperor. He feared torture and death at the hands of the Chinese and disgrace and shame if he ever returned home.

Once the Chinese had disarmed the captured Japanese, they were no longer treated as enemies. The Communists gave them the best treatment possible under frontline conditions, guarded them lightly, and asked them whether they wished to return to the Japanese Army. Those who did were fed, indoctrinated, and sent back to their units. The Communists knew that the returned soldiers would spread the word about how the Communists had treated them as prisoners. The captives who wished to remain with the Chinese were given Eighth Route Army uniforms. All except the seriously injured were routed back to subregion headquarters. There, after spot interrogation by the Japanese propaganda workers, they were left alone to rest and adjust to their new environment. These new prisoners had virtually complete freedom, although their actions were observed closely and were recorded. When the prisoners were deemed safe enough, Japanese or Chinese psychological warfare workers escorted them to Yenan, a twenty-day march. Upon their arrival the newcomers were given cigarettes and food comparable to that which members of the Eighth Route Army received. The prisoners saw that other Japanese moved around with very few restrictions.

After the food and good treatment had had time to take effect, the Japanese People's Emancipation League spokesman explained that the Chinese Communist Party had no hard feelings against the people of Japan and that the prisoner of war was a victim of military oppression. The spokesman told the prisoners that the best thing the Japanese could do was to hasten the downfall of the war-making regime in power in Japan so that a government dedicated to the interests of the common man could be installed in its place.[18]

The "workers and peasants" in the Workers and Peasants School belonged to the Japanese People's Emancipation League, which claimed branches throughout Communist-held territory. Students prepared propaganda materials, produced plays and variety shows, and held exhibitions and discussion sessions. Some of these were for the benefit of the Americans and dealt with subjects like the education of newcomers, propaganda preparation, and discussion of life in postwar Japan.

The Americans sometimes took part in the school programs. On December 7, Emmerson made a forty-five-minute speech in Japanese about prewar American-Japanese relations and the glories of American democracy. He showed his audience a recent copy of *Life*, which portrayed some of the positive elements in Japanese culture, and used the magazine to illustrate freedom of speech and press in wartime America. Ariyoshi told them about the loyalty of the Nisei. The listeners responded noisily, especially when annihilation of the militarists or the building a "new Japan" was mentioned.[19] An exhibit of 120 pictures also interested the prisoners of war. These were hung on the walls of the cave that served as a dayroom. The photos showed the skeletal remains of a Japanese soldier on the Salween front, B-29 production, and the liberation of Paris.[20]

On August 12, 1944, at a dinner and theatrical entertainment given by the Japanese People's Emancipation League for the U.S. Army Observer Section, Okano made a direct appeal for Allied recognition and support of the JPEL. Barrett had not been warned that such a speech would be made. He replied with a few general remarks, succinctly expressing thanks for the event.[21]

Such was the account that the Chinese Communists gave key American personnel of their activities with the Japanese prisoners of war in Yenan. Clearly they wanted to depict these activities as humane and constructive, and they largely knew what the Americans wanted to see. For his part, Emmerson would not have known what they had concealed. More interested in techniques used to convert the prisoners of war, Emmerson and Ariyoshi did not ask themselves whether the Communist activities aimed primarily to defeat Japan or solely to lay the groundwork for the looming confrontation with Chiang Kai-shek. Clearly, they saw Chinese Communist interest in Japanese prisoners of war as serving two purposes: it provided a way of undermining the

Japanese war effort, and it added to the number of those who could one day support their position in the ultimate struggle against Chiang Kai-shek.

The Americans had heard that Yenan harbored many prisoners from Southeast Asian countries in addition to the Japanese. Supposedly, the others were also being readied to direct the postwar destinies of their homelands. The Americans were never invited to meet any except the Japanese and were too busy to press the matter. The only other group with which the Americans had any contact with was the Korean Workers and Peasants School. Emmerson did not consider the people there to be of the caliber needed to run a country. Koji Ariyoshi, rather than Emmerson, was their principal interviewer.[22]

Ariyoshi noticed similarities in the propaganda techniques used by the Japanese People's Emancipation League and those of the Koreans. There were some interesting differences, however. For instance, the Koreans had a volunteer army that fought alongside the Eighth Route Army. Occasionally, the Korean volunteers also protected the Korean psychological warfare workers when they went into occupied villages or blocks. Furthermore, the Koreans carried on more extensive underground activity than the Japanese, enabling the organizations to keep in contact and work with revolutionary groups in Korea and Manchuria.

The Koreans in Yenan spent a great deal of time studying Korean-Japanese problems and the condition of Koreans living under Japanese rule in Manchuria and North China. They estimated that there were approximately 2 million Koreans in Manchuria and 200,000 in North China. In Manchuria, most were farmers, and the Eighth Route Army reported that they were doing poorly. In contrast, most of the Koreans in North China lived in the cities to which they had migrated after 1937, influenced by Japanese propaganda about the opportunities for advancement that they would find. The majority of the émigrés had been young, poorly educated men. When they were unable to open businesses, work in factories, or cultivate farms, many became opium peddlers, following the Japanese troops. When war broke out in the Pacific, the Japanese began oppressing the Koreans in various ways. The Japanese forced the Koreans to take Japanese names, forbade them to traffic in opium, and induced them to volunteer for the army and labor battalions by guaranteeing jobs and special treatment for their families.

Korean psychological warfare workers in North China capitalized on such situations. In their propaganda they urged their countrymen to ask why they were selling opium, why they were serving in army and labor battalions, and why they were fighting the Chinese. The workers encouraged these men not to work for the Japanese and to demand better pay, clothing, and food.[23] Ariyoshi also spoke with Korean deserters from the Japanese Army and concluded that American propaganda directed at Korea should play up incipient Korean nationalism with leaflets produced by the concerned Korean groups.[24]

Korean businessmen, actors, actresses, and musicians also found their way to various Eighth Route Army bases and with the others formed the Korean Volunteer Army and the Korean Independence League. The work of these agencies thus appeared to be encouraging people to take the risk of going over to the Chinese Communists.[25]

The Dixie Mission did not rely solely on Japanese and Chinese sources for information. After a few months, the OSS set up a microfilm lab and began training a Chinese to operate it. The Americans planned to establish other labs, first at Fouping, then in other territories, to film captured documents, newspapers, and magazines. They made arrangements with Okano to send men to Peking to buy periodicals in large quantities. Two copies were to be made of everything. The microfilm would then be sent to Chungking for transmission to Washington. This plan required building a photo lab to process the microfilm, but it was felt that there would be other important uses for an adequately equipped darkroom.[26]

Originally, one of the major justifications for sending observers to Yenan was that American air operations in the CBI Theater had increased during 1943 and 1944. The result had been more plane crashes and the need to rescue fliers downed in Japanese-occupied territory and in areas controlled by the Communists. The incidence of crashes especially increased after the introduction of the B-29. This aircraft, which carried a very large bomb load, had serious problems. When the planes were heavily loaded, the pilots considered taking off to be more dangerous than facing flak or enemy fighters. Even a partial loss of takeoff power from one engine almost invariably resulted in a crash. The feathering mechanism was dismally unreliable, and fuel quantity gauges were so inaccurate that a pilot on his way home from a bombing run could only guess whether he would run out of gas. Engine failure remained the worst problem, however, and the one that resulted in the most crashes.[27]

The Dixie Mission was expected to rescue survivors. The Chinese Communists, who had been involved in escape and evasion prior to the advent of the Mission, asked for instruction so that they could be of the greatest possible help in this activity.[28] The Communists were not the only Chinese engaged in rescuing American fliers, of course. When Air Corps General Gabe Disosway was shot down in Japanese-held central China, Nationalist guerrillas found him and got him out. Locals then hid him for weeks until he could be taken to a safe place. The Nationalists and the Communists cooperated with the Americans in these rescues, but they did not cooperate with each other. In these matters, as in its other contacts, Dixie dealt only with the Communists.

The American military unit most concerned with helping military personnel escape from the Japanese was the Air Ground Aid Service. First Lieutenant Henry C. Whittlesey was the first AGAS representative with the Mission. When he died in a Japanese ambush, Major Arnold Dadian replaced him.[29] AGAS believed its chief function was to make the Chinese understand that recovery operations were their responsibility and that the primary American function was liaison. Whittlesey and those who succeeded him wanted to find out about escape and evasion possibilities in the Communist-controlled areas and to bring that information to the Air Corps so that fliers would know how to place themselves in Communist hands if they went down. AGAS told the Communists that a considerable amount of information needed to be exchanged and that certain changes needed to be made, some of which had originated as suggestions made by fliers who had escaped. They suggested to chief of staff General Yeh Chien-ying that he form a Chinese AGAS committee with a representative from each of the Communist-controlled areas. Yeh agreed and appointed the committee. At a preliminary meeting, each member produced a map of his area showing "safe" and "unsafe" zones. Each then had an individual conference with Whittlesey to discuss his region in detail. Whittlesey found these men enthusiastic and well informed about their respective locales and judged them useful to the rescue effort.[30]

Whittlesey stressed the significance of this committee to escape and evasion work in his communications with his commanding officer in Chungking. He said that although Yenan had radio contact with all the Communist Army bases, the network did not appear to work well, and he gave examples. He considered the committee at Yenan vitally important because it could keep all of Communist-dominated China "on its toes." It could also develop plans to extend the safe areas in each base. Whittlesey speculated that the Chinese Communists and the Americans would exchange information about lost airmen through the committee and would evaluate new suggestions. Furthermore, at least until they worked out more direct means of removal, all evacuees would pass through Yenan to be interviewed. He hoped to extend AGAS operations. To further this objective he made a trip to the Shansi-Chahar-Hopei military region[31] with Peterkin, Ludden, Domke, Hitch, and Gress. They left Yenan on October 6, 1944.[32]

The case of First Lieutenant J. P. Baglio illustrates a Communist rescue. Baglio parachuted out of his plane near Taiyuan, Shansi Province, on June 9, 1944. He walked north of the Chengtu Railroad, where he met Communist forces, and spent three months traveling from central Shansi to Fouping and ultimately to Yenan.[33]

First the Communists escorted Baglio to the headquarters of the Shansi-Chahar-Hopei military region. Then, on July 16, 1944, they took him to visit an arsenal in Fouping. He later described it to Barrett, who thought that it sounded very similar to the Communist arsenal in Yenan in equipment and production capacity.[34] Baglio also confirmed statements that General Nieh Jung-chen, the commanding general and political commissar of Chinese Communist forces in the Shansi-Chahar-Hopei military region, had made to Barrett about military operations, enemy forces, and the Communist policy of using the people in the region. This validation further increased the confidence that Barrett and others felt in the truthfulness of information that they were receiving from the Communists.

To Baglio's surprise, the men of the Dixie Mission were also very interested in learning about things like banditry and about the People's Militia in the Communist-controlled areas. Baglio told them that he had heard no mention of bandits during his journey and that he did not see how there could be any when everybody was busy fighting and supporting the army. This comment intrigued the Americans, because banditry prevailed in the Kuomintang territories. John Service believed that if the Communists accomplished nothing more than the elimination of banditry they would have performed a great service for the common people of China.

Baglio's first contact with the Communists had been with the People's Militia (Min Pin), the 2-million-man support for the regular Communist forces organized from the Self-Defense Army, which had rescued him. Their quickness and efficiency had impressed him greatly, as did their intelligence work, which he thought was superb. Baglio's insights were especially interesting because he had known nothing about the People's Militia before landing in Shansi, nor had he been subjected to any propaganda in favor of the Chinese Communists. The Mission therefore regarded him as an absolutely unprejudiced observer. Both Baglio and Barrett were further impressed by the fact that the Communists had done everything for Baglio with no intention of claiming a reward, nor did they ask to be compensated for the expenses that they had incurred looking after him.[35]

Baglio's dramatic rescue attracted the attention of the newspapermen who lurked around Yenan in hopes of a story. Israel Epstein, reporting for *Time-Life* and the *New York Times,* wrote an article about Baglio, whom he met at the northwest Shansi Communist base. The American army censor at Forward Echelon headquarters killed the story, however, in accordance with a policy developed in the European Theater which stated that rescues from "enemy-occupied territory" were to be kept quiet. Service and other members of the Dixie Mission believed that Epstein's sketch, perhaps after Baglio's name and certain place names had been deleted for security reasons, could and should have been released, because it was good news, had human interest, and would have given the American public a vivid picture of actual conditions on the Chinese war front. Such a description of American-Chinese cooperation could have helped offset the gloomy news that the public received from the rest of China.[36]

Frequently Whittlesey and his Eighth Route Army AGAS committee were busy with rescues. On September 8, 1944, an Air Corps bomber crashed in East Hopei. Chinese Communists found seven of the crew members near Changli, Hopei, in the heart of an area of great strategic importance to the Japanese. Barrett believed the Chinese ability to recover these men gave credence to their claims that they, and not the Japanese, controlled East Hopei.[37] The seven fliers were brought out on foot, a journey that took several weeks. The radio message that the Communists sent was garbled in transmission, and so the men's names were not known until they were actually out.[38] Like Baglio's account, the reports of these men helped confirm what the Chinese had told the Mission.[39]

The downed planes were usually bombers that had been damaged or had developed trouble while on a bombing run. Often they were from the Twentieth Bomber Command. Plane 3363, for example, crashed while on a return flight from Mukden on December 7, 1944. The crew bailed out into the mountains between Lang Shu-yuan and Shih Cheng-chen at 1:00 P.M. Japanese forces in the nearby city of Lucheng saw the plane start to go down. The next morning they mobilized over a thousand Japanese troops and puppets, plus a hundred peasants, to transfer the loot they expected to find in the wreckage. The crash occurred so far from Lucheng that they did not reach the site until December 9. When they got there, they found that Chinese Communist troops had arrived fifteen minutes earlier. The Communists struck in a frontal attack, forcing a retreat. As they fell back, the Japanese were then attacked by the People's Militia. While they fled, they were caught in an ambush and were driven back to their starting point.

The crew from the plane had bailed out into the most rugged and craggy mountains in the region. The local population and all of the workers at a nearby clothing factory were mobilized and sent to the mountains as a search party. Because of strong winds, deep snow, and icy paths, however, they located and brought out only seven crew members that day. The local people worked throughout the night of December 7, making clothes and shoes for the rescued men.

When the Third District government learned that there were still four men missing, it mobilized everyone in its twenty-six villages. On the night of December 8 the entire mountain was illuminated by the torches of the Chinese scouring the region. The expedition netted three more Americans, but the fourth was not located until the third day. He had landed in between two cliffs and had been caught on a tree. The head man of the village, who was leading the search party, tied himself with ropes and had himself lowered down the side of the cliff so that he could untangle the man, tie him to his own body, and have the villagers draw them both up. The American had gone without food for three days, had injured his leg in his fall, and had been exposed to the cold. He could barely move and could not walk, so the village chief carried him on his back for over three miles, across the mountains to a doctor who gave him the necessary emergency aid.

On the evening of December 12, the eleven crew members were brought together at Chang Ling-tsun, where they were received warmly, and their trip back to friendly territory began. Everywhere during this trek the Americans were welcomed heartily, both by the Communist Army and by the ordinary people, who brought their best food. In every village people, some of whom had come great distances, lined up to greet the Americans. The villagers filled the airmen's pockets with peanuts, persimmon cakes, walnuts, melon seeds, and other morsels. An old farmer in one small town combed an area of several miles in a snowstorm to find eggs for the fliers. During this journey the group often traveled in the middle of the night for safety reasons. Even then, the people in the villages through which they passed would awaken on their own initiative to prepare food and water and present the rescued fliers with chickens. Once, when the frozen, slippery path across the mountain made it impossible to carry the stretcher bearing the wounded man, more than 200 peasants rushed to help.

The expedition arrived at the military region headquarters on Christmas Eve. The men were immediately feted at a celebration banquet and were provided with entertainment. Two days later the group left for the field headquarters of the Eighteenth Group Army.[40] George Varoff, the captain of this fortunate crew, was further honored by the

George Varoff, captain of the crashed B-29 crew rescued by the Chinese Communists. Courtesy of George Varoff.

Communists when they built an airstrip in the vicinity of the crash and named it Varoff Field.[41]

Not every American experience had a Hollywood ending, of course. In early January 1945, a plane carrying a cargo of gasoline took off from Kunming bound for Lao Ho Kow, Hupei. The crew members lost their orientation because of bad weather, and so they flew low in an effort to find their destination. Over Honan, four enemy planes attacked them, forcing them down. Fire destroyed the plane, and one of the crew died. In the process of arresting the other three, the Kuomintang wounded the lieutenant's arm while wrenching away his pistol. After spending ten days in detention, these airmen were handed over to the local troops under Wang Ta-kung. General Yeh, in his report of the incident, described Wang as a man connected to a traitor who had gone over to the Japanese. This man had once attacked a Chinese Communist Army Hospital and had murdered over twenty wounded troops. According to Yeh, his people often buried Chinese Communist functionaries alive. The Americans were in danger of being discovered and taken prisoner by the Japanese when the Communists liberated them.[42]

On February 2, 1945, Captain A. J. Humby of the Twentieth Bomber Command was returning from a photo reconnaissance mission over Korea when his plane developed engine trouble. His attempts to feather the propeller failed, and it began to windmill. The crew destroyed all classified material on board and jumped, leaving the crippled ship to crash and burn. When they reached the ground they were met by men who were either plainclothes soldiers of the local people's army or soldiers of the regular army. They were protected and gathered together quickly. Although a nearby Japanese garrison sent out a small force to capture them, the Chinese speedily repulsed it.

The local people provided food, shelter, and clothing to protect them from the cold and to disguise their identities. They refused payment and said that national government currency was of no value to them. AGAS observed afterward that inasmuch as rescue journeys usually took two to four months, fliers should carry items like watches, knives, sidearms, and trinkets, since it would be impossible to carry enough money of any kind to pay the expenses involved in such a trip.

The Humby crew was joined on its walk out by Lieutenant Wells, a fighter pilot who had bailed out about fifty miles from Peking. He told his compatriots that the first person he saw after landing was a farmer, whom he seized and to whom he showed the American flag sewed inside his jacket. The farmer took him to a guerrilla leader who arranged for him to join Humby and the others after a four-day walk. They traveled mostly at night in the dangerous areas, for the Japanese knew their approximate location. Battles were being fought close by, and they saw a Japanese reconnaissance plane. This party also had to deal with physical difficulties. Injured ankles, snow blindness, fever, and intestinal disorders plagued them, so an attempt was made to arrange for a drop of medical supplies at Fouping. After waiting for it for nineteen days, the group departed, leaving behind the man with the injured ankle and another man to keep him company.[43] In mid-April Lieutenant Louis Jones of the Dixie Mission drove to Michih, about 157 miles from Yenan, to bring out the nine members of the Humby crew. At that time the two who had been left behind were expected near the end of the month.[44]

To AGAS, this episode illustrated the problem of arranging drops or air evacuations when the Americans depended totally on Chinese communications.[45] It also meant that hauling a payload for a 314-mile round trip took eighty gallons of gas, a scarce commodity in that area.[46]

The above cases merely illustrate the Dixie Mission's direct or indirect commitment to the rescue of downed planes. There were also times when both the Chinese and the Americans were involved in salvaging aircraft. In April 1945, for instance, three men drove a weapons carrier to Michih to salvage a P-51 that had crashed nearby. Peterkin wrote to Dickey that he could use a couple of L-5s to make such work easier.

The Communists knew the importance of rescue and salvage to

the war effort. They continued to cooperate even when relations with the Americans were deteriorating. This effort cost them dearly. At the end of April 1945, they told Captain James C. Eaton, the AGAS man in Yenan at that time, that over 500 lives had been lost bringing out about 80 men.[47]

AGAS knew that the maintenance of way stations created a financial burden for the Communists too. Spaced conveniently along the roads and trails in the rear of the lines, the Eighth Route Army had established a series of "Chan Ping," or "Soldier's Stops." Each could quarter from about twenty-five soldiers to over a hundred. The Chan Ping were usually built in the form of a court. Along one side were cavelike rooms, each with a big heated k'ang, upon the end of which the soldiers slept. A window and a door were located at the front. Animals were lodged on one side; facilities such as cooking, living quarters for personnel, and storage were arranged on the others. Soldiers or government workers traveling at night were also put up and fed at these Chan Ping.[48]

In spite of their mutual interest in rescuing downed fliers, relations between AGAS and the Chinese were not always smooth. Conflict occurred mostly because AGAS told the Chinese how to run their rescue operations and the Chinese balked when they were not allowed to do things their own way. Peterkin believed that the Communists would continue to bring in the airmen however they wanted, regardless of AGAS. An American stationed at Varoff Field, in Peterkin's opinion, would have been able to do all the necessary coordinating. The Chinese did not like to be instructed about the urgency of finding downed fliers. They quickly informed Peterkin that they had rescued fliers before they even heard of AGAS and would continue to do so even if AGAS left. Peterkin told Eaton to stop lecturing the Chinese.[49]

AGAS did not minimize Chinese efforts. Indeed, AGAS not only recognized that every operation was costly but also noticed that every flier who came out was loaded with gifts. The debt incurred when Chinese soldiers fought and died to protect or rescue American personnel or equipment seemed incalculable. AGAS wanted medical supplies given to the Communists in return for the medical aid being provided to wounded Americans. The point was not only to replace what had been used but also to ensure better medical treatment in the future. In a communication directed to his AGAS commanding officer, Eaton noted that if AGAS could provide medicine and equipment on this basis, the central government might not have grounds to object.[50]

AGAS credited the Chinese successes in rescue operations to the Communists' high degree of organization and their strength in the areas they controlled. Still, suitable radio communications and greater facilities for air evacuation were needed. AGAS also recommended creating caches of medicine, food, and comfort supplies as well as providing medical assistance.[51]

In fact, medical supplies were made available to the Communists. In October 1945, theater headquarters arranged for diphtheria serum to be flown into Yenan to relieve an epidemic in one of the Chinese nurseries.[52] The Chinese appreciated such humanitarian gestures and reciprocated as they could. They presented Colonel Yeaton, for example, with a set of splendid woodcuts.[53]

The Chinese sometimes asked the Americans for items like pamphlets and seeds.[54] They sought books of all kinds, wristwatches and clocks, playthings for children, bottles of multivitamins, and special edibles like candy, Yunnan hams, brandy or whiskey, and, of course, American cigarettes. Frequently, Dixie requested items that could be used as presents. Gifts to Communist dignitaries and others who had been of great assistance needed to be special, like sheepskin-lined parkas or fountain pens. Parker pens were sometimes specified because the Chinese considered them the best kind, and anyone receiving one gained face.[55]

The War Department had no problem providing AGAS with certain trade and gift objects for issue to deserving Chinese. The department also sent some small arms and ammunition to be given to Chinese who provided information. Not all of AGAS's wishes were granted, however. Theater disapproved a July 1945 request for certain arms and ammunition to be given to individual Chinese, for example, on the ground that no authority existed for the gratuitous issue of such equipment. General Clayton L. Bissell explained that the previous April AGAS had proposed issuing some arms and ammunition to guerrillas in eastern China "for a means of defense" and as a "just reward" for assisting in the safe return of Americans evading the Japanese. At that time, the implications of filling such a request had been carefully considered, he said, and it was determined that no exceptions could be made to the policy of not authorizing diversions of equipment.[56]

Peterkin's irritation with AGAS and with Eaton, whom he found rude and a troublemaker, illustrates on a small scale the kind of rivalry that existed among the branches of the military even in a unit as small as the Dixie Mission.[57] Even after the war ended, Wedemeyer had to remind the navy that, although the navy seemed to think otherwise, meteorological stations needed to be operated jointly, inasmuch as the weather information they obtained was equally valuable to both services.[58]

The Tenth Weather Squadron provided all of the weather service for the China-Burma-India Theater. It had eleven men attached to Dixie

Weather operations at Dixie. Moland Breland (left) and Charles Dole operate the weather balloon. Courtesy of Jack Klein.

at one time or another responsible for gathering weather information and training Chinese Communists behind the lines so that they could take temperatures, assess the cloud cover, and send data back at a scheduled time. The Communists had had no weather network earlier,[59] but as soon as Dixie arrived they asked to be instructed so that they could provide as much help as possible.[60] Both men and women were assigned to train as weather observers. Instructors who encountered women were sometimes surprised, having expected to be working with males. As at the dances, the padded cotton suits worn by both sexes made it difficult to tell them apart.

Working together with the Chinese, the Americans occasionally had opportunities to witness the sometimes surprising ways in which the East blended old customs with new. One day Major Young walked into the room where some Communist soldiers were being taught how to operate a weather station. One was using an abacus but not very well. He eventually began using a slide rule for his calculations. The others teased him about not being able to use an abacus, so that he had to rely on a foreign invention. The speed with which some of the Chinese performed long division on the ancient tool amazed Young.[61]

The first man placed in charge of weather observation at Yenan was Major Charles R. Dole. Soon after his arrival, Dole recommended that a Class A weather observation station be established as soon as possible. Master Sergeant William E. Cady, Dole's assistant, began instructing a class of twelve radio operators from the Eighteenth Group Army in October 1944. The courses ran for three to four weeks. Graduates were then sent into the field to improve the quality of radio reports and to set up new observation stations. In addition, the daily weather reports received from Fouping, Hopei, and Yenching were transmitted to Chengtu, together with observations taken each day in Yenan.[62]

In April 1945, the Chinese began construction of a power plant and a building to house weather equipment and provide working space for the weather personnel. The weather building was eleven feet by twenty feet and cost about $7,000 in gold.[63] It was located on an unguarded hilltop above the compound. Almost everyone had access to it. Prior to Yeaton, the commanding officers had not worried much about security.[64]

Originally, the weathermen had no equipment to share with the Communists. Then Colonel Richard Ellsworth, the Tenth Weather Squadron officer to whom the Dixie Mission weathermen reported at theater headquarters, arranged to send equipment to Yenan that could launch air balloons to obtain high-altitude atmospheric data. The weathermen trained the Chinese to use these balloons, and twenty-four-hour-a-day weather watching began. The Americans supplied the Chinese with hydrogen generators to fill the balloons. By observing the balloons through a transit, one could calculate the winds. A balloon was filled with a certain amount of hydrogen gas. Knowing its rate of rise, one could calculate what the winds were at, say, 2,000 or 5,000 feet. The person on the ground tracked the balloon and determined its velocity by noting how fast it moved laterally as it climbed. When the balloons reached a certain height, they exploded.

In other places, where the Chinese were better trained, an instrument was sent up that would radio back to the receiver on the ground the temperature and pressure at various altitudes. This information was useful in forecasting, but because the Communists at Yenan never received this training, visual methods continued to be used. Tenth Weather trained Chinese to go out into the field and send information back that was then transmitted to Chengtu via the Dixie Mission radio. Weather Central valued this information and added it to the reports that pilots sent about temperature, pressure, wind, and cloud cover.

In particular, Twentieth Bomber Command relied on this information because it not only flew bombing raids but also ferried gasoline from India, the Twentieth's home base, to Chengtu.[65] Chengtu had four nearby airfields that had been hand built by peasants. This weather information was also important for the long bombing runs from Chengtu to Japan that began on June 15, 1944. These raids were expected to cripple Japanese production, but according to postwar assessments, the Twentieth Bomber Command B-29s operating from China reduced Japan's steel supply by less than 2 percent.[66]

By the end of 1944, weather reports composed most of the Yenan radio traffic, which was expected to increase. News went regularly to Chungking headquarters, Twentieth Bomber Command, Chengtu, and OSS headquarters in Kunming. It was anticipated that Yenan would soon have contact with fifteen agents equipped with sets.[67] In early January 1945, the Tenth Weather Squadron submitted a plan for installing weather stations all over China.[68] By May of that year it seemed likely these stations would be flown or dropped in, a procedure that AGAS regarded as offering a splendid opportunity to set up long-awaited caches of supplies for downed fliers.[69]

But sometimes the dropping exercises did not work out well. In June 1945, for example, Peterkin received word that eleven of thirteen bundles had been partly or completely destroyed. About 80 percent of the equipment in the drop was damaged beyond repair, including weather apparatus as well as AGAS equipment. Improper packing had caused this particular disaster,[70] and the blame was laid on Lieutenant Winston Guest, who had been the supervisor.[71]

As in other areas, there were rivalries among those who collected weather data. About February 25, 1945, Colonel Ellsworth brought two AACS sergeants and a transmitter to Yenan. He also brought each man in the Mission a pound of sugar, a welcome gift. Earlier that month, a Signal Corps station and crew had been put into operation to collect weather information. They continued to do so even after AACS arrived. Finally, Lieutenant Klein, the Signal Corps officer in charge, ordered the AACS men to stop loafing and set up their equipment. Until then they had dodged all fatigue duty by saying that AACS men were allowed to do only AACS work. Even after they had set up their equipment, the Air Corps men continued to use Signal Corp equipment when theirs was out of order.

This situation inspired Peterkin to write Dickey that, in his judgment, the Signal Corps had adequate men and gear to do the job without AACS. He recommended to his superiors that AACS be pulled out of Yenan. The job could be done best by the Signal Corps alone, he said, because fuel, buildings, and transportation were at a premium and because housing and messing facilities were overburdened. Last but not least, he regarded the AACS men as malcontents and troublemakers. He made these comments as weather paraphernalia, AGAS cache supplies, and medicines were being dropped in the Fouping area to service three new weather stations to be manned by Chinese. Additional Signal Corps weather personnel were also being sent to Yenan.[72]

When the Mission was first established, an air of incipient cooperation and goodwill existed between the Americans and their Communist hosts. As the war drew to a close, however, the Chinese became less and less willing to cooperate with the weather people without receiving something in return. Once Major Spilhaus, the Tenth Weather expediter, called a meeting that was attended by Colonel Wong, chief of Red communications; Huang Hua, the interpreter; Lieutenant Demetrius Russell of Tenth Weather; and Lieutenant Remenih of OSS communications. The meeting aimed to clarify the details of the weather radio network that Spilhaus had been installing and organizing in North China.

Colonel Wong suggested that since there had never been any definite statement of policy regarding the nature of cooperation between the American army and the Chinese Communist Army, there should be an understanding that the weather network would be treated as a separate project, independent of any other project that might be installed in the future. He said he preferred that the weather radio stations work through the Chinese Communist network rather than through the American one set up for this purpose, because this arrangement would facilitate administration of the Chinese personnel involved.

The Americans then offered Wong the Tenth Weather radio equipment to use as he pleased when it was not broadcasting the twice-daily weather report. Wong declined on the ground that the stations should broadcast only weather; otherwise the security of his own communications system would be compromised. He said that when the Observer Section had first arrived in Yenan, he had been led to believe that radio gear would be sent to the Chinese Communists to relieve their overcrowded network. In fact, the Communist nets were now more crowded than ever. Nevertheless, he still preferred to have weather and all the related administrative traffic go through his network rather than through the American one.[73]

When Colonel Peterkin learned that Spilhaus had agreed to all of Wong's points, he was displeased. He wrote Dickey that Spilhaus was "long on promises, short on performance, and never stayed in one place long enough for his unfulfilled promises to catch up with him."[74]

As the war moved into its final months with no determination of the future relationship between the Chinese Communist Party and the United States, both the quantity and the quality of weather intelligence received from the Communists fell off. Peterkin considered the decline in information a reflection of the passive, noncooperative attitude that the Chinese were adopting because the Americans had not responded to their requests for a better-defined relationship.[75]

Nevertheless, as late as August 1945, plans to expand the Yenan Observer Group continued. Yeaton sent a memo and a chart outlining them to the chief of staff of the Eighteenth Group Army. The proposal was in two parts, one marked in blue, for immediate expansion, and the other in red, a longer-range plan.[76] At the time the war ended, OSS planned to extend a radio network into all parts of North China, with the Yenan Observer Group as its signal control center. At that point the group's objective was changed: it now functioned as a liaison between the Communists and the China Theater forces and performed this task even as overall relations with the Communist Chinese deteriorated.[77] While the blueprint was never finalized, weather apparatus continued to be flown in as late as 1946. In January of that year, a C-46 brought in 2,000 pounds of supplies from Shanghai for the weather station, much to the delight of the Chinese Communist weathermen.[78]

The main military contributions of the Dixie Mission can thus be seen as recovery of downed fliers and weather reporting. While these activities may not have influenced the final outcome of the war, they were certainly valuable services performed at small cost to the American taxpayer.[79] Some of the other information that the Mission gained was useful too, if only because so little was known about the Japanese units north of the Yellow River and in Manchuria. Otherwise the Mission seems to have benefited the United States mainly as a point of contact with the Chinese Communists, whose commitment to defeating the Japanese enemy the members of the Dixie Mission do not appear to have questioned.

Unfortunately, the men of the Dixie Mission received virtually no feedback from Chungking about whether the information they had acquired was considered valuable or whether it was acted upon. For this reason some of them believed that their efforts served only to corroborate what was learned from other sources. Raymond Ludden suspected that the various intelligence agencies involved in China had created a hopeless situation. All of them were empire building but mostly in disorganized fashion. In addition, much OSS information came from Kuomintang sources or from puppets or warlords who served their own ends.[80] Thus Dixie's main accomplishment was to establish an American presence in the Communist-held parts of China.

4

Communications

The Dixie Mission's radio connection with Chungking was its life line. In the beginning, responsibility for the link rested with the signal communications officer, Captain Paul Domke. OSS provided his radio and technical personnel, Sergeants Tony Remenih and Walter Gress. Domke and Remenih brought the radio and generators with them on the first plane to Yenan. By the time Gress arrived on the second plane, they had already selected one of the adobe-type houses on the hill behind the caves as the site for their operation.[1] The Communists supplied the electricity, a one-lung (one-cylinder) diesel engine. Remenih, a longtime amateur radio operator, considered the setup very primitive and said that he had better gear in his home.[2]

They worked out a simple plan to establish regular communications with Chungking, 1,000 miles away, and transmission was usually very good. At first it was all in Morse code, as they did not have sufficiently sophisticated voice radio equipment, but later the lighter radio transceiver equipment that had been developed for OSS was sent up.[3]

In the beginning, the men improvised everything. Remenih thought it strange that he had not been given a generator on what was supposed to be an important mission. Using what he had, he taught some of the Chinese guerrillas how to operate the hand-powered equipment that Signal Corps supplied in quantities adequate only for training. He also invented codes that the Chinese used behind the lines. In general, he considered his job with the Mission nothing more than his ham radio experience in action, especially when he had to go out in the field and operate or repair equipment with nothing more than his hands and his wits. He put his skills to use the first day the Mission arrived in Yenan, when the receiver burned out and had to be fixed during its maiden transmission, the one that was to notify Chungking of the men's safe arrival.

A hand-operated radio. The Yenan pagoda is seen in the background. Courtesy of Col. Wilbur J. Peterkin.

Besides having regular communications with Chungking and occasional contact with Kunming, the Yenan radio, code named Yensig, also received and relayed data from American navy personnel in the Gobi Desert. The navy was in the desert to monitor the weather as it flowed from Siberia toward Guam, and Remenih had to be on a certain frequency at a particular time to receive naval information.

If possible, the radio men were to determine whether any radio traffic took place between Moscow and the Yenan Communists. This was a difficult assignment, because Dixie lacked the proper equipment for isolating such radio signals, and Remenih knew the Chinese could have secreted a set that he could not see. More than once, he scanned the band to determine whether such a link existed but to no avail. He did know that the Communists had other installations. One was located ten miles from Yenan, and when his generator went out, the only way he could keep to his 8:00 A.M. transmission schedule was to mount a Mongolian pony and ride ten miles to use it.

The special codes that Remenih prepared for men who were heading behind the lines were machine codes, simple and complex transpositions, both of which were used at various times to contact him.[4] Encrypted messages coming in from the field were usually forwarded to the relay station in Chungking, where theater decoded them. Order-of-battle information was handled this way but not messages for individual OSS members, which were handed to the person for whom they were intended in an encoded state. The recipient then did his own decoding.[5]

The Yenan radio maintained contact with men behind the lines as well as direct connection with Signal Corps, Chungking. Rather quickly, Remenih learned that the really "hot stuff" was not sent over the air but communicated in letters or written reports that the frequent visitors to Yenan hand carried back to Chungking. Since Yenan had no regular courier service, most of the messages sent there were routine, for example, who would be arriving for the weekend. From the security standpoint it was wise not to use the radio for genuinely important news, since Yenan transmissions could be picked up as far away as San Francisco.[6]

In the beginning, according to Jack Klein, post security was lax. Anyone, including the Communists, could walk into the radio shack at any time and read the messages as they were being sent. When Klein joined the Mission in early 1945, however, procedures began to be tightened. Klein set up a small repair shop to maintain Dixie's radio paraphernalia and got Colonel Peterkin to put in an S maze entry. The transmitter was located so that outsiders could not see the codes. The radio transmitted on seven megahertz, approximately forty meters, and everything that came in and went out was encoded. Klein was also concerned because people like Michael Lindsay, Dimitri Yellacich, and some of the Chinese lingered near the radio. He felt that too many people who had no business there loitered around the message center, chatting and perhaps picking up information.

As previously noted, there were rivalries between the two services that operated radios in Yenan. The Signal Corps ran one of the American radios, and the Air Corps operated the other, which unlike Signal's simple arrangement was quite a sophisticated setup. It was to be used for sending weather reports, and it sometimes worked when Signal's did not. AACS would not allow Klein, or those who performed similar duty, to use the AACS radio, however, even when Yenan radio might otherwise be off the air for as long as twenty-four hours. Yeaton went along with this policy and decreed that the Signal Corps equipment should be used for sending intelligence information and the AACS gear for weather. So the Signal Corps operators kept patching up their old gear while the AACS apparatus stood idle three-quarters of the time.[7]

Communist radio operations also interested Dixie. Because it was necessary to move their equipment frequently, they had developed small, efficient, and highly portable sets. Very soon after the Mission's inception, Barrett sent the commanding general a report stating that each

Red army regiment or corresponding unit was in contact with subdistrict headquarters by radio, that subdistrict headquarters had telephone and/or radio connections with area headquarters, and that all areas had connections with Yenan.[8]

Michael Lindsay prepared a thorough report on the Eighteenth Group Army's communication system. He noted that the operations of the Eighteenth Group Army and the New Fourth Army extended from Kansu in the west to Shantung in the east and from south of the Yangtze into Jehol and Manchuria. Only the area west of the Yellow River, which included Yenan, was safe from Japanese attack, he observed. There were thirteen separate areas east of the Yellow River, the largest broken up into subareas. Under these main base areas were eighty-two military subdistricts that controlled the local regiments or guerrilla units. Lindsay divided the territories into four categories: (a) stable base areas, located mostly in the mountains, that the Japanese could attack only with large force; (b) semistable base areas with a complete Chinese organization that were liable to surprise Japanese raids because they were small or lacked natural defenses; (c) guerrilla areas in which Communist forces operated regularly that had large numbers of Japanese forts and garrison points and were intersected by motor roads and blockade ditches; (d) and the Japanese-controlled areas, mostly along the railroads, which Communist forces penetrated only on raids or in undercover operations.

In all these areas, said Lindsay, radio equipment had to be lightweight and easily transported. In the stable base areas, a station might be able to stay in one place for six or more months, but more commonly there were approximately three months during the year when the Japanese could be mopping up. During this period, the men on the station's team, frequently marching at night over difficult terrain, would carry out all the equipment on their backs. Heavy apparatus could be used in quiet periods, but it had to be safely buried when there was any threat of a Japanese attack, and it would be out of operation for several months each year.

In the semistable areas, all stations had to be ready to pack up and move, sometimes with only ten or twenty minutes' notice. In guerrilla areas, the gear had to be both portable and small, so that it could be carried without attracting attention. Quite often the stations operated in villages garrisoned by the Japanese.

Wherever they might be located, the sets needed to be capable of communicating regularly with Yenan over distances of up to 1,000 miles. Even the smaller units, which were used to contact local headquarters, had to transmit and receive over a hundred miles or more. Reliability also

Left to right, kneeling: Swenson, Dadian, and Cady; standing: Domke, Stelle, and Remenih. June 1945. Courtesy of Col. Wilbur J. Peterkin.

was essential, as sets that could not be maintained by their operators might have to be sent across several Japanese blockade lines for repair.

The Communists often changed frequencies to avoid Japanese detection and interference. Crystal-controlled transmitters were therefore unsuitable for general use. In August 1944 the Eighteenth Group Army and the New Fourth Army had a total of 657 operating stations. Of these, 322 obtained power from hand generators, 19 (all located in the Shensi-Kansu-Ningsia region) from an alternating current (AC) power supply, and the rest from batteries.

Little of the Communist radio equipment was up to date. The Communists did not start producing small hand generators until 1944, and few were in use at the time Dixie began. Lindsay found the transmitting equipment fairly satisfactory, although the receiving equipment with three type 30 tubes was nonselective. Nonselectivity was a serious disadvantage in equipment that had to work with very low power front-line stations. Also, the oscillating detector caused some radiation, and the note of a receiver searching for a signal made nearby stations easy to detect. Then too a shortage of batteries restricted the use of the radio. Batteries generally had to be brought in from the outside, as Yenan made only a few dry cells. Batteries consequently became harder and harder to get. Wet cells were used to some extent in telephone work, and some experimenting was done in making "B" batteries from small storage cells, but these were not portable and could be used only during noncombat periods in stable base areas.

The problem was that the Communists lacked a sufficient amount of communication equipment. Lindsay believed the Americans should provide them with field radios so that they could cooperate better with American intelligence. The exact number of sets they would need depended on the military situation, but a full program would mean 400-500 stations with large hand generators (fifteen to twenty watts output), 1,000 or more stations with small hand generators (two to five watts output), and perhaps 1,500-2,000 small battery-operated stations (two to three watts output). In August 1944, 322 hand generators were in use.

Lindsay also recommended introducing radio telephones as a way to speed up communications, since only the best operators could send or receive standard Chinese telegraph code without having to look up most of the characters in the codebook. Although a telephone network could be set up only in the main stable areas, he believed that much of the Eighteenth Group Army operating area offered geographical conditions in which ultra high frequency apparatus might be useful. In some locales, such as along the Pinghan Railroad, the Communists controlled the high mountains to the west, and line-of-sight communication was possible. This would involve small apparatus, would not require separate antennae, and would be difficult for the Japanese to intercept, as doing so would require a very large number of monitoring stations.

Barrett transmitted Lindsay's report, together with his own notations, to Dickey in Chungking. His notes reflected Barrett's belief that this suggested survey of required signal equipment would save time if assistance were given to the Communists later. He deemed such American support to the Communist intelligence-gathering activity appropriate, not to help the Communists, but to assist the U.S. Army in acquiring intelligence and weather information and to facilitate AGAS work. Colonel Dickey, who sent Lindsay's report to Stilwell, editorialized that it was "obvious from the outset that the information and aid which can be obtained from the Communists will depend on the speed and efficiency of their radio, telephone and telegraph network which, while a miracle of ingenuity in the mere fact of its existence, is precariously short of equipment."[9]

At the time Dickey sent this memo, the Communists had, in addition to the above-mentioned sets operated from hand generators, the following regular sets in operation: 19 (all at Yenan) on AC, 316 battery-operated sets, and over 500 other battery-operated sets not in use because they lacked batteries. The Communists were ready to put every ounce of supplies to immediate use and, according to Lindsay, could transform their entire communications system with 100 tons of materials.[10]

Some of the other Communist communication techniques were more primitive than their radios. They included: horse- or mule-mounted messengers, bicycle riders, military post, and secret couriers. Units below regiment used foot, mounted, and bicycle deliveries, especially in the plains areas. Army post offices were operated by the military and government jointly and served as an important supplement for daily communication within the bases. Secret couriers profited from good relations with the local population. They provided an important supplementary means of communication within a base or between bases.[11]

The Americans felt that the courier service could be improved by setting up schedules between regular stations. The existing service was irregular and slow, and couriers traveled only when they had sufficient messages to make a trip. Often, messages were sent only when a special party was making a trip from one base area into another. Consequently, important documents could be delayed for months before they reached central headquarters at Yenan.[12]

Sometimes the Communists used flags and flares to show the location of units and to signal the front or rear. At the front, they placed flags at the end of a long pole, which worked well in daylight, as did smoke signals. At night, they used native or locally made flares and beacon fires to signal the location or progress of a unit. Panels that would have allowed ground troops to indicate the location of various targets or particular enemy military units to American planes were not used, as there were no supporting aircraft.

The Chinese also kept in touch by shouting and blowing bugles. Men stood on hills or mountaintops and called to one another, passing information along. News often traveled at a rapid rate in this way. The stable base areas used bugles year-round, but in the semistable base regions they were used only during the quiet periods, when the enemy was not mopping up. Bugles were more effective in the mountains than on the plains, where enemy patrols could easily hear them. In cities or villages, inhabitants rang ancient bells as air raid alarms or to signal the approach of enemy planes. In army units, bugles supplemented this method.[13]

Frequently, local people used a human telegraph system. Two young saplings or poles of medium height were placed six to eight feet apart on the summits of high hills or mountains or were located on vantage points on ridges. Often the poles carried white or red flags at the staff end, a bundle of straw, or a peasant's garment. If trees were used, all the branches were trimmed off except those within a few feet of the top. The trimming left a noticeable plume that could be seen easily for miles down the valley. One or two local villagers, usually old men, young boys, or women, were stationed near the mountain or ridge with these signal devices, and they alerted the people down the valleys in agreed-upon ways.

Both flagpoles and upright standing trees signified that there was no danger. If the enemy left its stronghold and headed in the general direction of the people in the valley, the watchers would lower one pole or tree, to signal the possibility that the enemy was entering the area and the people should prepare to leave. The same signal also told members of the People's Militia to prepare to lay mines or otherwise to anticipate defending their area. The lowering of the last pole or tree indicated that the enemy was in the immediate vicinity. The inhabitants then needed to scatter to the mountains, and the People's Militia knew to take up their positions and complete their mine laying and other defenses. The signals were usually placed in advantageous positions so that the warnings could be relayed in a matter of minutes from one pole or ridge to another down a long valley or from one valley to another.

In conjunction with such visual means, old temple gongs, bells, or lengths of railroad steel were hung from a tree or frame. These were placed near the visual signals but usually down the slope at the foot of the mountain, near the village or a peasant's courtyard. By beating the gongs or bells, the sentries drew people's attention to the visual signals on the mountain peaks. When the enemy drew close, the signals sounded constantly, until everyone had made a getaway. The signaler was usually a member of the People's Militia or the Self-Defense Army.

A third type of signal was used mainly at night but sometimes during the day when no visual or sound means was available. It consisted of a single hand grenade, which was thrown when the scout or sentry saw the enemy approaching or had other definite information that the enemy was in the immediate vicinity. This warning advised the people to leave quickly without taking anything with them. One night Peterkin's group from the Observer Section crossed the railroad and made their way up a streambed near a village. An alert sentry threw a hand grenade to warn the sleeping populace because he had mistaken the observers and their accompanying troops for an enemy column.

The Communists did not communicate with dogs or pigeons as the Japanese did. They had captured many specimens from the enemy, but because they lacked experience in using them and fought a highly mobile type of warfare, birds and animals were never used.[14]

After consulting with the Communists, especially with Wang Chen, the director of the Yenan Radio Department, the Americans concluded that the Chinese facilities were so overloaded that any added high priority traffic that American military intelligence might request would slow it down and would further decrease its efficiency. The observers proposed expanding the network and designed one that could transmit intelligence from subordinate points through main bases to a central collection point at the headquarters of the Eighteenth Group Army at Yenan. Wang Chen told them that the Chinese could support such an expanded network best by providing operators and a few technicians. Most of the headquarters stations would be able to operate into Yenan using sets with an output of fifteen to twenty watts powered by hand or foot generators. Motor-generated equipment was not advisable, because it sometimes became necessary to move quickly, and such equipment was difficult for the soldier-operators to transport, he said.

The plan became known by its code name of Yensig 4, after the memo on which it was first proposed to Chungking. The scheme envisioned a minimum of three to five separate transmitter and receiver stations, to be set up in Yenan for sending, receiving, and coordinating all the traffic handled over the proposed network. As a first step, caves were to be prepared to house the personnel and equipment. Once the stations were up and running, they would operate twenty-four hours a day from locations in the hills. They would be placed some distance from the city of Yenan as a precaution against possible air raids.

Regular gasoline-powered generators could supply power for the Yensig equipment as long as a good grade of oil and some standard octane gas was made available. The gasoline obtainable in Yenan was of wide fraction and could be used with fair results, but the oil produced locally from castor beans was not suitable for lubricating high-speed motors, and so oil for the purpose had to be brought in from the outside. All motor maintenance in this part of China was complicated by the presence of quantities of fine loess dust in the air in the winter, spring, and summer.

Domke recommended that Americans operate the stations at central headquarters in Yenan, in close cooperation with the radio men of the Eighteenth Group Army. The Communists would assume the initial responsibility for setting up the intelligence collecting field stations, and their upkeep would be the Communists' responsibility.[15]

Radio reports from Yenan well served those interested in prosecuting the war, particularly the Twentieth Bomber Command and AGAS. In a report dated September 12, 1944, Colonel Foss of Twentieth Bomber Command noted that during the current week three reports of more than ordinary interest had been received. The first stated that on July (date jumbled) four aircraft had bombed the railroad yards at Cheng-Hsien, killing seventeen Japanese and frightening the survivors so much that antiaircraft protection had been increased. When the local people saw the American planes, they "clapped their hands with joy." A second message, dated August 22, stated that there were over eighty enemy planes, apparently practicing maneuvers, on the airfield at Shi Chia Chiang.

The third report, from the east coast of central China, included a telegram signed by Yeh Chien-ying and mentioned the crash landing of Twentieth Bomber Command aircraft 26264. It described how one of the planes in a very large formation had suddenly burst into flames and fallen. Troops from a Communist independent brigade rushed to the rescue. On the way they collided with 200 enemy troops, whom they repulsed after two hours of bitter fighting. The Chinese lost five men and the enemy more than ten in this encounter. At the time this radio message was sent, they had undertaken a wide search for the parachuted crew. Five were located on September 1, although one had gone down in enemy territory. Naturally, Twentieth Bomber Command was pleased to have a detailed report of this incident, especially since it included the aircraft's number.[16]

AGAS also liked the idea of expanding the Communist net but preferred to have a few small sets located in spots vital for obtaining information pertinent to the rescue of downed fliers.[17] In addition, AGAS believed that a radio net should be established to collect information concerning prisoner of war camps. Conceivably, such a net might aid prisoners of war and might be able to help evaders in northeast China, Manchuria, and Korea. Also, radio contact would minimize competition and duplication of effort.[18]

Emmerson thought that an augmented Chinese radio net could broadcast to Japan, Korea, and Manchuria and could be used to spread defeatism and reduce resistance when the home islands were invaded. He suggested setting up a transmitter in a Communist base area such as Shantung Province, where the Japanese People's Emancipation League had a strong unit and was establishing a school. He noted that the Communists had trustworthy Japanese personnel to operate such a station and that additional trained personnel could be recruited from the school in Yenan. Emmerson thought that the broadcasts would have immeasurably greater effect if the station were identified with a "Free Japan" group rather than with Americans, who were the enemy.[19]

Everyone agreed that although the Communists lacked experience in gathering the kind of intelligence that the United States wanted, they were anxious to please and eager to improve. Their one deficiency was that because they had no air force, they had paid little or no attention to air intelligence. More than one American thought that helping them get a good radio net would be the first step in maximizing their potential in the war effort.[20] As it was, radio communication was so halting and slow that messages prepared by Sergeant Nakamura in the field took three weeks to arrive in Yenan, making order-of-battle people feel that it was not possible to keep up to date on Japanese troop movements.[21]

Eagerness to cooperate did help the Chinese overcome some limitations. They secured long questionnaires from Dixie on various types of military intelligence, translated them, consulted the Americans about details, and then radioed them out to their forward areas. Many Dixie members were impressed with the accuracy of the Communists' statements and their potential for intelligence, which was revealed by items received from the field. Stelle of OSS thought the Communists important enough that the Mission to Yenan should be made permanent.[22]

It was the expectation of establishing a political modus vivendi that led to the ambitious Yensig 4 project.[23] Stelle, anxious to get the net operating and agents trained "before the bandwagon began to get cluttered up," left for Kunming via Chungking on October 5, 1944, with Barrett's approval. He arranged for radio equipment, which Tenth Weather Squadron was to fly directly to Yenan via Chengtu at the end of the month.[24] Stelle considered the approval of this transfer of goods to be the first really important operational development since the section's inception.[25]

By November, however, it was evident that political negotiations would be long and drawn out, so that immediate theater action on the OSS project would be stalled. Again with Barrett's blessing, a much more modest plan was concocted. It called for the procurement of materiel, the training of operators, and the setting up of a central station in Yenan to work twenty to twenty-five field stations. This plan was presented as a joint OSS–Tenth Weather project, since Tenth Weather was eager to get reports from the field more quickly than the limited Communist network could provide them. Colonel Dickey approved the project with the understanding that it would be under the direction of the commanding officer of the Dixie Mission and would be coordi-

nated with the larger project if it was ever approved. By January, training was far enough along that equipment for setting up the central
station at Yenan could be secured. The men involved believed that the
new equipment would implement the plan, would help potential OSS
operations, and would create goodwill with the Chinese by relieving
some of the burden on their network.

Then, while Stelle and Remenih were in Kunming assembling
equipment, they learned that General Wedemeyer had unexpectedly
approved the Yensig 4 plan. The two men expected a good deal of time
to elapse before arrangements could be made for the equipment for the
larger project. They also felt that it would be valuable for some OSS
radio gear to be taken promptly to Yenan, if only for local goodwill.
Accordingly, they proceeded with the smaller project, believing that
the initial network would be incorporated into Yensig 4 when that system was ready to go into operation.

Meanwhile, Colonel Peterkin had replaced Barrett as commanding officer. He bustled around Chungking and Kunming and reduced
by at least a couple of months the time required to ready the Yensig
equipment for Yenan. By the time Stelle had returned to Yenan, equipment for the large project was on its way, and by the time Remenih
returned with the remainder of the OSS gear, several planeloads of Yensig
paraphernalia had arrived.

It seemed obvious that going ahead with the small setup would
be wasted effort, especially since theater was considering turning over
administration of Yensig to OSS. Common sense demanded that there
be only one unified network in the forward areas held by the Communists. A better policy appeared to be pooling the small amount of OSS
equipment with the large amount of Yensig gear and starting the whole
thing as a unit.[26] Heppner spoke to Wedemeyer about this plan. The
commanding general wanted to talk to Hurley and the Generalissimo
before giving OSS the go-ahead on its project. He was concerned about
the type of personnel to be sent to Yenan, so Heppner advised confin-
ing OSS personnel there to Special Operations (SO) and Secret Intelligence (SI), since "these types will be, I hope, least subject to political
influences and less likely to dabble in movements."[27] (The purpose of
SO was to effect physical subversion of the enemy by conducting sabotage operations and supporting resistance groups. SI obtained information by secret means not available otherwise.[28])

As a result, a directive from General Wedemeyer gave control of
Yensig 4 to OSS on April 25, 1945. The memo noted that 14,000
pounds of an estimated 58,000 pounds of equipment for the project
had already reached Yenan and was in storage. This materiel had been

diverted from other projects and was not to be turned over to the Communists for their private use. It could be used only for the collection and transmission of intelligence for American agencies.[29] At a later date OSS expected to be authorized to do intelligence and sabotage work in the same area.[30]

By May 1945, there were twenty-five trained Chinese radio operators in Yenan, along with a sizable quantity of radio and weather equipment for simple field observations. Starved for equipment, the Chinese were impatient because everything that had arrived sat idle. Tenth Weather was also irritated at having to wait around while theater decided how Yensig was to be established. The Chinese reported the location of Japanese and puppet-controlled radio installations, some of which were quite large and employed up to sixty men. Often they could give the Americans drawings or charts of these installations. The information they provided about Japanese communications and order of battle was evaluated for reliability and was ranked as to its value. This work was especially important when an agent had no technical radio or electrical background.[31]

In the meantime, the Dixie Mission radio had all it could do to keep up with the Chungking administrative and intelligence traffic and the considerable weather news transmitted to Chengtu. Peterkin asked that Captain Malsbary of the Signal Corps be sent to Yenan to install Yensig. He anticipated having at least three collecting stations operating within a month. One would be at Chin Sui, and others would be located at Tai Hang (near Varoff Field) and Fouping.[32] Peterkin planned to tie all weather stations and order-of-battle operations into this system. He replaced the two American radio operators in the field with Chinese radio operators whom Lieutenant Remenih had trained.[33]

The plans for the expanded radio net did not work out to the satisfaction of either the Americans or the Chinese. The Communists believed that the radio equipment had been sent to relieve their overloaded communication net. In fact, the effect was the opposite, and the Chinese nets were more jammed than ever once they began carrying weather information.[34] By early June the Dixie Mission had to inform OSS headquarters that the Communists were unwilling to allow a communications net to be set up prior to the formal presentation of an overall plan for intelligence and other operations. The Communists wanted to know what the Americans planned for their area. Peterkin thought the situation called for a visit from a high-ranking representative of the commanding general, someone who could officially present and discuss an overall plan.[35]

Attempting to break the stalemate and get Yensig underway,

Peterkin, Stelle, and Swenson conferred with General Yeh. They requested permission to set up a radio monitoring station, to send order-of-battle people to Tai Hang, to send an American weatherman to Chin Sui, and to have American order-of-battle people meet with the local statistics committee. When the communications plan was outlined, Yeh said too many soldiers from the Eighteenth Group Army would be necessary to protect the Americans. The Americans told him that they neither needed nor wanted protection. Then, in a departure from his usual custom, Yeh asked to postpone any decisions until after he had consulted with his superiors.[36]

While this Communist balking did not materially delay operations, Americans could not be placed in the Communist forward areas without their agreement. Yensig would have to wait until someone with authority came from theater and assured the Communists that the United States respected their capabilities in the war against Japan. Such a meeting would also serve to offset the general informality that existed in the relations between the men of Dixie and their Communist hosts.[37]

Japanese prisoners were another source of news. A captured soldier, for example, described how carrier pigeons and their handlers were trained.[38] Also, the Japanese had used dogs prior to 1942 to carry messages from one strong point to another or between blockhouses. They curtailed this practice when the Eighteenth Group Army successfully captured the dogs.

Both Japanese and puppets used pigeons extensively in the plains areas, especially in central Hopei and Shansi Provinces. They helped units going out on mopping-up campaigns to report back to their bases. They were useful in emergencies too, for example, when wire communications were destroyed between blockhouses and strong points. Early in the war, each Japanese infantry company maintained a loft of forty to fifty birds. For their part, the Communists considered birds unreliable for communication because they had been able to intercept, capture, and kill so many of them.[39]

While Dolan was at the Ninth Sub-District headquarters in central Hopei in January 1945, he discovered that puppet troops used pigeons. A unit of Japanese and puppets had attacked the headquarters before dawn. Dolan and members of the staff bolted into the village's underground tunnels, where they remained all day. They later escaped under cover of darkness. A week later, on January 27, members of the Eighteenth Group Army captured a carrier pigeon just outside another puppet strong point. The pigeon carried a message intended for one of the garrisons. It warned that a foreigner, probably an American, was traveling southwest with the Eighteenth Group Army. Dolan learned of the bird's capture and the message it carried a few days later when he and his party reached a small village about thirteen miles to the east.[40]

In addition to using pigeons and dogs, the Japanese employed pyrotechnic signals, both for ground communication and for air-ground liaison. Prearranged signals incorporated red, green, and white flares either singly or in combination. The Japanese in North China also used prearranged smoke signals from smudge fires or smoke candles. They had a visual communication system that used lanterns and the Japanese national flag or two small cloth flags, one red and one white.

The Eighteenth Group Army had given Japanese communication intelligence little or no tactical or technical attention during the eight war years prior to the Americans' arrival. Tactically, the type of guerrilla warfare the Communists fought did not force them to learn much about enemy communications. Their only interest had been in cannibalizing enemy equipment to supplement their own insufficient and inadequate supply stocks for both wire and radio communication. With the exception of some wire equipment, enemy gear had seldom been used without partial or complete modification. It was either too heavy or too clumsy for the small, quick-moving bands of regulars and partisans whose strength lay in surprise and clever, rapid tactics of deception.

The Yenan men of the Signal Corps were able to send headquarters captured coded documents that had been translated and microfilmed.[41] The Japanese used various codes interchangeably. In North China, the majority of the cryptographic systems they used in the field stations were numerical, including those using signal flags, signal lamps, and signal panels.[42] They did not use these devices to warn of impending air raids, however. As soon as an air alert was given, they closed all the main trunks in the telephone net to other traffic and gave air raid announcements urgent priority.

The Americans learned about the Japanese air alert system from a captured document. The same document ordered military radios to transmit warnings within three minutes of sighting enemy planes, including the time necessary for encoding. Commercial radio stations also reported these alarms to the populace, and stations in Peking and other large cities gave a warning note, announced the approach of enemy planes, and urged inhabitants to take necessary precautions.

According to General Yang, some of the main enemy airfields had sound detectors mounted on high towers like "mechanical ears." These were able to detect enemy planes at 100 kilometers. When the general was quizzed about the possibility that these "ears" might be radar, he said he thought they were probably sound detectors and that neither he nor his men knew what radar was or what a radar installation looked like.

Railroad security presented the Japanese with special problems. Trains running on the main railroad systems in North China had no way of communicating with the railroad stations while they were underway. Many times trains left a station only to be intercepted by Allied planes whose presence had not been reported prior to the train's departure.[43]

The security of the Chinese codes concerned the Americans somewhat, but in general they felt confident about them. They were concerned after a number of messages were sent regarding the observer party that traveled behind the Japanese lines, because the capture of that group would have been a major prize for the Japanese. Furthermore, radio messages were always sent to Yenan regarding fliers who had been forced to bail out almost in the teeth of the enemy, and these men were usually evacuated without being captured.[44]

Any comprehensive evaluation of the information-gathering network that operated in North China during the period of the Dixie Mission must assess both the Communists' effectiveness and the viability of the plans for Yensig 4. Considering their out-of-date methods and equipment, the Chinese achievements were impressive. They operated all along the China coast. It was theoretically possible for them to relay information from as far away as Canton or Hainan by radio, messenger, or other means. No sure way to check this information existed, however, and sometimes the radio messages arrived garbled or too late to be of real value. Yensig 4 had been planned to correct these problems. Had the war lasted longer than it did, Yensig might have gone into operation and might have supplied a more complete flow of information.[45]

The Chinese Communists, however, came increasingly to feel that their efforts were not going to be recognized and would not gain them a voice in determining China's future. As a result, they became less and less willing to take part in programs that they believed would benefit others more than themselves. One such program was the expansion of the communications net that the Americans had planned without telling the Communists exactly how it was to be used.[46]

On August 8, 1945, Colonel Ivan D. Yeaton, then commanding officer of Dixie, sent General Yeh two plans to "increase the quantity and quality of intelligence transmission." The plan for immediate expansion of the communication system was marked in blue and was therefore called the Blue Plan. The other plan, known as the Red Plan, was longer range and presupposed that the United States would remain in North China. The Blue Plan provided for immediate expansion of the communications net, including the addition of two to five more operators and repairmen and an understanding that further new stations would require additional personnel. Other services, like AGAS, would also need extra staffing as their roles became more prominent. At the close of his memo describing these two schemes to Yeh, Yeaton made statements implying that the Blue Plan would open the way to an important increase in the volume and speed with which vital enemy intelligence could be transmitted. He stressed that both the Blue Plan and the Red Plan had been drawn up in accordance with military requirements for defeating Japan, and neither planned or contemplated hidden or subversive activities.[47]

Preparation of the Blue and Red Plans coincided with America's dropping of two atomic bombs on Japan and the rapid ending of hostilities in Asia. These actions eliminated any further need to expand the network or to continue the information-gathering activities that had been the reason for expansion in the first place. Tenth Weather was subsequently authorized to reduce its personnel to the minimum and to use the Chinese as operators.[48] AACS was told to relinquish all AACS equipment to any American unit, pack up, and leave on the next plane.[49] Still, regular radio schedules were maintained with Shanghai and Peking, and even after all the equipment on the post had been turned over to the Communists, the Americans continued to keep the radio operational.[50]

In the end, more than ninety new radio sets remained in crates in a storeroom. These were field operations radios with hand-cranked generators. Clifford Young, Dixie's last commanding officer, asked theater what to do with them. He also needed to dispose of the transmitter that guided aircraft, the photograph and signal equipment, the generators that produced electricity, and the vehicles.

At the time it was closing down, the Mission possessed two weapons carriers, two jeeps, and two three-quarter-ton trucks in addition to the items mentioned above. There was also a radar weather device located on top of the hill. Theater instructed Young to dismantle the radar equipment and ship it back but to declare all other equipment surplus and do whatever he wanted with it. Since he would have needed planes to fly everything out, which probably would have cost more than the gear was worth, Young turned everything but the radar over to the Communists. They were elated. The OSS had trained them on the apparatus, and they were familiar with it. This was the only equipment the United States ever gave them outright.[51]

5

Diplomacy, Differences, and Patrick J. Hurley

As previously noted, the United States did not always find Chiang Kai-shek the most agreeable wartime ally. His long-standing differences with Mao Tse-tung clearly indicated that a civil war between the Nationalists and the Communists would inevitably follow the close of international hostilities.

Chiang also squabbled with General Stilwell. In July 1944 he bypassed the general and asked FDR to send an influential man to China, someone who would enjoy the president's full confidence and with whom he, Chiang, could collaborate on all political and military matters. He wanted someone farsighted, with political ability and vision, for he believed that military cooperation had to be built on cooperation in other spheres.

The suggestion of a direct liaison dovetailed with Roosevelt's penchant for doing business through personal representatives.[1] Roosevelt had told Wallace the previous May that he believed an American arbiter might be able to "knock some heads together" and engineer a political compromise, which Roosevelt wanted in this case because he feared that the Russians might attempt to grab Manchuria if a civil war erupted in China.[2]

On August 10, the president informed Chiang that he had chosen Major General Patrick J. Hurley for the job.[3] The sixty-one-year-old Hurley was a self-made millionaire lawyer-investor from Oklahoma who prided himself on his negotiating ability and had, in fact, negotiated a favorable settlement for Sinclair Oil with Mexico just before the war.[4] Donald Nelson, the former head of the War Production Board, who was being sent to Chungking to help the Chinese government plan and organize production, was to travel with Hurley.

Hurley's selection originated in the War Department. In the be-

ginning there was apparently no particular difference of opinion between him and either the War Department or State regarding the purpose of his mission.[5] In marked contrast to many American officials in
the China Theater, whose language ability and cultural knowledge
prompted them to take sides on China's domestic issues, Hurley viewed
himself as representing only the interests and objectives of the United
States. He strove to act from this position regardless of his personal
convictions.[6]

According to General Hurley's report to the Department of State,
his instructions from the White House dated August 18 specified that
he was:

1. To serve as personal representative of the President to the
   Generalissimo;
2. To promote harmonious relations between Chiang and
   General Stilwell and to facilitate the latter's exercise of
   command over the Chinese armies placed under his direction;
3. To perform certain additional duties respecting military
   supplies;
4. To maintain intimate contact with Ambassador Gauss.[7]

Once Chiang had agreed to accept Hurley and Nelson as Roosevelt's spokesmen, FDR pressed the Generalissimo to put Stilwell in
charge of all Chinese forces, under Chiang's direction. In a message
proposed by Marshall on August 12 that was sent on August 23, FDR
urged Chiang to act "at the earliest possible date [as] extended delib-
erations and perfection of arrangements may well have fateful consequences in the light of the gravity of the military situation." The president understood the political difficulty of installing an American officer
in the desired command position but felt certain that Hurley and Stilwell
between them could adequately comprehend the political problems.[8]

Hurley began his journey to China as personal representative of the
president on August 18, 1944. He and Nelson flew to Chungking via
Moscow, where they discussed the Chinese situation with Russian foreign minister Vyacheslav M. Molotov. According to Nelson, he explained
that his main business in China involved economic matters, while Hurley's
concerned military affairs, that Chinese cooperation in the war was of
"vital importance," and that to achieve this cooperation the U.S. government must support the Generalissimo and effect complete unity in China.

Nelson requested a Soviet opinion on this subject. Molotov replied that the Chinese had shown little interest in strengthening relations with Moscow, which had deteriorated in recent years. The Rus-

sian then spoke of the impoverished conditions of the Chinese people, some of whom mistakenly called themselves Communists when they were merely expressing dissatisfaction with their economic condition. They would forget this political inclination when their situation improved, Molotov said, and the Soviet government should not be associated with or blamed for these "communist elements." In fact, the Soviets would be glad if the United States aided the Chinese in unifying their country, and in improving their military and economic condition, choosing the best people for this task. Molotov made it clear that until Chiang Kai-shek tried to improve Sino-Soviet relations by changing his policies, the Soviet Union had no interest in Chinese governmental affairs.

This conversation was critical to Hurley's developing position, as shown by his frequent references to it in later reports.[9] His treatment of the internal divisions in China reflected his confidence that without Soviet support, the Chinese Communists would respond positively to proposals for creating a unified national government.[10] He believed that if the Russians supported Chiang, or at least remained aloof, the Chinese Communists would be dissuaded from pursuing an active revolutionary line in China. Then Chiang would feel more secure and might be prepared to accept some sort of meaningful compromise with the Communists.[11]

Hurley arrived in Chungking on September 6 and spoke briefly with John Service in mid-October. Hurley had never read any of Service's reports, nor was he interested in listening to the Foreign Service officer's comments. Shortly thereafter, Service went to Washington to participate in policy discussions and to report on his stay in Yenan. While he was there, he advised Harry Hopkins, Roosevelt's longtime adviser, that Clarence Gauss planned to resign as American ambassador to China. Gauss's decision reflected distress at Hurley's flamboyant manner and discouragement about Chiang's refusal to compromise with the Chinese Communists. In his opinion, Service warned, it would be disastrous to replace Gauss with Hurley.[12]

Meanwhile, back in Chungking, Hurley brimmed with self-assurance. Optimistic and favorably inclined toward Stilwell, with whom he had established a rough-and-ready rapport, Hurley conferred with Chiang on September 7. He then radioed FDR that Chiang was prepared to give Stilwell actual command of all forces, plus his complete confidence, but "we have not yet ironed out any of the details, some of which will undoubtedly be difficult to solve."[13]

Hurley told Chiang what Molotov had said, expecting in this fashion to dispel the Generalissimo's belief that the Chinese Communists were controlled from Russia and to lessen his fear of dealing with them. But Gauss believed that both sides doubted each other's motives. He questioned whether it was possible to eliminate their mutual distrust on a broad basis, although he thought a limited solution might be reached. Such a resolution could provide for special groups or parties to be represented, perhaps in a council formed to meet the serious war crisis that China currently faced. Secretary of State Cordell Hull agreed with Gauss's suggestion. He urged the ambassador to persuade Chiang to arrange a meeting between himself and Chou En-lai, the Communist representative in Chungking, so that the Communists could be told that unity was urgent. Gauss should inform Hurley, Stilwell, and Nelson that he was doing so and possibly take one or more of them with him to see Chiang.[14]

In *Dragon by the Tail*, John Davies recalled how Hurley had an expansive nature and was not content to deal solely with those matters that the president had defined as his mission, namely to harmonize Chiang-Stilwell relations and to facilitate Stilwell's exercise of command. On September 12, he presented the Generalissimo with a ten-point agenda. Only the last four points bore directly upon Stilwell's powers. The first six were essentially a prospectus for the transformation of China:

1. The paramount objective of Chinese-American collaboration is to bring about the unification of all military forces in China for the immediate defeat of Japan and the liberation of China;
2. Co-operating with China in bringing about closer relations and harmony with Russia and Britain for the support of the Chinese objectives;
3. The unification of all military forces under the command of the Generalissimo;
4. The marshaling of all resources in China for war purposes;
5. The support of efforts of Generalissimo for political unification of China on a democratic basis;
6. Submission of present and postwar economic plans for China.

Later in the month, Hurley laid two more documents before Chiang. One was a draft appointing Stilwell field commander of the Chinese ground and air forces. The second was a draft directive from Chiang to Stilwell that instructed the American field commander to "proceed at once with the reorganization and relocation of ground and air forces." This document ordered Stilwell to activate and equip new units, to disband old units, and to transfer individuals and units from one command to another without regard to existing jurisdictions. Finally, Stilwell was to improve the troops' living conditions and to requisition supplies, for which receipts would be given that the Chinese government would redeem.

Hurley would have been shocked if he had understood the implications of what he was asking from the Generalissimo. His two documents, which reflected Stilwell's wishes, could have brought down Chiang's rickety power structure if they had been put into effect. Most officers would have rejected even the proposal to better the lot of the troops; the existing system habitually and deliberately underfed, exploited, abused, and profited from its soldiery. If the officers' objections were overridden, the inflation-logged economy would be swamped. Nor could the Chinese treasury afford to pay for supplies requisitioned by army units.[15]

Almost every day, and sometimes more than once a day, the Generalissimo and Hurley discussed ways of augmenting Stilwell's command powers that might be mutually satisfying. In the meantime, the military situation was deteriorating. Chiang wanted the Y Force moved from the Burma border (where it had just taken Tengchung and needed to take only Lungling to control the entire trace of the Burma Road) in order to protect Kunming. Stilwell reported this request to Marshall, who was meeting in Quebec with Churchill, Roosevelt, and the Combined Joint Chiefs of Staff. They were planning the complete recovery of Burma, and withdrawal of Chiang's troops from the border would upset this plan.

On September 16 the president sent Stilwell a stinging message to hand carry to Chiang.[16] It was written in the first person and was transmitted in special code so that a literal copy, not a paraphrase, could be delivered. It stated the president's conviction, after reading the last reports on the situation in China, that Chiang was faced with disaster unless he proceeded at once to (1) reinforce the Chinese armies in the Salween area and have them press their offensive and (2) place Stilwell "in unrestricted command" of all his forces. The president said he trusted that the Generalissimo, whose farsighted vision had guided and inspired the Chinese people during the war, would see the need for these steps. The president had stated his thoughts with complete frankness, the note ended, because "it appears . . . that all your and our efforts to save China are to be lost by further delays."[17]

Hurley was at the Generalissimo's house on the afternoon of the nineteenth when Stilwell arrived with the president's message. Stilwell declined Chiang's invitation to join the various men who were meeting there and instead asked Hurley to step out of the room. He then showed Hurley the president's message. Hurley wanted to deliver it himself.

The Dixie compound in the spring of 1945. Courtesy of Col. Wilbur J. Peterkin.

He told Stilwell, "You shouldn't now, because of this firm language, pile it on him at the time when he has felt compelled to make every concession that we have asked. . . . he is ready to bring troops down from the north to reinforce you on the Salween front; he is going to appoint you commander-in-chief."[18]

Certainly, it would have been better politically for the president's representative rather than Stilwell to have delivered the message, since the Generalissimo found no one more repellent than Stilwell except possibly Mao Tse-tung. Also, by delivering the news during a conference that involved Chiang, Hurley, and senior members of the Chinese high command, Stilwell heightened Chiang's embarrassment.[19] When the Generalissimo read the Chinese translation of the message, he looked, according to Hurley, as if he had been hit in the solar plexus, but showing no emotion, he merely said, "I understand." He then reached over to his teacup and put the cover on upside down. Stilwell, in Chinese, said, "That gesture still means, I presume, that the party is over." Someone said yes, and Stilwell and Hurley walked out.[20]

Stilwell was so pleased with what he regarded as a final victory that he wrote a verse commemorating the occasion. But Stilwell and others had misjudged the power of the United States to compel the regime of Chiang Kai-shek to perform. If Chiang did not wish to act, all he had to do was stall and go limp, as in fact he did.[21] Hurley advised him to take time to put his thoughts and feelings in order as they continued to talk about the terms and ways of implementing the president's proposals. Chiang's revulsion to Stilwell so impressed Hurley, however, that when Hurley prepared the next report for the president, it seemed to Stilwell to be recommending that he be relieved. Hurley revised it but found the Generalissimo no longer willing to consider *anzy* program that would leave Stilwell with authority in China.[22]

On September 24 Chiang and Soong sent Hurley a message for transmission to Roosevelt. It reiterated that, while Chiang had accepted the principle of an American commander in charge of his army, he could never accept Stilwell in this position. To force him to do so would be to "knowingly court inevitable disaster." Hurley added his own comments: Stilwell himself had become the central problem in China.[23] Only his removal could remedy the damage already done. Furthermore, no progress would be made in resolving other questions until FDR appointed a new American supreme commander.[24]

Finally, on October 5, the president radioed Chiang that although he would replace Stilwell as chief of staff and as distributor of lend-lease supplies, he wanted him retained as commander on the fighting fronts of Yunnan and Burma. Chiang stood by his original request that Stilwell be relieved. On October 18, in a cool and businesslike communiqué, FDR informed him that Stilwell would be recalled immediately. Henceforth, the China-Burma-India Theater would be split into two theaters, with India-Burma under Major General Daniel I. Sultan and China under Major General Albert C. Wedemeyer.[25] The latter was appointed commanding general of the U.S. forces in the China Theater. He was also authorized to accept the position of chief of staff to the Generalissimo. Sultan was to have the same post in the India-Burma Theater, with actual control of the Chinese troops fighting in Burma. Sultan and Wedemeyer were mutually enjoined to work closely together.

Some of Stilwell's staff thought that Wedemeyer had been selected in part because he had established himself as someone who could get along with the British, who were often as difficult for Stilwell to deal with as was Chiang.[26] The new arrangements made Wedemeyer's command relationships much simpler than those under which Stilwell had tried to operate.[27]

Wedemeyer left for China with great misgivings. In Washington, where he had been serving as a planner on Marshall's staff, he had heard terrible things about the Generalissimo. He had listened to Stilwell's opinions about Chiang's dishonesty and lack of knowledge in military matters. Wedemeyer assumed that Stilwell was the top American authority on China, so it surprised and displeased him to arrive in China and find that the general had departed. Wedemeyer had expected Stilwell to brief him truthfully, as a "fellow American," but instead Stilwell had left in a huff on October 21. Wedemeyer did not discount the possibility that Stilwell was not only angry at being removed for what he considered to be political reasons but also resentful at having been replaced by a man fifteen or twenty years younger than he.

General Claire Chennault, commander of the Fourteenth Air Force, met Wedemeyer in Kunming, where he arrived after flying the Hump. But Chennault had not been on speaking terms with Stilwell for a while. As a result, Wedemeyer had no one to tell him exactly what dispositions Stilwell had made as theater commander or what kind of directives he had given to the far-flung outposts. China was approximately the same size as the United States, and Wedemeyer, at headquarters in Chungking, felt much as if he had been in Chicago and had been charged with administering to people in Florida and New England using poor roads and limited communications.[28]

Wedemeyer, who took command of the newly designated China Theater on October 31, 1944, was temperamentally different from Stilwell. He usually relied on flexibility and conciliation rather than rigidly insisting on essentials. His directive specified that:

1. With regard to U.S. combat forces under his command, his
   primary mission was to carry out air operations from China;
2. He was to continue to assist the Chinese air and ground forces
   in operation, training and logistical support;
3. He was to control the allocation of Lend-Lease supplies

delivered into China, within priorities set by the Joint Chiefs-
of-Staff;

4. In his relationship with the Chinese forces he was to advise
   and assist the Generalissimo in the conduct of military
   operations against Japan;

5. He was not to use American resources to suppress civil strife
   except if necessary to protect American lives and property.[29]

To men like John Service, who had been in China for much of the
war, Stilwell's recall marked another downward step in American-Chinese relations. Chiang had used Stilwell's delivery of the unwelcome
message to retract his promise to put Stilwell in command; because
Stilwell had delivered the message, he remained Chiang's subordinate.
In a "confidential" talk to the Kuomintang Central Executive Committee that "leaked out," Chiang then threatened to continue fighting
without American aid. The combination of Stilwell's temperament, the
fact that there had been complaints about him from many sources,
Chiang's insistence on his own prerogatives as chief of state, and Hurley's
pro-Chiang stance had resulted in FDR's decision to recall Stilwell.
The episode may have had greater importance in that it reflected China's
declining military importance and Washington's realization that China
would not become a great power after the war.[30]

Long afterward, John Davies concluded that the command crisis
over Stilwell was the inevitable result of two illusions. One was America's
romantic image of China, which embodied an element of self-reproach
because America had not sprung to the rescue when the Japanese first
invaded. The other illusion was the belief that the United States could
significantly shape the course of events in China.[31] At the time, however, the president responded to questions about Stilwell's recall by
treating the change in command as merely a "case of personalities." It
did not involve matters of strategy, distribution of supplies, or relations
with the Chinese Communists, he insisted. Clearly, the personalities
had clashed, for though Stilwell knew China well, he was not one who
suffered military malingering gladly. He had grown impatient because
of all the frustrations he had experienced trying to make Chiang take
the field against the common enemy.

For his part, Chiang never tolerated opposition to his political
scheming from his entourage, and so he certainly would not put up
with an antagonistic foreigner, especially one who only a short time
before had been a mere colonel. After Stilwell's departure the Generalissimo was subjected to fewer rough American admonitions. He still
had to remain mindful of American judgment, however, since the change
left the American government greater freedom to decide where to send

the resources he needed for his armies. Furthermore, his triumph was not as complete as he might originally have thought, since he lost the opportunity to have the Nationalist Army remade into an effective, modern fighting machine at American expense.[32]

It is not correct to label Stilwell—as did many of those who worked with him—a clairvoyant and selfless hero, the potential savior of China. Indeed, when compared with Americans like Chennault and American naval officers such as Admiral Milton E. Miles, who assisted Tai Li's secret police, he did seem almost saintly. Beyond his idea of developing a strong, efficient American-oriented Chinese army, however, Stilwell had little to offer China. His reforms focused on training a client army under close American supervision, an experiment later tried in Vietnam, where it proved disastrous.[33] According to journalist Theodore White, he was a political innocent, too proud and too old-fashioned to dissemble. He was the first American in China to insist that the furtherance of U.S. interests required the political elimination of a major foreign chief of state. When Stilwell made this demand, he failed to perceive that what was good for America, and in this case for the war effort, might be bad for other people.[34] Nevertheless, the withdrawal of General Stilwell as theater commander just after the United States had established contact with the Chinese Communists in Yenan seemed to place America on the Kuomintang side of China's domestic conflict. Many who sensed the growing power of the Communists felt that if the United States lined up against them, it could find itself in endless trouble.[35]

The change of command also affected the status, purpose, and future of the Dixie Mission. It had, after all, been created to serve as liaison with the Communists. The Communists saw Dixie in relation to Stilwell. Without him, they thought, Dixie could do little more than thrash around. The Communists knew that the Mission acted on orders from Chungking. They continued to extend courtesy to the members, who were, the Chinese saw, out and working with their hands. They especially respected the weather officers, who carried their own water and equipment, and the signal men and officers, who appeared to have a definite job to do. They increasingly sensed, however, that American policy was not to work with them at all. They therefore wondered why Dixie needed so many men, noting that nearly every plane brought more Americans.[36]

Once the appointment of Wedemeyer had resolved the Stilwell crisis, Hurley undertook to solve the problem of the Communists. When he went to Chungking in September, he had concluded that the success of his mission "to unify all the military forces in China for the purpose of defeating Japan" depended on the negotiations already underway for the unification of Chinese military forces. Accordingly, shortly after his arrival he undertook active measures to mediate between the Chinese Nationalist government and the Chinese Communist Party.[37]

On September 23, when he still believed Hurley supported him, Stilwell had proposed to Hurley that they jointly confront Chiang. Stilwell wanted to travel to Yenan, where he would make "proposals to the Reds." The Communists would be asked to acknowledge Chiang's nominal authority while accepting Stilwell as an actual field commander. Communist forces would then be deployed north of the Yellow River and would be given supplies to equip five divisions. Further aid to Chiang's armies would be granted only after delivery had been made to the X, Y, and Communist divisions.

Also in September, General Chu Teh had invited Hurley to visit Yenan. At first, the president's representative did not want to go, but Lin Tsu-han and Tung Pi-wu, the Communist representatives in Chungking, met with him on October 23 to seek his aid in building a true coalition.[38] John Davies also urged Hurley to visit, and radioed him from Yenan that it was "of such immediate and long-range strategic importance that it warrants your personal visit [as] info . . . can be obtained here which you cannot get in Chungking. . . . you can take significant information and proposals back to the president that vitally affect the war and future balance of power in Asia and the Pacific, if you will visit Yenan."[39]

Hurley, accompanied by Sergeant Smith, his secretary, flew to Yenan on November 7, 1944. In his memoirs, Barrett relates his impression as Hurley appeared at the door of the plane after it landed. Tall, gray haired, soldierly, and extremely handsome, he wore one of the most beautifully tailored uniforms Barrett had ever seen, and "on his chest were ribbons representing every war in which the United States had engaged except possibly Shays Rebellion." No one had informed Barrett, or anyone in Yenan, that Hurley was coming, so the crowd that greeted him at the airstrip was just the usual bunch of Chinese and Americans who turned out for the week's most exciting event, the arrival of the plane. Chou En-lai asked Barrett who the distinguished visitor was. Barrett recognized Hurley, whom he had seen once in New York when Hurley was secretary of war. Chou left quickly to get Mao, and soon the two of them appeared in the only vehicle the Communists had at that time, an old beat-up truck that had once seen duty as an ambulance. Behind them came a company of infantry, evidently mustered at a barracks close to the airfield. They lined up in guard-of-honor formation, and Hurley reviewed them after Mao had greeted him ceremoniously. Hurley returned the salute of the officer commanding the company, then he drew himself to his full, impressive height, "swelled up like a poisoned pup," and to the great astonishment of everyone present, let out a Choctaw war Whoop.[40]

Mao, Chu Teh, Chou En-lai, Yeh Chien-ying, Hurley, Davies, Barrett, and Theodore White then piled into the old ambulance and drove to the Dixie Mission compound. A mule on the road swerved into their path. When the driver clubbed him, Hurley yelled, "Hit him again; hit him on the other side"! He then told Mao that he had been a cowboy in his youth and knew about animals. Mao responded that he had been a shepherd. As the ambulance rolled along, Mao explained how the gully waters rose and fell with the rains, so that there was sometimes a torrent and at other times a dry gulch. Hurley responded by telling him that in Oklahoma during the summer you could tell when a school of fish was swimming upstream by the cloud of dust they raised.[41] In his memoirs, Barrett noted that he translated all this, sometimes with difficulty owing to the saltiness of Hurley's remarks and his unusual language,[42] but White thought Barrett's command of Chinese was exquisite in tone, nuance, slang, and decorum. Then the ambulance arrived at the Dixie compound, and everyone had tea and swapped stories about history.[43]

As soon as he had settled down, Hurley went to the cave where the Mission radio was located. He told Remenih, the radioman, "I have an important message for the President of the United States. As soon as you establish contact with Chungking please let me know and we will give you the message and you will encode it and send it to the President."

As luck would have it, that day was the only time during Remenih's year in Yenan when he could not contact Chungking. Later he learned that a violent electrical storm had created so much static that his little transmitter could not be heard. Not knowing of the storm, he kept trying for thirty-six hours. Every couple of hours General Hurley's shadow fell into the cave door. "Sergeant, no contact yet?" he would say, "Why not?" Remenih had no explanation. After some hours Hurley exhibited his infamous terrible temper. "Sergeant," he said, "back in Washington I can talk anywhere in the world just by picking up the telephone. I don't understand this." Remenih, who was especially concerned because he now knew the nature of Hurley's mission, was relieved when Chungking finally answered. He ran to where the general was sunning himself and said, "General, I have Chungking on the line." Hurley said "Good." He walked into the cave and gave Remenih this message: "Mr. President: Congratulations on your election victory."[44]

Hurley and Theodore White talked privately the afternoon of the day Hurley arrived. White told the general that a few days earlier Mao had said there was no way to "untie the knot," meaning that there was no way to negotiate a peaceful end to the coming civil war unless America recognized the existence of a de facto Communist government and accepted it as an independent ally in the war against Japan.[45]

Hurley was billeted in Lieutenant Louis Jones's cave for the duration of his stay in Yenan. At that time Jones had the only "bed" in the Mission, which he had rigged by laying three two-by-twelve-inch boards across two sawhorses. He then placed an inflatable rubber mattress across the boards and slept in a sleeping bag on this improvised bed. At that time everyone else slept on a k'ang. For General Hurley, the Chinese made up Jones's bed with a pillow, sheets, and blankets. They also put new rice paper over the doorway. For the duration of Hurley's stay, Jones bunked with the weather officer, about eight caves away.

In the middle of the night, one of the guards stationed at the entrance of General Hurley's cave awakened Jones. Jones had apparently forgotten to take to his new quarters the German shepherd he had acquired in Yenan. The dog preferred to sleep on the foot of his master's bed no matter who was in it. By the time the guards sent for Jones, Hurley had kicked him out twice. The second time the dog growled, and so they fetched Jones. The next day Jones apologized to the general, who acted like a good sport and asked to see the dog in the daylight.[46]

The next morning Hurley conferred with Mao, Chu Teh, Chou En-lai, Ch'en Chia-k'ang (Chou's secretary), and a newspaperman named Yu Kwang-sen. The latter explained that he was there not as a newspaperman but as a friend who wanted to make everything clear to both sides. Barrett, Hurley's secretary, Sergeant Smith, and Lieutenant Eng, an interpreter, were also present. Hurley explained that he had come as FDR's personal representative, with the consent and approval of Chiang Kai-shek. The United States did not wish to become involved in Chinese politics, he stated, and his goal was to unify the Chinese military forces for the defeat of Japan in cooperation with the United States. The Generalissimo had offered to legalize the existence of the Communist Party and all other political parties in China and would consider placing Communists on what Hurley called the Supreme War Council of China.[47]

Barrett thought Hurley leaned over backward in these introductory remarks to be fair to both the national government and the Communists. He then presented Mao with a statement that he said represented the basis on which Chiang Kai-shek was willing to come to an agreement:

1. The Government of China and the Chinese Communist Party

will work together for the unification of all military forces in China for the immediate defeat of Japan and the reconstruction of China;

2. The Chinese Communist forces will observe and carry out the orders of the Central Government and its National Military Council;

3. The Chinese Government and the Chinese Communist Party will support the principles of Sun Yat-sen for the establishment of a government of the people for the people and by the people. Both Parties will pursue policies designed to promote the progress and development of democratic processes in government;

4. There will be but one national government and one army in China. All the officers and soldiers in the Communist forces . . . will receive the same pay and allowances . . . and equal treatment in the allocation of munitions and supplies;

5. The Government of China recognizes and will legalize the Chinese Communist Party as a political party. All political parties will be given legal status.

Brusquely, Mao asked whose ideas the five points represented. Hurley replied that they were his but that they had been worked on "by all of us," which Barrett assumed meant the Generalissimo and his advisers in addition to Hurley.[48]

When the group reconvened later that day, Mao told Hurley that China needed unity but that it should be based on democracy. He noted that China at the time was divided into three parts: the Japanese-occupied districts, the liberated areas held by the Chinese Communists and their supporters outside the Party, and the territories ruled by the Kuomintang. He railed against Chiang and his poor military showing. When Hurley quickly drew his attention to recent Kuomintang victories, Mao responded by saying, "What I have said has already been said by Roosevelt, Dr. Sun Fo, Churchill, and Madame Sun Yat-sen. Do you consider these people to be enemies of China?"[49]

Barrett thought that Hurley responded skillfully to the situation. The general said he had misunderstood the tenor of the Chairman's remarks. He acknowledged that there was some corruption in the national government. Mao then minimized the significance of the Generalissimo's offer of a seat on the National Military Council. Hurley asked on what terms he would be willing to join in a coalition government. The two men then agreed to discuss the subject the following afternoon.

The next morning, Barrett took Hurley in the Mission jeep for a sightseeing tour of Yenan and its environs. That afternoon, the Communists submitted their proposals to Hurley, who said he found them fair but not broad enough and took them back to his quarters for revision. With his modifications, they were presented on the morning of November 10. I will henceforth call them the Five Point Plan. Hurley suggested that both he and Mao sign the document. He left a blank space below for Chiang Kai-shek's signature over his typed name:[50]

1. The Government of China, the Kuomintang of China and the Communist Party of China will work together for the unification of all military forces in China for the immediate defeat of Japan and the reconstruction of China;

2. The present National Government is to be reorganized into a coalition National Government embracing representatives of all anti-Japanese parties and non-partisan political bodies. A new democratic policy providing for reform in military, political, economic and cultural affairs shall be promulgated and made effective. At the same time the National Military Council is to be reorganized into the United National Military Council consisting of representatives of all anti-Japanese armies;

3. The coalition National Government will support the principles of Sun Yat-sen for the establishment in China of a government of the people, for the people and by the people. The coalition National Government will pursue policies designed to promote progress and democracy and to establish justice, freedom of conscience, freedom of press, freedom of speech, freedom of assembly and association, the right to petition the government for the redress of grievances, the right of writ of habeas corpus and the right of residence. The coalition National Government will also pursue policies intended to make effective the two rights defined as freedom from fear and freedom from want;

4. All anti-Japanese forces will observe and carry out the orders of the coalition National Government and its United National Military Council and will be recognized by the Government and the Military Council. The supplies acquired from foreign powers will be equitably distributed;

5. The coalition National Government of China recognizes the legality of the Kuomintang of China, the Chinese Communist Party and all anti-Japanese parties.[51]

David Barrett observed in his memoirs that this document pleased the Chinese Communists. He records that after the signing, everyone left for the airfield. On the way, Hurley reminded Mao that he could not guarantee that the Generalissimo would accept the terms. Chou En-lai suggested that they be communicated directly to Chiang without first being seen by T. V. Soong or other national government officials. Five men—Hurley; Chou; Ch'en Chia-k'ang, Chou's secretary; Theodore White; and Barrett—then boarded the plane and took off for Chungking. Mao had declined Hurley's invitation to accompany them.[52]

The next day, Hurley sent T. V. Soong a copy of the Hurley-Mao protocol. Soong immediately went to Hurley and told him he had been "sold a bill of goods" by the Communists. "The National Government will never grant what the Communists have requested," he declared. Two days later, Hurley told John Davies that he was mediating the negotiations between Chou and Chiang, that he considered the proposals he had brought back from Yenan eminently fair, and that if there was a breakdown in the parleys it would be the fault of the government, not the Communists.[53]

Chiang refused to sign the agreement. Hurley was furious. He said he thought that the men around Chiang were sabotaging him. They seemed to be telling the Generalissimo one thing and Hurley another. At the moment, Hurley's anger was directed at Chiang, but soon his frustration led him to blame both sides.[54] He told Davies that the negotiation of an agreement with the Communists had been part of the bargain over Stilwell's removal.

In the meantime, as Service predicted, on November 1 Gauss resigned as ambassador. Contrary to Service's advice, FDR appointed Hurley in his place. Hurley immediately accepted, ordered a Cadillac to be flown in to him, and described to John Davies his plans to redo the ambassador's residence.[55] The new ambassador presented his credentials to Chiang on January 8, 1945.[56] A few months later he outlined his understanding of his mission and of U.S. policy in China:

1. Preventing the collapse of the National Government;
2. Sustaining Chiang Kai-shek as President of the Republic and Generalissimo of the Armies;
3. Harmonizing relations between the Generalissimo and the American Commander;
4. Promoting production of war supplies in China and preventing economic collapse, and;
5. Unifying all the military forces in China for the purpose of defeating Japan.

The national government, however, was having no part of the

Hurley Five Point Plan. Instead, they submitted a counterproposal, their own Three Point Plan:

1. The National Government, desirous of securing effective unification and concentration of all military forces in China for the purpose of accomplishing the speedy defeat of Japan, and looking forward to the post-war reconstruction of China, agrees to incorporate, after reorganization, the Chinese Communist forces in the National Army who will then receive equal treatment as the other units in respect of pay, allowance, munitions and other supplies, and to give recognition to the Chinese Communist Party as a legal party;

2. The Communist Party undertakes to give their full support to the National Government in the prosecution of the war of resistance and in the post-war reconstruction, and give over control of all their troops to the National Government through the National Military Council. The National Government will designate some high ranking officers from among the Communist forces to membership in the National Military Council;

3. The aim of the National Government to which the Communist Party subscribes is to carry out the Three People's Principles of Dr. Sun Yat-sen for the establishment in China of a government of the people, for the people and by the people and it will pursue policies designed to promote the progress and development of democratic processes in government. In accordance with the provisions of the Program of Armed Resistance and National Reconstruction, freedom of speech, freedom of the press, freedom of assembly and association and other civil liberties are hereby guaranteed, subject only to the specific needs of security in the effective prosecution of the war against Japan.[57]

On November 21 Chou received the Kuomintang's disappointing proposals. To make matters worse, his discussions with Hurley and Wedemeyer, who insisted that the Three Point Plan had some things in its favor, troubled him. He decided to break off the talks and return to Yenan. Hurley requested that Barrett, who had participated in the meetings, accompany Chou to try to keep the door open for further negotiations.[58] They planned to leave on November 28, but bad weather forced a delay. On December 4 Chou met with Hurley; Barrett; Wedemeyer; Wedemeyer's chief of staff, Major General Robert B. McClure; and Ch'en Chia-k'ang, Chou's secretary, who acted as interpreter. The Americans tried unsuccessfully to persuade Chou to accept the Nationalists' Three Point offer. Finally, on December 7 the weather broke. Barrett and Chou left for Yenan. It was an eventful flight. The pilot got lost and flew toward Tibet until Chou pointed out the error to Barrett, who translated for the pilot.

The next day, Barrett met with Chou and Mao, whom he described as recalcitrant.[59] In essence, Mao said he had nothing left to talk about with Chiang. Hurley had recommended that Mao's followers accept representation in the National Military Council as a way of getting a foot in the door. The Chinese Communist leader called this suggestion worthless advice. A foot in the door meant nothing if their hands were tied behind their backs, he said. They had already told Hurley that they would cooperate with Chiang on the basis of the Five Point Plan. They could not be expected to give up their army and place themselves at Chiang's mercy.

Chiang, Mao went on, was a rotten shell. If the United States wanted to keep propping him up, that was its privilege, but Chiang was doomed to failure in any case. As for the Communists, they did not need to be propped up by any nation, although they would be sorry if the United States abandoned them. They had welcomed the Observer Section and had done their best to cooperate with it. If it stayed, they

Special Presidential Emissary Patrick J. Hurley and Mao Tse-tung. Courtesy of Jack Klein.

would be happy, if it left they would be sorry, and if it left and later returned, they would welcome it back. Since Chiang was refusing to form a coalition government that afforded the Communists decent participation, the Communists considered the talks ended. The Communists were proposing to the People's Political Councils of the various regions under their control that a "United Committee" be formed as the first step in forming a separate government.

Coldly and calmly Chou reinforced Mao's angry words. The latter shouted that his people would not yield further, that Chiang was a turtle's egg whom he would have cursed to his face if he had been present. The diatribe left Barrett feeling that he had talked in vain to two clever, ruthless, and determined leaders with absolute confidence in the strength of their own positions.[60] Ultimately, Mao closed in a cooler tone, reminding Barrett that both he and Hurley had signed the Five Point Plan and that in the future the Communists might show the document to the Chinese and foreign press.

The next day Barrett told Hurley that Mao had mentioned showing the signed copy of the Communist terms to the press. The furious ambassador yelled, "The motherfucker, he tricked me!"[61] Hurley then wrote Chou En-lai that he did not want the five points published "while the negotiations were pending," to which Chou replied that they would wait, but when the appropriate time came to pressure the government, the document would be made public. His letter went on to say that the Communist Central Committee and Mao appreciated Hurley's enthusiasm in trying to unify China to defeat Japan and to rehabilitate China.[62]

Throughout all of this mayhem, Hurley had remained optimistic about his chances for bringing the two sides together. His communications to FDR had implied that success was on the horizon. On November 29 he wrote Roosevelt, "What looks like an agreement between the National Government and the Communist troops has been pending for two weeks. . . . Both parties now seem anxious for settlement. . . . The recent delay in getting action has been due largely to weather. . . . Before reaching final agreement Chou En-lai must return to Yenan and get the consent and approval of Mao Tse Tung and the Central Committee of the Chinese Communist Party."[63]

Even after the war ended, Hurley remained confident that the Communists would come to understand that reaching an agreement with the national government would serve their cause better than continuing to oppose it. The Sino-Soviet Accord of August 14, 1945, pledged Russian support of the national government as the only government of China. General Order No. 1 essentially said that the United States, the United Kingdom, and the Soviet Union agreed that as Allied commander in chief in the China Theater, Chiang Kai-shek should receive the surrender of the Japanese armed forces in China. In the wake of these documents, Hurley urged Chiang to invite Mao to Chungking. Chiang agreed, and an invitation was sent on August 16.

At that time the Communists were claiming the right to share fully in accepting Japanese surrender and in the settlements that would follow. Mao therefore declined Chiang's invitation. Hurley urged the Generalissimo not to take no for an answer, to show that he could lead the nation well and generously in peace as in war.[64] Then Hurley heard that the Chungking government would not guarantee Mao's safety. He sent Mao word that he was willing to fly to Yenan, fly back in the same plane with the Communist leaders, and take personal responsibility for their lives while they were in Chungking. Mao responded that he was willing to go but that he would send Chou En-lai first for consultation. According to Mao, however, Chiang had indicated that Chou might not be in a position to make firm commitments, and the Generalissimo therefore wanted Mao himself. Furthermore, he felt that the time had come for them to settle their differences.[65]

Colonel Ivan Yeaton commanded the Dixie Mission at the time all these communications were going back and forth. Just before leaving for Yenan, he had told Hurley that the Communists were interpreting the invitation to go to Chungking as a sign that the Chinese and the American governments needed them. The Communists thought that a position within a coalition government would enable them to take control of China. Still, Yeaton thought it might be possible to work out a transient arrangement under which the control of China would be loosely divided by regions among the government forces, the Communist forces, and local warlords, all of whom would cooperate under some sort of flexible central administration.

Hurley spent only one day in Yenan on this, his second and last trip there. All parties expressed personal friendliness. When he flew back to Chungking on August 28, Mao Tse-tung accompanied him. Negotiations between the Communists and Nationalists continued throughout the rest of August and into September in a more friendly manner than they had in the past. Hurley, who mediated, firmly believed that in the end both sides would see the need to make concessions.[66] He took credit personally for the willingness of Chiang and Mao to negotiate. It was, he said, "a source of gratification to us that we have been able to maintain the respect and confidence of the leaders of both parties."[67]

On September 22 Hurley returned to the United States for medical reasons and for guidance. He informed the State Department that as the conference advanced, there seemed to be a rapprochement between the two leading parties in China, and rumors of civil war were abating. Chiang, anxious that Hurley continue to sustain him, asked President Truman to return the ambassador to Chungking. On October 20 Truman said he would do so, because he had confidence in General Hurley's judgment and ability.

Hurley, however, did not wish to return. On November 26 he handed Secretary of State James F. Byrnes a lengthy letter of resignation. Truman tried to talk him into continuing but on the twenty-seventh Hurley told the press that the Foreign Service men he had worked with in China had undermined official American policy. The president interpreted his words as an insult to his administration and accepted the ambassador's resignation.[68] No one replaced Hurley as ambassador until July 11, 1946, when Leighton Stuart was appointed to the post, although Truman designated General George C. Marshall as presidential envoy almost immediately.

Even after he resigned, Hurley continued to offer explanations of what had gone wrong. He expressed his willingness to appear before any public hearing and was quickly asked to testify before Congress on American policy in China. With great attention from the press, he spread the blame for America's "failure" in China far and wide, attributing some of it, perhaps inevitably, to the Dixie Mission and those who supported it. The observers had told him things he had not wanted to hear, that the problem he believed he could solve was, in fact, unsolvable. They had predicted a civil war when he thought one could be avoided, and they had foreseen that the Communists' strength would continue to increase while he was backing the other side.[69] Hurley always treated people like military subordinates. His biggest mistake may have been that he did not rely on the advice of his advisers. At any rate, Washington policymakers ignored both his advice and that offered by members of the Dixie Mission who, after all, could share unique insights.[70]

As previously mentioned, the Dixie Mission had originally been part of Stilwell's plan to bring all Chinese troops, Communist and Nationalist, under his leadership. The Communists were willing to cooperate with this plan, and on September 13, 1944, two of their representatives in Chungking met with Stilwell. Stilwell wanted to provide them with arms to facilitate their participation. The Dixie Mission had been formed with an eye toward closer cooperation.[71]

Although not everyone noticed it at the time, with Stilwell's removal the Mission's status began to decline, as did that of the individuals associated with Stilwell who had encouraged its formation. At the time of his removal, when he thought he was going to be put in charge of all the Chinese forces, Stilwell had been planning a trip to Yenan.

Wedemeyer, his successor, whom Stilwell described as "the world's most pompous prick,"[72] never made such plans even though Mao Tse-tung and Chou En-lai invited him. Wedemeyer has said that Hurley had asked him not to go because he thought the commanding general's presence might compromise his own efforts. Wedemeyer noted a physical resemblance between Hurley and his own father.

Wedemeyer also said in retrospect that the Oklahoman had not been a good choice to represent the United States to the Chinese. Generally, Wedemeyer had had cordial relations with Hurley, but the ambassador seldom took the theater commander into his confidence. When the two men spoke, Hurley expressed optimism and occasionally shared a few of his experiences in trying to bring the Nationalists and Communists together. Nor did Hurley ask for help, which Wedemeyer thought particularly strange, since Hurley knew nothing about China or Marxism and Wedemeyer considered himself an expert on Marx. Wedemeyer claimed to have enjoyed "marvelous conversations" on Marxism with Mao and Chou when they stayed at his house during the negotiations.

It is possible that the flamboyant, politically ambitious Hurley, unwilling to share the limelight, was jealous of Wedemeyer. Nevertheless, the latter believed that he had bent over backward to please the ambassador, for instance, by giving him the theater commander's Cadillac with the American flag in front to use until Hurley's own car arrived. Hurley liked riding around in the showy car.[73]

Hurley noted in his letter of resignation that there had been a great discrepancy between American objectives in China and the conduct of foreign relations. The United States began the war, he stated, with the principles of the Atlantic Charter and democracy and in the end bolstered imperialism and Communism. This shift was the responsibility of those career Foreign Service men who had advised the Chinese Communists that his (Hurley's) efforts to prevent the collapse of the national government did not reflect U.S. policy. Those men had told the Communists that they should decline to combine their army with the Nationalist Army unless they were given control.[74]

John Davies was the first of the four Foreign Service officers affiliated with the Dixie Mission to catch Hurley's wrath. On December 19, 1944, Hurley, influenced by T. V. Soong, told Davies to transfer to Moscow. Davies arranged to do so, but three days later the two men had an explosive argument. Hurley accused Davies of sneaking off to Yenan to sabotage his negotiations. Davies believed that Hurley was no longer thinking clearly and that the maelstrom of intrigue going on around him had confused him. At a Christmas party Hurley seemed to be trying to patch things up, but on January 9, when Davies stopped on his way to Chungking airport to say good-bye to him and to Wedemeyer, Hurley became highly agitated at something Davies said, and another yelling match took place.[75] During the exchange, Hurley accused Davies of being a Communist. Years later Wedemeyer expressed doubts about the ambassador's true beliefs. Wedemeyer himself assumed that Davies, Service, Ludden, and Emmerson reflected the "spirit of Stilwell," that the reports they wrote were less pro-Communist than anti-Nationalist, and that they were young, dedicated, and perhaps overly enthusiastic about what they saw. Davies begged the ambassador not to ruin his career. Nevertheless, Hurley screamed that he was going to have him thrown out of the State Department.[76]

Wedemeyer prevented Davies from being discharged, but there were other times when the Foreign Service officers' enthusiasm for what they had seen behind the Japanese lines led to conflict with Hurley, causing trouble that would not go away. In February 1945, for example, Raymond Ludden flew to Chungking to see Wedemeyer. By coincidence, Ludden flew to Chungking on the same plane as Chou En-lai, who was on his way to see Hurley. Morris DePass, the language officer who had filled in as Dixie's commanding officer from the time Barrett left until Peterkin took over, was also aboard. DePass told Ludden how much he admired Hurley and predicted that Ludden would find him an inspiring leader.

In Chungking, Ludden spoke to Wedemeyer alone. He told of his reaction to the 1,200-mile trip that he, Peterkin, and other members of the Mission had made behind the Japanese lines.[77] Excitedly, he described a fight he had witnessed between the Japanese and the Communists. In it, the Communists had fought courageously, capturing many Japanese. They ought to be given more arms and equipment, Ludden said, so that we can take advantage of their capabilities in the war effort.[78] Later, Ludden held a briefing session about his experiences in Yenan and his trip behind the lines for Hurley. Admiral Miles also attended this briefing.[79]

Ludden's observations greatly interested Wedemeyer, who expressed no anti-Communist sentiments during their conversation. Nor was the commanding general hostile when Ludden urged him to go to Yenan to see for himself what the Communists were doing. Ludden's remarks also intrigued General Robert McClure, Wedemeyer's chief of staff, when Wedemeyer brought him up to date. The commanding general, however, believed he knew more about tactics than Ludden or the other Foreign Service men. While he wanted to use their expertise, especially to help determine the character of the Communist leaders and the capabilities of their forces, he did not receive Ludden's recommendation with as much enthusiasm as Ludden had hoped to see.[80]

In fact, at the moment of their meeting, Wedemeyer was preparing to return to Washington to discuss overall policy matters. He ordered Ludden to go too, on a top priority, so that he could be available for consultation. Ludden did not suspect that once there, Wedemeyer would release both him and John Emmerson to the State Department "because of pressure he could not withstand."[81]

Before Wedemeyer left Chungking, Ludden and Service wrote a memorandum summarizing Ludden's observations. Essentially, it said that the Kuomintang had less interest in defeating Japan than in preserving its own power and that political disunity had caused China's military failure. The safest and sanest course of action for the United States would be to judge all parties and factions by their readiness to fight the enemy and not by their ideologies.[82]

A few days later George Atcheson, the man in charge of the embassy in Hurley's absence, decided to give the State Department a more realistic report of the situation in China than had been possible when Hurley was there. He and the embassy staff put together a telegram proposing that President Roosevelt inform the Generalissimo that military necessity required supplying and cooperating with the Communists and other suitable groups. Doing so was a good idea, the message said, not only to win the war, but also to keep the Communists on our side instead of casting them into the arms of the Soviet Union when the USSR entered the war.[83]

When Hurley learned the contents of the telegram, he was livid. As ambassador he had tried to bring members of his staff into line by censoring their dispatches. He had once even drawn a pistol on Arthur Ringwalt, second secretary of the embassy, after Ringwalt showed him a critical telegram that had already been sent. He said, "I know who drafted that telegram—Service. I'll get the SOB if it's the last thing I do!"[84]

Hurley was even angrier when he was "called on the carpet with a full array of the pro-Communists in the State Department as my judges and questioners to defend the American policy in China against every official of the American Embassy in China." He believed that his staff had gone "behind his back," as indeed they had, by waiting until he was out of Chungking to send their telegram. In retaliation, he had Atcheson transferred to another post and Service moved from General Wedemeyer's jurisdiction to the embassy's jurisdiction and returned to the States.[85] The action showed Roosevelt's support for his ambassador against the State Department.

Back in Yenan, the Communists noticed the recall of John Davies, who had worked tirelessly to lay the foundation for cooperation with them. They concluded that pressure from Chiang Kai-shek's government had forced out all four State Department men.[86] In fact, Hurley and his staff both mistakenly assumed that the Kuomintang and the Chinese Communists could be reconciled.[87]

Hurley took an even more negative attitude toward the Dixie Mission and its purpose when he learned that in his absence General Robert B. McClure, Wedemeyer's hard-drinking, poker-playing chief of staff, together with his good friend Colonel David Barrett, had indicated to the Communists that direct aid from the United States might be forthcoming. Hurley was furious because they had acted without informing him. Ironically, in this instance he was in a position similar to that of the Foreign Service officers assigned to his staff, who had complained that he had refused to tell them about his negotiations with the Chinese Communists.[88] Nor had the ambassador rushed to share information or consult with Wedemeyer, although he had agreed to do so.[89]

Actually, Hurley was upset with everyone who had gone off to Yenan. He would surely not have agreed to the establishment of such a group had he been on the scene when it was formed. Yet even after the McClure/Barrett fiasco he did not go so far as to suggest or demand that the Mission be disbanded.[90] But people who had seen his Wild West style in Yenan reported to Wedemeyer that the Communists thought Hurley was a clown. When Domke heard him speak in Chungking, he wrote Peterkin that the White Moustache was innocuous, like someone in the States running for office.[91]

When Ludden went to see Hurley after his trip to Fouping, the only thing Hurley asked was why he had been ordered to go to Yenan in the first place. Ludden had brought the ambassador a fine saber from Yenan as a gift, but he was so put out at the ambassador's lack of interest that he gave it to George Atcheson so that he would not have to hand it to Hurley himself. Ludden assumed that the many charmers who operated in the Chungking government had hypnotized Hurley.[92]

Service considered Hurley an obsessive talker. When Service returned to Chungking after three months in Yenan, he spent about an hour and a half with Hurley. The ambassador spent most of the time telling Service about his talks with the president and how people had accused him of being pro-Chinese and anti-Stilwell. In reality, he said, he understood Stilwell's problems and just thought him not the right man for the job. Hurley said he certainly was going to get arms for the Communists. "That's what I've come here for, sir, is just to get them arms and they're gonna get them. I know they're gonna be tough to deal with, I know. People keep telling me and they don't realize I've had a lot of experience, they think I'm a child." Service wanted to tell him that the Communists were going to be *very* tough and that there were certain things they would insist on, but Hurley was not a man to question.[93]

Service had been destined for some time to be a particular target of Hurley's rage because of his reports from Yenan. Even Barrett had warned him, saying, "You are hanging yourself as high as Haman with those reports, sonny boy." Service had replied, "David, if they don't like them they can say so. I'm merely reporting what I think is the truth."[94]

In December 1945 when Hurley testified before the Senate Foreign Relations Committee about his reasons for resigning as ambassador, he accused both George Atcheson and John Service of sabotaging his efforts to unify China. Service, whom he could not control because "he said he was serving under General Stilwell," suggested in October 1944 that the national government be allowed to collapse, Hurley testified. Furthermore, he continued, "During the war the imperialistic powers were Germany and Japan. Today they are Great Britain, France, the Netherlands, Belgium and Portugal." When *Pravda* reported on the hearings, the Russian newspaper labeled Hurley "the mouthpiece of imperialistic elements in the United States."[95]

Hurley erred in thinking that once he had the ball rolling he could bring the two sides together. Possibly he convinced himself, when he saw the contrast between the Communists as they were living in Yenan and Chiang as he lived in his palace in Chungking, that the Nationalists were better people, more "his kind of people."[96]

Hurley often spoke about "our policy" in China and sometimes contradicted himself. On the one hand he said that the Communists were not "real Communists," and on the other hand he declared that the United States had to support the Nationalist government. His inconsistencies caused Emmerson, for one, to see him as an opportunist who bent with the wind and as an ill-informed man who regarded the Nationalists and the Communists as if they had been Republicans and Democrats, equally able to serve together in the same government.[97] Hurley said, "I can handle these fellows, they're just like Mexicans and I can handle Mexicans."[98]

Dole, present when Hurley arrived in November 1944, believed that the legend of the ugly American began with Hurley. Right after Hurley's arrival, a small tea party was held in a little shack not far from the airstrip. Hurley, standing in a group of six or seven men, leaned over to Chou En-lai and said, "Say, what is it *you* do here?"

Still, not all of those associated with the Dixie Mission fared badly at Hurley's hands. John Colling got a career boost from his association with the Oklahoman. He left the Dixie Mission and became Hurley's assistant attaché. Colling thought he could give the ambassador information that would shorten the war. He also believed that mistakes usually attributed to Hurley were actually Roosevelt's. The president, after all, had picked an emissary who was totally ignorant about China and was more concerned with his own image and political future than with diplomacy.[99] And Hurley, who departed with a war whoop that was returned by Mao and Chou En-lai, was very effective at reducing things to basics.[100] Some of the men who had been left behind quickly noted that Colling, too, was an opportunist.[101] He had originally brought himself to Hurley's attention by taking a large number of pictures that included him. The photographs earned him an invitation to accompany Hurley on his private plane back to the States for Christmas.[102]

Hurley's belief in "personal diplomacy" made him a poor choice to deal with the delicate and complex situation that existed in China. The comment "When I think I can risk telling the Generalissimo a dirty joke, I'll feel I'm getting somewhere" reflected his style. His war whoops led the Communists to brand him a buffoon, an impression he reinforced by calling Chiang "Mr. Shek" and Mao Tse-tung "Moose Dung." For their part, OSS gave *him* the code name "Albatross."[103]

Hurley's brashness may have covered up a persecution complex. He told MacCracken Fisher, who spent some time in Dixie for the Office of War Information, "Mac, you are the only one in this outfit who hasn't spit on me."[104] His mercurial personality made the United States officials in China contemptuous. The Embassy staff called him "Colonel Blimp" and accused him of "crass stupidity," of being a "bungler" and a "stuffed shirt playing at being a great man." His staff saw him as "50% bull or more." They and the Chinese referred to him as the "Big Wind" and a "paper tiger."

If nothing else, Hurley was a politically ambitious, contradictory egomaniac with a bad temper that many of those associated with Dixie experienced. His insecurity led him to throttle dissent and lash out against his critics. Still, although he was shallow, he was not stupid, and some historians believe that his ignorance regarding China may have caused no harm. He remained hopeful when those with more sophistication, like Gauss, became cynical and negative. Probably no one could have resolved either the dispute between Stilwell and Chiang Kai-shek or the struggle between Chiang and Mao.[105] The latter, after a brief "honeymoon," decided he was not trustworthy.[106]

Some historians have called Hurley a bumbling fool, an incompetent who played at being great, acted without sufficient authority, and thereby preempted official policymaking. He was vain, pompous, ignorant of China, and not above lying to his superiors, or at least telling them what they wanted to hear. Yet he and the presidential emissaries who had preceded him—Laughlin Currie, Wendell Willkie, and Henry A. Wallace—were in the mainstream of American policy toward China, while Stilwell and his supporters, including those associated with the Dixie Mission, were not.[107]

When the Dixie Mission went to Yenan, the Communists were optimistic. The positive feeling gradually gave way to dismay and anger, however, when they did not get what they had expected. Hurley's failures coincided with the Communists' reassessment of what they needed to achieve their goals, either with or without Dixie's aid. In a sense, although harmony was not attained, both Hurley and the Dixie Mission were effective insofar as they delayed the inevitable civil war. Confronted with American negotiators, both Yenan and Chungking were temporarily forced to negotiate. The resultant grace period helped maintain the China front until Allied victory in the Pacific was achieved.[108]

6

The Communist Attempt
to Bypass Hurley

Patrick Hurley's assignment in China had been to bring the Kuomintang and Communists together. He started his task in an even-handed manner, but when negotiations collapsed, he revealed himself as a partisan of the national government. In response, the Communists changed their approach to the United States. From mid-December 1944 until early January 1945, they tried to circumvent Hurley and Chiang and to collaborate directly with Americans they considered friendly. During this period, however, many of the Americans who supported cooperation with Yenan lost influence. The Communists then sought direct routes to Washington. They also expressed interest in offers of military assistance made by men in OSS and attached to the Dixie Mission or to theater headquarters. The Communists apparently remained convinced that sooner or later the United States would recognize their contribution to the war effort. But despite some conciliatory gestures, American policy continued to focus almost solely on minimizing Communist power, either through cooperation with the Soviet Union or by bolstering the Kuomintang. This trend continued until June 1945.[1]

In Yenan, one midnight in early December 1944, Mao, Chou En-lai, Chu Teh, and Doc Ma secretly met with Lieutenant S. Herbert Hitch of the Dixie Mission. They asked him to deliver a message personally to Admiral King in Washington.

Hitch responded, "Well now, Mr. Chairman, I'm not the head man of the Navy out here. I have a boss down in Chungking. And my boss has a boss. We have to go through channels in the United States Navy and in the Armed Services. My boss has got to get permission from General Wedemeyer to let me do this."[2]

Mao erroneously thought that Hitch did not want to run the errand, but Hitch was happy to carry the letter and suspected that he knew its contents. He said, "Seriously, this is an important matter to you and it will also be a very serious matter with the United States government. I must get this permission." The Chinese said they understood his position but emphasized that what they wanted him to do must be kept secret from others in the Dixie Mission, including Barrett.[3]

John Davies, whom Hitch felt he could trust, happened to be in Yenan at this time. Hitch went to him and said, "John, I've got something I have to talk to you about and you can't tell this to anybody, not to Colonel Barrett or anyone. I can talk Captain Jarrell into this but I don't know General Wedemeyer at all because he came to China after I left for Yenan and I need your help with him."[4]

Davies replied that he was going back to Chungking and they could fly there together. Hitch then went to Barrett and asked permission to go, saying that he had something to discuss with his superior officer. Barrett told him to go, so Hitch, carrying a draft or synopsis of the Communists' letter, boarded the next flight out of Yenan. When he arrived in Chungking he told Jarrell what the Communists wanted him to do, and the Captain gave his approval. Hitch then got in touch with John Davies and together they went to see Wedemeyer. The three of them chatted for about three hours.

At this time, the Japanese appeared to be making a thrust through China in retaliation for Allied attacks on their coastal shipping. This campaign worried General Wedemeyer, who talked about taking an escape route out of Chungking through the north and Tibet if the Japanese captured his headquarters in the process of trying to take Chungking. In discussing these events with me, Hitch speculated that Wedemeyer's concerns in this area made him especially receptive to the idea of conveying Mao's message personally.

Wedemeyer wrote an introductory letter in Morse code, saying that while he did not know Hitch personally, John Davies spoke well of him. He asked Hitch how soon he could leave, to which Hitch replied that he needed to go back to Yenan and tell Mao that he had permission to deliver his message. Wedemeyer said, "Well, I'm going to give you the very highest priority I can, and I want you to get it [the letter] there as soon as possible."[5]

Before he left Chungking, Hitch wrote Jarrell a lengthy report detailing his impressions of the Communists in Yenan. He described his trip behind the Japanese lines, the military conditions he had observed in the area, the Communists' weaponry and communications, their treatment of prisoners, and their intelligence potential. He closed with the following evaluation:

Brooks Atkinson of the *New York Times* . . . expressed the sage
observation that "these people are disarmingly frank and outspo-
ken." This is unquestionably true and is perhaps one of the reasons
why they have unfailingly impressed all who have had an opportunity to know them. That they are hard as nails and ruthlessly realistic is also true, though not as apparent. Slowly but surely are
coming over to their ranks those in Occupied China who are not
afraid of a life which is physically at least difficult, and who, though
they may not agree entirely with the Communist dogma, yet pre-
fer being free men and women again, to either Japanese control or
Central Government corruption. The Chinese Communists are and
will continue to be a potent factor in China's internal political setup
because of their self reliance and fearlessness and because the movement has for one reason or another attracted many of the ablest
men in North and Central China.

Even their severest critic[s] cannot deny the organizational
ability of the "men who made the long march" or the discipline of
the Communist leaders and party members. Today we can use them
to advantage in helping to save hundreds of American lives, tomorrow for many reasons this may not be true. Future relations
between America and China may also be dependent upon the course
followed by our government now in dealing with them, or in perhaps failing to count them in.[6]

It took Hitch a couple of days to write his report. When it was
finished, General Wedemeyer provided him with a plane for his flight
to Yenan. Hitch made the journey in his dress uniform, which he thought
appropriate garb for saying good-bye. Mao gave him two copies of the
letter, one in English and one in Chinese. "You keep the English copy,"
the Chinese leader said. "Deliver the one in Chinese and let them translate it." Hitch then returned to Chungking, packed his clothes, called a
few friends and was on his way. He expected to return in a month or so
with an answer from the Navy Department.

He arrived in Washington on about December 23. He spent one
entire afternoon talking with Secretary of the Navy James Forrestal[7]
and met with John Carter Vincent of the State Department on December 29. Both men had seen the letter from Mao, which had been dupli-
cated and was being circulated to appropriate parties.

Hitch told Vincent he was convinced that effective use could be
made of the Communist troops with two provisions: (1) they needed
to be supplied with demolition equipment and Japanese ammunition,
since the Communist troops were equipped almost entirely with captured Japanese small arms, and (2) they had to have some assurance of

Left to right: Chu Teh, Stelle, Mao Tse-tung, and Hitch. Photo taken on the day Hitch left for Washington in November 1944. Courtesy of S. Herbert Hitch.

continued support in the form of recognition of the role they could play in defeating Japan. He explained that the Communist troops were loath to increase their activities against Japanese troops unless they could be assured of continued support from the Americans. Sporadic attacks brought terrible retribution to the villagers without commensurate military advantages. The Communists were very short of ammunition, Hitch reported, and they wished to have sufficient supplies to enable them to hold the strategic areas alongside the Japanese communication lines they attacked.[7]

Hitch also mentioned the aid that the Communist troops could give American landings at almost any point along the North China coast down to Shanghai. He cautioned that the Communists could not afford hinterland protection longer than two days unless they were immediately supplied with ammunition and other military equipment. He informed Vincent that his experience in Yenan had left no doubt in his mind that the Chinese peasants wholeheartedly supported the Communists, that the Communists were sincerely anxious to cooperate with Chungking on a basis which recognized their strength in China, and that the Communist leaders sympathized more with the United States than with Russia. He added that the much heralded "democracy" of the Communists had not impressed him much, but their popularity and the relative progressiveness of their administration were unmistakable.[8]

On January 6 Hitch met with the Joint Chiefs of Staff, who had sent him a formal request to appear. He talked with the twenty or thirty assembled men for about twenty-five minutes. Hitch was anxious to have this meeting, because he knew that Admiral Miles of SACO would have learned somehow about the purpose of his trip to Washington (see chapter 7).

Hitch began by telling his audience how he had been sent on detached duty. Then he described the situation in China:

> China is currently held by several different forces. The Japanese control all the interior lines of communication between north of the Yangtze River and portions south of it. The Chinese Communists have imbedded themselves in caves in Yenan, Shensi Province, where the Japanese can't readily attack them. Around the Border Region area patrolled by the Chinese Communists are perhaps half of Chiang Kai-shek's best troops, who watch to see they don't escape or come south and make contact with other Chinese.
>
> On a particular date I was relieved by my commanding officer, Captain Jarrell, and permitted to go to Yenan with a small group designated by the President of the United States. (They sat up a little when I said that, because they had not known the President had designated the Dixie Mission.) We were to stay there for two weeks, or longer if the situation seemed to demand it. While up there, myself [*sic*] and some others were requested by the leader of the Chinese Communists to make a trip into the interior, behind the Japanese lines. This was to evaluate the fighting capability of the Japanese and to determine what intelligence the Communists could provide for us. They claimed to have radio communications with all parts of China, including the Shantung Peninsula and Manchuria. We traveled some 900 miles and while we had some brushes with the Japanese, the Chinese Communists always saw to our safety. I was very much impressed with the fact that they seemed to have the complete respect and total cooperation of the peasants. This indicated to me that at the same time the Chinese Communists were helping the peasant defend himself against the Japanese, they were establishing a solid friendship with him. The peasants comprise 82% of the population and if their hearts and minds are captured, as appeared to be the case in all the areas we visited (where they shared their food with us and did all these other things), we had better take a second look at our policy in China.

I do not believe any force the Nationalist Government can put together, with or without our help, is going to be very effective in the long run. Not that I like Communists: I don't. I never saw a real live Communist until I got up there, but whatever they are they'll have to be reckoned with. We'd do well to further our relations with them, which so far have been very good, because no matter how much money we spend to help the Chiang Kai-shek regime, ultimately the Chinese Communists are going to take over all of China. The Chairman claims it could be in five years. It could take ten or twenty-five years, but he has no doubt that they will take over all of China.

When he concluded these remarks, Hitch noticed very little reaction on the part of the audience, which surprised him. After a few days he asked Colonel Bales, head of the China Division of the Office of Naval Intelligence, when he could expect to receive his orders to return to China. Much to his surprise Bales said, "We don't know if we're going to let you return to China." Later, Hitch learned the probable reason. While no response had been made to Mao's offer, the Office of Naval Intelligence (ONI) had copied and circulated the report he had written for Jarrell. Miles's people had seen it and, even though the document was classified secret, they had undoubtedly given it to Chiang Kai-shek's military attaché. Hitch believed that the Nationalists did not want a man who wrote such a report to return to Chungking.

In the meantime, a small group in the ONI, including Colonel Bales, was interested in testing the Chinese. In order to authenticate Hitch's report and determine whether Mao was sincere, they began working on a scheme to send Hitch back to China without Miles's knowledge. To accomplish this objective, ONI people in Chungking needed to contact the Chinese Communists, after which Hitch and a small band of marines would be landed from a submarine onto the Shantung Peninsula. This place was deemed suitable for a major American landing, should one take place north of the Yangtze River. If Hitch could land there, they figured that 1,000 marines could too. These men would then put in radio gear and do other things; the specific details would be worked out in the future. A great deal of effort went into formulating this plan, which involved Hitch's leading the crew and paddling ashore in a rubber boat, to be met by the Communists.

Hitch kept asking Bales when the plan would get underway. Bales would reply, "Well, I just don't know, Herb," until one day he said, "By the way, they need someone at the Philippines desk. Can you go over there?" Hitch continued to receive private letters in the diplomatic pouch from Jarrell asking when he would be coming back. Nevertheless, and in spite of his own desire to return to China, Hitch spent the rest of the war on the Philippines desk of Naval Intelligence. He was responsible for monitoring what the Philippines newspapers said about the Japanese, for watching the Philippines economy through agents, and for filing weekly reports. The plan to land him in a submarine on the Shantung coast was never implemented.[9]

As previously noted, in the months preceding Stilwell's recall, some Americans had contemplated providing lend-lease to a Chinese army that might include Communist forces. The change of theater commanders had not altered the views held by these people, and the Japanese threat to the Kunming-Kweiyang-Chungking area led others in theater headquarters to think that the Chinese Communists might be very useful in stopping the Japanese. An example of such thinking was the plan created by Barrett and Major General Robert B. McClure, Wedemeyer's chief of staff after November 28, 1944.

Three other ideas also emerged at this time. The earliest and simplest involved supplying the Communists with munitions, but when Wedemeyer mentioned this possibility to the Generalissimo on November 27, the Chinese leader immediately rejected it. Then word arrived that Donovan was planning to visit China, so McClure and Wedemeyer began to shape more comprehensive plans. The idea was to present them to the OSS chief, pending Chiang's approval. It seemed prudent to get Donovan's support, because one of the nascent plans involved guerrilla warfare, something in which both OSS and the Communists specialized.[10]

David Barrett suggested the first plan. Three Communist infantry regiments, approximately 5,000 men, would be organized in Yenan. The U.S. Services of Supply would arm and equip this force. An American officer supported by ten liaison officers would command it. They would move into Nationalist territory, either southwest China or the Tung-kuan–Hsian area of Shensi Province, near where the Chinese Nationalists were blockading the Communists.[11]

On December 15, 1944, after McClure had assured him that the errand he was about to run had been cleared with Ambassador Hurley, Barrett flew to Yenan. Lieutenant Colonel Willis G. Bird of OSS accompanied him. John Davies traveled on the same plane. Barrett (as he later wrote in his memoirs) thought that Bird was going to Yenan to consult with Communist leaders concerning the extent and nature of the cooperation and support they were prepared to offer American forces in the event of a landing on part of the Shantung coast that was under Communist control.[12]

Barrett carried a message from Hurley to Chou En-lai thanking the Chinese leader for the hospitality extended to him during his brief visit to Yenan. The note also expressed the ambassador's understanding that the five points contained in Mao's offer of settlement were to form the basis of discussions, like the three points that Chiang had offered in response. Hurley went on to say that he hoped Mao would not publish his offer of settlement, as Mao had threatened to do when negotiations broke down, because doing so would close the door to further discussions.[13]

While they were in Yenan, Bird and Barrett consulted with Mao, Chu Teh, Chou En-lai, and Yeh Chien-ying. The Communist leaders asked searching questions about what might be expected of them. Barrett had the impression that in general the prospect of operating in concert with American forces pleased them, as such action would greatly enhance their position vis-à-vis the Kuomintang.[14]

Barrett flew back to Chungking on the seventeenth, carrying replies from Chou and Mao. Chou's letter stated once again that the Communists did not want to close the door on negotiations, although they believed that the Kuomintang were insincere. They had originally agreed not to publish the five points, but they would do so, they said, when it became necessary to inform the people, as a way of pressuring the government to change its position. Mao also reminded Hurley that when he had congratulated FDR on winning reelection the previous month, the president had expressed his willingness to cooperate with *all* anti-Japanese forces in China.[15]

Then McClure prepared a plan which specified that American airborne units totaling 4,000 to 5,000 well-trained technicians should be sent to Communist-held territories to demolish and sabotage Japanese installations.[16] Wedemeyer approved the concept,[17] and so McClure presented his scheme to General Chen Cheng, the national government's minister of war. McClure said he spoke not just for himself but also for General Wedemeyer; as "practical soldiers" they believed that the United States had the right to fight its enemies anywhere in the world.[18] Following this conversation, McClure ordered his good friend David Barrett to speak with the Communists. Barrett was to say that after the defeat of Germany, an American paratroop division then serving in Europe might be sent to China to take part in the final attack on the Japanese islands. Barrett was to ask the Communists whether, following the establishment of a beachhead, they could supply the division, except for arms, ammunition, and other munitions of war, until regular army supply procedures began functioning.

The planned beachhead was presumably to take place on the shores of Shantung, an area already under Communist control. McClure told Barrett to impress upon the Communists that this talk was purely exploratory, since it had not yet been decided whether the American division would be sent to China after the defeat of Germany.[19] Barrett was also to make sure that the Communists understood that national government approval would be necessary before anything could be put into motion. For the United States to do otherwise would be a flagrant breach of diplomatic etiquette and tantamount to recognizing the Communists as a legitimate government in China.[20]

Barrett made his last trip to Yenan on December 27, 1944, carrying contingency plans for cooperation that had supposedly been drafted by McClure.[21] In his memoirs he wrote that this trip qualified him for the Order of the Broken Back. He talked again with Chairman Mao, Chou En-lai, General Chu Teh, and General Yeh Chien-ying and again made it clear that nothing was definite. The Communists seemed receptive to the idea of having a large American force in territory they controlled but did not appear to be as pleased as Barrett had expected. They asked whether they would be consulted about the operations of the division in the event that it arrived and acknowledged that they could supply it until regular American army supply agencies assumed the task.

Barrett returned to Chungking on December 29 and attended a dinner party that evening. Hurley was present, but Barrett did not mention his recent excursion to Yenan. A few days later, Barrett went to Kunming to assume his new post as chief of staff to the newly created China Combat Command under General McClure. Shortly thereafter, he learned that Kuomintang intelligence agents in Yenan had reported back to Chungking that he had offered the Chinese Communists an American paratroop division. T. V. Soong had instantly demanded an explanation from Hurley. Hurley, according to Barrett, had told Soong that he knew nothing about either the trip or the plan, and he bitterly reproached Wedemeyer, who had been out of Chungking when McClure acted so presumptuously.[22] The ambassador hit the ceiling when he learned that while Wedemeyer was attending a conference at Myitkyina, personnel in his headquarters had allegedly prepared a plan to bypass the Generalissimo and use Communist troops.[23]

As soon as Marshall received Hurley's report, he sent Wedemeyer a message demanding to know what was going on. Marshall sent it to Kunming, because Wedemeyer was visiting the Salween front, far from any spot that could provide secure communications. To receive Marshall's urgent query, Wedemeyer had to fly 800 miles to Kunming, then fly back to Chungking to deal with the problem.

Once in Chungking, Wedemeyer immediately contacted the ambassador. He expressed disappointment that Hurley had not shown him the report to the president before it was dispatched. Wedemeyer also reminded Hurley that when he had taken over command of the China Theater, he had said explicitly that he did not want to be involved in political matters as his predecessor had been. Wedemeyer recalled his promise to keep Hurley fully informed if political complications emerged accidentally.[24] He now noted that for the three months Hurley had been in China he in turn had kept the theater commander posted on the progress of his negotiations with the Communists and Chiang Kai-shek. He had used American army officers as emissaries to the Communist headquarters in Yenan. Each of these men had had explicit instructions and knew that it was Wedemeyer's policy to support the national government. Consequently they could not negotiate with persons not recognized or approved by the Generalissimo or assist in any way with other Chinese activities.

Wedemeyer believed that McClure and Barrett had followed these instructions, he continued, although it was true that several plans had been discussed in theater headquarters. Some of these plans had contemplated the employment of Communist troops, but only if and when the Generalissimo approved. Since McClure had assured him that his instructions had been followed, Wedemeyer took issue with Hurley's charges. It was possible, he admitted, that the Communists might have learned about these plans, but in his opinion it would not have been because an officer in his command had revealed them. Indeed, Wedemeyer suspected that T. V. Soong and General Chen were the sources of the leak.

In view of the fact that Hurley had made no specific charges against individuals, and given the absence of factual data, Wedemeyer recommended that Marshall take no further action on the matter.[25] Hurley's wrath, however, cost Barrett the star he had hoped to earn by serving in the Dixie Mission. Wedemeyer had recommended the promotion, but Hurley forced him to withdraw it. McClure did not suffer as many repercussions as Barrett, perhaps because he already had his star—or perhaps because at a cocktail party he had seized Hurley, grasping him by the front of his suit, and told him what he thought.[26]

Marshall followed Wedemeyer's recommendation. No official investigation of McClure's and Barrett's overtures to the Communists took place. Nevertheless, there were hard feelings among Wedemeyer, Barrett, and McClure and between all of them and Hurley. During a cocktail party at Wedemeyer's house, Hurley exchanged bitter words with McClure and, livid with rage, challenged him to a fistfight. Wedemeyer broke it up because he thought that the powerfully built

McClure might kill the ambassador with a single blow. Wedemeyer then closed the episode. He sent McClure to faraway Kunming. Wedemeyer also reduced Barrett's responsibilities to give him fewer chances to make mischief.[27]

Thereafter Hurley did not speak to Wedemeyer for days. The silence was particularly awkward because Hurley had been living in Wedemeyer's house ever since a bomb behind his own house had hurled a boulder into the kitchen, killing a man.[28] Although the ambassador and the commanding general made up, after this episode Hurley moved into housing for the embassy people, displacing them so that they all had to find new quarters on very short notice, not an easy matter in wartime Chungking. Wedemeyer, perhaps calculating that FDR would back Hurley, subsequently decided to avoid further disagreements with the ambassador and try to get along with him.[29]

The demise of McClure's plan to supply and equip the Communists sharply affected the careers of several of the direct and indirect participants. It altered the relationships that some Foreign Service and staff personnel had with Hurley. It also influenced the Dixie Mission, whose continued existence was tied to the idea of ongoing and expanded cooperation with Mao and his followers. If the United States had gone on to do any of what the McClure Plan envisioned in North China, Dixie's scope and responsibility would have been expanded. As it was, the number of men assigned to the Mission increased, but its functions remained the same.[30]

Independent of Barrett but on the same day that the McClure Plan was presented, Lieutenant Colonel Willis Bird, the deputy chief of OSS China who had flown to Yenan with Barrett, entered into negotiations with the Communists on behalf of the OSS.[31] Wedemeyer, of course, knew that OSS was in his theater and in the Dixie Mission, but he did not know everything about the extent of the organization's involvement with the group.[32]

He knew that OSS continually cooked up plans, however. In 1944, for example, Joseph Spencer of OSS's Research and Analysis branch worked on one for many months with Stelle, Rosamond Frame, Major Philip Crower, who was acting chief of the Secret Intelligence branch for CBI, Lieutenant Guy Martin (OSS/SEAC liaison with the British planners in Delhi), and Lieutenant Tom Davis (then SEAC, later to serve as Heppner's aide). They presented this plan to Bird,[33] a thirty-six-year-old graduate of the Wharton School of Finance who had been an executive of Sears Roebuck in Pennsylvania and New York before Donovan had recruited him into OSS. His fellow officers thought Bird a "con-man," an "operator," and a vain man who reportedly carried a set of pearl-handled revolvers.[34] While in China he had an affair with an OSS woman whose parents, much disturbed, wrote Wedemeyer about it. Theater had not authorized his contacts with the Communists at this time,[35] but such omissions were not unusual for OSS.

Bird first met with General Chu Teh on the morning he and Barrett arrived. Barrett told Chu that Bird was there at the request of the U.S. Army staff in Chungking to discuss what would and could be done, pending approval by the American government. After much conversation on this subject, another meeting was called for that afternoon with the chief of staff, General Yeh. In the course of almost five hours, several items were discussed and agreed upon:

1. Special Operations branch men with their units would be placed in the Communist-controlled areas to destroy Japanese communications, airfields, and blockhouses and generally to raise hell and run;
2. OSS would fully equip Communist units that assisted and protected Americans engaged in sabotage work;
3. In general, points of attack were to be selected by Wedemeyer. Details would be worked out in cooperation with Communists in their territory;
4. OSS was to provide complete equipment, except for food and clothing, for up to 25,000 guerrillas;
5. Schools would be set up to provide instruction in the use of American arms, demolitions, communications, etc.;
6. An intelligence radio network in cooperation with the Eighteenth Route Army would be established;
7. The People's Militia would be supplied at least 100,000 Woolworth one-shot pistols;
8. In return, when Wedemeyer decided that strategy required it, the Communists would give the complete cooperation of their army of 650,000 and People's Militia of 2½ million.

After the formal discussion, General Chu talked about whether the Generalissimo might approve the plans. When he asked Bird's opinion, Bird intimated that he and those he represented were very hopeful. Chu also wondered whether Bird thought the government of the United States would approve the plans. Bird responded that while there were many people who would recommend them as a good way to kill Japs in North China, it was not possible for him to predict what Washington would or could do in view of commitments made to the national government.

Later, Bird recalled that General Chu had then asked what would happen if the United States approved but Chiang did not. Everyone, including himself, had laughed at the question, Bird reported, and Bird had said something to the effect that army personnel obeyed orders and would do whatever they were instructed to do. More questions along the same line followed, but Bird always maintained that everyone understood clearly that the entire program had to be passed upon by the highest authorities in the United States before any steps could be taken. The talks closed with General Chu stating that whether or not they received one rifle or one round of ammunition, the people of North China looked upon the United States as their best friend and upon General Wedemeyer as their commander in chief, whose military orders they would follow if he chose to give them.[36]

Bird had apparently managed to reach tentative agreement on matters of the highest importance in an afternoon. Yet Wedemeyer's reports on the subject suggest that he did not know about Bird's activities until January, when McClure told him he had sent Bird to Yenan in order to forestall a proposal by General Donovan, who was expected in China momentarily. In his January 27 report to General Marshall on the matter, the theater commander stated that he had informed all officers under his command that "we must support the Chinese National Government" and that there would be no "negotiations with or assistance of other Chinese activities or persons not approved or recognized by the Generalissimo." Wedemeyer believed that Barrett and Bird knew about these orders. He added that he had not been told that Bird was going to accompany Barrett to Yenan. By quoting Bird's message to Washington, he implied that he had not known of Bird's discussions.[37]

The Communist leaders, who undoubtedly wanted to believe that both Barrett and Bird spoke on behalf of high American authorities, took new hope from the aforementioned encounters. Sensing that they could work with a different American faction, they rejected Hurley's renewed demand that Chou fly back to Chungking for further negotiations. When Davies, who on December 15 had traveled to Yenan on the same plane as Barrett, returned to Chungking on December 17, Hurley accused him of persuading the Communists to break off further political discussions.[38]

During his two-day stay, Davies had been "reimpressed by the evident supremacy of Mao over all of the other Communist leaders." He subsequently reported that General Yeh had asked him whether he thought it would be a good idea for a Chinese Communist representative to visit the United States. Davies replied that to him the suggestion seemed academic, as he could scarcely see the national government issuing the necessary visa. The question gave Davies the impression that Yeh wanted to go to the United States.[39]

Perhaps related to the conversation that Yeh had with Davies, or perhaps because he had received no response to the letter sent with Hitch, in January 1945, Mao offered to go to Washington in person, with Chou En-lai. The acting chief of the Dixie Mission, Major Ray Cromley transmitted the original proposal to Wedemeyer's headquarters in Chungking on January 9:

> Yenan Government wants to dispatch to America an unofficial rpt unofficial group to interpret and explain to American civilians and officials interested the present situation and problems of China. Next is strictly off the record suggestion by same: Mao and Chou will be immediately available either singly or together for exploratory conference at Washington should President Roosevelt express desire to receive them at White House as leaders of a primary Chinese party. They expressly desire that it be unknown rpt not known that they are willing to go to Washington in case Roosevelt invitation not now forthcoming. This to protect their political [sic] vis-à-vis Chiang.

Cromley interpreted this request as follows (I paraphrase):

1. Evidence indicates highly important conferences here between important Communist Chinese leaders;
2. Outright statement indicates a decision has been reached that Chiang will not compromise with the Communists;
3. Subordinate officials here say that the Yenan government is actively preparing for an imminent large- scale civil war, but highest officials avoid this subject;
4. Our liaison openly declares that all south and southeast China behind Jap lines will be completely in Red hands within six to twelve months;
5. Organizers and army leaders are reported to be leaving Yenan areas not for item 4;
6. It is reported that the Red army as such will total 1 million troops by the end of this year;
7. Doctor Ma, who apparently has the complete confidence of the highest Yenan leaders states, "Time for decision between Chiang and Communists is now. We will have either ballots or bullets now. If America bolsters Chiang with arms and economic help and not us, America will suffer the responsibility for results within China and our future relations with her;"
8. I definitely think that Yenan's tone toward Chiang and

America has hardened the last few days, with sharp anti-
Chiang editorials in the local press;

9. Because of remarks by my liaison and the chief of staff's
reticence to explain an allegedly planned Jap attack against
Yenan and Sian, local people believe Chiang will collaborate
to join such an attack soon, although there is no evidence of
such an impending attack;

10. Liaison today suggested that either Wedemeyer or McClure
come here now. [40]

Chou requested air travel to the United States if Roosevelt issued
him an invitation, but the message, received in Chungking on January
10, was not forwarded to the "highest U.S. officials" who Mao and
Chou had hoped would see it. Instead, Hurley, with the concurrence of
General Wedemeyer, held it in Chungking[41] and only mentioned it on
the fifth page of a six-page letter sent to FDR on the fourteenth. In that
communiqué, Hurley tied the offer made by McClure and Barrett to
the breakdown of negotiations between the Kuomintang and the Communists. His letter does not indicate that he knew about Bird's plan.
Hurley wrote the president: during Wedemeyer's absence "certain officers of his command formulated a plan for the use of American para-
troops in the Communist-held area. The plan provided for the use of
Communist troops led by Americans in guerrilla warfare. They predi-
cated the plan on the United States and the Communist Party reaching
an agreement and completely bypassing the National Government.
American supplies were to be furnished directly to the Communist
troops, which gave the Communists exactly what they wanted, recognition and Lend-lease supplies for themselves and [the] destruction of
the National Government." Hurley claimed that while he had some
inkling of the "plot" (plan), he never knew it had been presented to the
Communists until they tried to have Wedemeyer arrange transportation so that Mao and Chou could meet with Roosevelt. It irked Hurley
that they had asked Wedemeyer to keep it secret from the national government and from him.[42]

At the time he informed Roosevelt about these developments,
Hurley knew that the Communists had tried to circumvent him, but he
didn't believe they knew that he knew. Nevertheless, he claimed he was
prepared to continue negotiations and to persuade Chiang to make
every possible concession so that the Communists could participate in
a unified government. He hoped that at the forthcoming Yalta meeting, the Big Three would endorse the immediate unification of all military forces in China and would advocate a free, undivided, democratic

China after the war. Then complete plans for uniting the military forces of China, for recognizing the Chinese Communist Party as a legal political party, for the representation of all parties in the administration of the Chinese government, for the liberalization of the Chinese government, and for the promotion of democratic processes and the establishment of fundamental individual rights and the reconstruction of a free, united, democratic China could be placed in Chiang's hands. At that time, Hurley felt, the president should offer to meet with both Chiang Kai-shek and Mao Tse-tung on the condition that they, prior to the meeting, agree between themselves about the unification of China, which would be the subject of the meeting.[43]

According to some historians, Hurley's attitude toward the Communists changed when he found out that Mao and Chou were scheming to go to Washington without his knowledge and when he learned that McClure and Barrett were making overtures and were engaging in other activities that he regarded as attempts to evade him. Certainly, the Yenan leadership had tried to bypass the ambassador through the Foreign Service officers and had tried to secure American aid for themselves by means of rumors that the Kuomintang were going to make peace with the Japanese. They were afraid to tell Hurley about Chiang's supposed capitulation, because they knew he would not believe it.[44] Also, they made a direct though unsuccessful appeal to Donovan for a $20 million loan through Chu Teh. The money was to be used "to strengthen subversive activities among puppet troops." It would be strictly accounted for and was to be paid back as soon as the war ended.[45]

These startling proposals reveal the lengths to which the Communists were prepared to go in their efforts to win American support and a measure of international legitimacy. Clearly, Mao and Chou believed it necessary to maneuver around Chiang and Hurley in order to put their case directly to their American "friends" and the "progressives." They apparently thought that they could appeal to the president's reason, hence their interest in approaching him directly. What the result would have been if they had succeeded is an interesting matter for speculation. The journey by Mao and Chou to Washington would probably have placed additional distance between Yenan and Moscow while making the Communists appear less like an insurgent group than like an equal player in the joint war effort.[46]

Indeed, it is interesting to speculate whether history might have been different if *any* of the overtures made to or by the Communists had been pursued. In the past, some historians have suggested that the three years of civil war following the Japanese surrender might have been shortened or entirely averted. Many considered the Communists' cooperation critical to the defeat of Japan. In 1944 and through at least part of 1945 one did not automatically become "pro-Communist" ideologically if one entertained this conviction. Those who did look beyond military expediency and hoped that American aid to Yenan might lead to the overthrow of the Kuomintang did so in the belief that such a change would benefit China. One did not necessarily see a rigid Communism replacing the current regime, possibly because so few believed that the Chinese in Yenan were "real" Communists. To them Mao and his group represented the triumph of a truly peasant-oriented movement rather than ideological hard-liners.[47] This theory presupposes that Mao's victory over Chiang might not have been accompanied by antagonism toward the United States because of the latter's assistance to the Kuomintang. The different policy, therefore, might have meant less harassment of American consular officials and others by the Communists as well as earlier American recognition of the Communist regime in China.[48]

In September 1945, just before he left Yenan, Arnold Dadian talked with Mao through the interpreter Huang Hua. Mao asked how Dadian had liked Yenan, then expressed concern about the future of relations between the Communist Chinese and the United States. He could not understand why the American public and American foreign policy were so negative, given that the Chinese people backed his revolution, he said. Dadian explained that Americans had a long-standing tradition of opposition to communism and did not differentiate between communism in Russia and communism in China. Mao then replied, "Why do the Americans persist in referring to us as agrarian reformers? We believe in the basic tenets of Marx." Dadian reported this conversation to Dickey, who suggested he need not include this in his report.[49]

The secret mission to Washington never took place, of course, but Hurley jumped to the conclusion that subversive plots against his authority had led to Communist intransigence and that disloyal Americans had persuaded Mao and Chou to seek direct support from Washington rather than accepting the compromise he was trying to work out between them and the Kuomintang.[50] Word of the secret mission to Washington had repercussions. Wedemeyer's increased knowledge of unconventional operations in the Dixie Mission and OSS prompted him, on December 29, to assert control over all OSS clandestine, guerrilla, and intelligence activities by Americans in China.[51]

OSS remained intact, however, perhaps because Donovan reached Chungking in time to mollify the angry Hurley. He also received a warm

Huang Hua, the interpreter for Dixie, and his wife, Ho Li-liang, in the summer of 1945. Courtesy of Col. Wilbur J. Peterkin.

greeting from Wedemeyer and was invited to attend a joint intelligence conference with British and SACO representatives. There Wedemeyer announced that he would no longer tolerate the chaotic state of the Allied secret services in China. He said he had received information that British MI-6 had recruited several thousand agents in China whose primary mission was to spy, not on the enemy, but on the Chinese government. Wedemeyer criticized Miles and Tai Li and declared his intention to have Washington abrogate the 1943 SACO agreement.

In a sense, then, OSS emerged victorious, because Wedemeyer assigned responsibility to Heppner's unit for the training of twenty Chinese commando-guerrilla units, a function that Miles had coveted. Nevertheless, Miles and Tai Li continued to allege that OSS supplied and collaborated with the Communists.

What if OSS arms and supplies had actually reached the Yenan armies? Their postwar oratory notwithstanding, Hurley, Wedemeyer, and Chennault all had words of praise for the Communists in spring 1945. Even Curtis LeMay, in charge of the Twentieth Bomber Command, exchanged gifts with Mao and later remembered that "everything was smooth as silk in our mutual relations." OSS probably had better justification than any other agency in China for establishing closer operational contacts with Yenan, because Donovan's men had been charged with gathering intelligence from any and all sources. If they had done so, and had used the Dixie Mission in the process, would our stance vis-à-vis Moscow have changed? Some historians have concluded that FDR's willingness to compromise on Stalin's political demands at the Yalta Conference of February 1945 partly reflected his belief that we needed the Russians to fight a massive Japanese army in Manchuria. OSS infiltration of that area would have revealed that the enemy force had been depleted. Possibly such knowledge might have meant less emphasis on Russian assistance in Asia and an altered balance of power during the cold war.[52]

7

Intelligence Gathering in Yenan

Most of the men in the Dixie Mission were affiliated with the Office of Strategic Services, the Office of War Information, or Army Intelligence (G-2). Each man's primary responsibility was to his parent agency. There was much rivalry among these organizations, and so empire building frequently took precedence over defeating the enemy.

The OWI, created by executive order on June 13, 1942, served as a clearinghouse and coordinating agency for wartime news and information both inside the United States and overseas. Directed by journalist Elmer Davis, it was part of the Office for Emergency Management. Within the United States the OWI, through its Domestic Operations branch, disseminated all official news relating to the war and maintained morale by promoting appropriate educational programs. The Overseas Operations branch carried on psychological warfare in enemy territory, using radio broadcasts, leaflets, and newspapers. F. MacCracken Fisher, who spent about three weeks in Yenan, ran the OWI office in Chungking. Koji Ariyoshi, a newspaperman from Honolulu affiliated with OWI, served with the Dixie Mission for a year.[1] As noted previously, he and John Emmerson interrogated Japanese prisoners. Ariyoshi also briefed Yeaton on the Communist leaders, and provided him with an assessment of the Red army's strength, the morale of party functionaries, and other matters related to the impending civil war.

From Yenan, Ariyoshi made several trips to Chungking to see General Wedemeyer, who told him that America planned to fly freshly trained, well-equipped Nationalist troops into Communist China to defend "Free China." Ariyoshi predicted a Communist victory in the coming struggle, which displeased Wedemeyer, who told him to repeat his prediction to Hurley. At the embassy, the ambassador greeted the former newspaperman in his stocking feet, shirt, and BVDs. He was trying to tie his bow tie and continued to do so while telling Ariyoshi that *he* knew the facts about China. He had removed the career Foreign Service officers who had knifed him in the back, he said. He knew how to cut more deeply and twist his blade. He claimed that Mao Tse-tung reported directly to him, and he knew which Americans in Yenan were loyal to him and which were not.[2]

F. MacCracken Fisher often found his job as frustrating as his encounters with Hurley. Often he had to rely on Davies, Service, and Ludden for information to use in press releases. The cozy relationship between these State Department men and the journalists stemmed in part from Stilwell's confidence in them. To a large degree it continued under Wedemeyer, because he was preoccupied with other matters.[3]

Stilwell had told Fisher that he and Service were responsible for anything having to do with psychological warfare, and so Fisher went to Yenan in late August 1944, to check on rumors that the Communists treated their Japanese prisoners well. Until that time, no one but the Communists had been able to capture Japanese soldiers alive. Either the Nationalists killed them, or the Japanese committed suicide. Fisher interviewed Okano, who told him about the Japanese Communists' plans for the country after the war. Fisher passed this information on to Service, who was interested in political matters.

Fisher also investigated the activities of the Japanese People's Emancipation League. He learned that the Communists had captured some Japanese Signal Corps people, had tapped into some of the Japanese communications, and had even called Japanese garrisons and talked to the troops on the telephone. During this trip Fisher brought the Communists some newsreels and pictures.[4] Before leaving Yenan, Fisher initiated arrangements between the Americans and the Communists for cooperative action on propaganda, including American monitoring of the Yenan shortwave and Communist distribution of American propaganda through their own channels.[5]

Wedemeyer believed that information provided by G-2 would help win the war. Colonel Joseph Dickey headed G-2 at theater headquarters. Colonel Thomas Van Natta served as G-2 officer at the Combat Command, reporting to General Robert McClure. Van Natta saw the role of G-2 as twofold: what it was supposed to do and what it did for publicity and training purposes.[6]

Strictly speaking, Dixie was a G-2 operation, and so its commanding officers addressed their reports to Dickey.[7] In addition to filing official reports, Peterkin carried on an informal correspondence with Dickey, who was enthusiastic about the Mission. Peterkin's letters usually contained the same information as his reports but also included his comments on things important to him as commander: notes about personnel who drank excessively, who were difficult to handle, or who were not doing their jobs; some insights into the daily problems of running the post; and his personal reaction to exchanges with the Communists.[8]

At one point, a peculiar situation existed in Dickey's office in Chungking. The Chinese G-2 officer was a Cantonese who spoke no Mandarin. All of the Chinese interpreters spoke English and Mandarin, which was very different from Cantonese. One officer spoke good Cantonese and good Japanese, however, so Dr. Alfred Burden, an American doctor assigned to G-2 because of his fluency in Japanese, acted as liaison. Translations between the Americans and the Chinese thus passed through two interpreters. Burden had expected to be one of the original Dixie group but had been held back because Wedemeyer said his language talents were needed in Chungking. He did manage to make a trip to Yenan in August or September of 1944, when he stayed about a month, observing the Mission and talking to some of the Japanese prisoners, usually in clusters.[9]

Much of what China Theater G-2 accomplished resulted from successful sorting out and evaluation of order-of-battle information or combat intelligence. General Thomas Van Natta thought those who went "down the garden path of enemy intentions" made this part of his job more difficult, because they based their assessments on how they believed the enemy was going to behave rather than on the facts. Before an attack, some Japanese deserters would almost invariably slip across the lines and drop their rifles. The first job of the G-2 officer who interrogated them was to determine from which unit they had deserted. Often this was the only piece of really valuable information that he could obtain. G-2 considered new units more dangerous and less predictable than experienced ones, but a competent combat intelligence officer could usually warn his men two hours before an attack. In fact, the ability to evaluate incoming intelligence was of paramount importance, since a G-2 officer who accepted every piece of information uncritically soon found himself inundated with useless data.

Rivalry existed within the structure of military intelligence. Frequently, Combat Intelligence received incorrect information from theater G-2, reports that placed Japanese troops at locations where men in the field knew they were not. According to Van Natta, after a few such mistakes the Combat Intelligence people discounted most of the information sent by Dickey's office. Combat Intelligence had little to do with the Dixie Mission, which it considered nothing more than a small team sent out to keep in contact with the Chinese Communists. In the fall of 1945, after G-2 had finished its study of the Japanese Army's order of battle, an order of battle of the Chinese Communist Army was developed. This was justified on the ground that the Communists had set up an operational organization in Japanese-held territory using skeleton commands.[10]

In addition to its communications with Combat Intelligence, G-2 in Chungking regularly received information from OSS. There was so much conflict between what Combat Intelligence said and what OSS said, however, that Dickey's people generally dumped the OSS messages in the wastebasket. Often the discarded information seemed ridiculous to the man evaluating it in Chungking, whose perspective differed from that of the OSS operative who had sent it.[11] Sometimes field operatives even picked up rumors that the Morale Operations (MO) branch had spread and fed them back to OSS as legitimate information to be acted upon.[12]

Duplication of effort led to problems of concern to everyone in the Chungking headquarters. Frequently, Dickey commented on the similarity of messages sent by different persons in the field who had contact with the Communists but not with each other. He also noted that the Communists' morale and tactics uniformly impressed the field men.[13] OSS teams were impressed too. The Chili Team reported that, as they marched through the mountains or sat at mess, they heard soldiers singing songs about how the farmers and the Eighth Route Army worked for each other. In at least three instances the Americans saw Eighth Route Army soldiers working in the field with farmers. Instead of raiding the peasants' food like the Kuomintang, the Communists tried as much as possible to grow their own food on large farms they maintained for this purpose. Nowhere did the Chili team see the red star or the hammer and sickle displayed. Instead, all propaganda slogans appeared under the circular pointed star of China.[14]

Duplication also concerned Dickey. On January 10, 1945, he sent a memorandum to Wedemeyer stating that no more than one agency should be going to the Chinese G-2 officer for information concerning the Japanese and their installations in enemy-occupied territory. Only one agency should turn material over to the Chinese, he said. He complained that G-2, the American military attaché, and the British military attaché all competed to be the first to give the Chinese the weekly battle order from Washington.

Dickey believed that the military attaché caused much of the unnecessary duplication. For example, he wrote, besides himself, the military attaché had three air attachés and two ground attachés attempting to glean information from the Chinese. Furthermore, Dickey learned that the military attaché intended to open a branch office in Kunming and was buying a house for $26 million (in Chinese Nationalist currency), a needless waste of American dollars. Kunming already had a multitude of American intelligence agencies, he said.[15]

The most significant rivalry between intelligence-gathering services was that between Major General William J. Donovan's OSS and Vice Admiral Milton E. (Mary) Miles's Naval Group, China. Created shortly after Pearl Harbor, Naval Group, China, began functioning in early 1942. In late December of that year Miles and General Tai Li, head of Chiang Kai-shek's "Gestapo," created the Sino-American Cooperative Organization. Tai Li was the commander, and Miles was the deputy commander, with each having a veto over operations.[16] SACO's powers were independent of the theater commander, and its supplies came through the navy rather than lend-lease. SACO had originally been given an allocation of 150 tons per month, but by early 1945, it was flying planes carrying several hundred tons of military supplies monthly,[17] mostly small arms ammunition, semiautomatic arms, and high explosives.[18] These "tools of terrorism" often went to Tai Li's "Gestapo" and were used to suppress dissident Chinese.[19]

Miles's official title was U.S. naval observer attached to the Chungking embassy. His orders were to gather intelligence and "harass" the Japanese.[20] Marine Colonel James McHugh served as naval attaché, and the assistant naval attaché was Lieutenant S. Herbert Hitch. Naval Group, China, as such, supplied meteorological and ship movement data to the U.S. Pacific Fleet. In another capacity it also functioned as part of SACO, training and equipping guerrilla fighters and assisting guerrilla operations.

Naval Group, China, was independent of Wedemeyer, who nevertheless found it a potential source of embarrassment.[21] A relatively low-level operation, it had a unique opportunity to sponsor political and military activities within China. Contrary to the political moderation that most knowledgeable Americans in China advocated, it bolstered the most reactionary and anti-Communist faction within the Kuomintang coalition. It enjoyed firm support from Admiral King and the Navy Department, not simply because of its political program, but also because it gave the navy a chance to exert influence in the army-dominated China Theater. Naval Group, China, provided weapons to the secret police, trained counterinsurgents, and supported Chiang in his disputes with Stilwell. In wartime China's highly unstable political and military situation, SACO's politicized personnel played a pivotal role that affected both the current policies and the future expectations of the two contending Chinese factions. SACO's direct involvement in China, its willingness to become a conduit for secret military programs, and its dedication to the destruction of revolutionary movements allowed it to have a disproportionately large impact on American-Chinese relations.[22]

General Tai Li's flair for assassination helped him become Chiang Kai-shek's chief of security. Chiang called on Tai when he wanted someone watched, investigated, arrested, or killed. Miles had become involved with Tai through his friendship with Major Hsiao Hsin-ju, the assistant military attaché at the Chinese embassy in Washington. This man explained to OSS China specialists in Washington that Chinese patriotic humiliation over the unequal treaty system of the past was still so great that sending any American to China who reminded the Chinese of past shame would be intolerably insulting. Miles became an intimate friend of Hsiao and was acceptable, but Colonel Hsiao made sure that others in Naval Group, China, were innocent newcomers, ignorant of Chinese speech and writing.

After visiting India in July-August 1942, Miles began developing a sabotage training center, known as "Happy Valley," that was located about eight miles outside Chungking. The Americans lived there in Chinese style and worked closely with Tai Li's men on terms of real equality.[23] The naval mission's position seemed strengthened when General Donovan named Miles head of OSS China in September 1942.

Chiang Ching (Mrs. Mao Tse-tung) in September 1944. Courtesy of Col. Wilbur J. Peterkin.

Donovan took this step in order to avail himself of Miles's political connections, but Miles resented Donovan's maneuver as an attempt to limit his own special relationship with Tai Li.

Tai vigorously opposed expansion of OSS activities in China. He thought the organization was a foe of the Kuomintang.[24] Both he and Miles believed that OSS should seek SACO's permission for any missions it undertook. In fall 1943, when the Morale Operations branch of OSS, which disbursed "black propaganda," wanted to send a team of officers to Chungking, Tai Li withheld his approval. Not until the MO branch chief for the Far East reminded Tai that he had the full support and backing of General Donovan, adding that he was prepared to suggest to the president of the United States that the whole question of American aid to China should be reviewed, did Tai agreed to let MO operate in China.[25]

Miles never regarded himself as an OSS officer, nor did he feel responsible for defending the agency and its operations.[26] The creation of SACO, which was signed into being by President Roosevelt on April 15, 1943, ensured that the operation run by the navy and Tai Li would remain independent of OSS as well as of the theater commander, and at the end of 1943 Miles ceased to be in charge of OSS China.[27] At Gauss's request his title was changed from naval observer to commander, Naval Group China. Gauss did not want Miles to have diplomatic status, and Stilwell, concerned about the connection with Tai Li, did not want any of his representatives at his headquarters.

Miles's new title did not involve a change in his relationship with Stilwell, but by this time a number of the naval activities that he controlled had become closely identified with Chennault's command. In June and July 1944, Naval Group, China, acquired twelve additional senior naval officers. They were to collect and evaluate information pertaining to the South China Sea coastal and insular areas and to plan for utilization of Chinese ports as fleet bases. The Chinese were told that the officers were being added to Miles's staff in recognition of the growing importance of his project and to assist in the formation and operation of amphibious, lake, river, and harbor guerrilla raiders, which the Generalissimo had recently approved.[28]

The power of Naval Group, China, lay in its ability to play off the various contending Chinese and American factions against one another. Stilwell's recall and the Communists' subsequent efforts to work secretly with the army and with OSS gave them added opportunity to do so. Furthermore, in early October 1944, Miles persuaded Hurley to use SACO's radio facilities for his communications with the president. As a result, the most important cable traffic between Chiang and Hurley passed through SACO headquarters, where it probably became available to Tai Li's agents. Copies of many crucial reports sent by the OSS and information sent by the Dixie Mission to Washington and Chungking headquarters found their way almost immediately to Miles. Yet even though Kuomintang intelligence in Yenan may have made sure that Miles and Tai Li knew in advance about all possible challenges to their policy,[29] SACO never had an agent stationed in Dixie.[30]

Both Stilwell and the embassy staff worked to curtail Miles, who hoped to "provoke the Reds" at the very time Stilwell was trying to get both sides to "bury the hatchet." The replacement of Stilwell with Wedemeyer marked the "beginning of the end" of Miles's power.[31] As mentioned before, Wedemeyer did not like the various intelligence agencies within the theater to be independent of his headquarters, nor did he have anything but contempt for Tai Li, the "Chinese Himmler."[32]

Wedemeyer locked horns with Miles right after Wedemeyer took over. At a staff meeting he asked Miles to provide some intelligence in order to answer certain questions. Wedemeyer said to Miles, "What is the answer? What do we do now?" Miles replied, "I can't tell you." "Why not?" asked Wedemeyer. Miles said, "Don't you know? I might know, but I work for General Tai Li and I would have to get his approval." Furiously, Wedemeyer retorted, "Since when does an American flag officer not respond to a question from the Theater Commander?" Miles just smiled.[33]

Later, Wedemeyer talked at length with Miles about why the navy was running so many guerrillas. "I just stumbled into this," Miles explained. "Admiral King gave me a green light after I had Stilwell's permission, and now the guerrillas really are beginning to pay off." He said he hoped SACO's Hump tonnage might be increased to 500 tons, but instead Wedemeyer limited it and also ordered SACO not to train and equip Tai Li's units except when they were directly involved in anti-Japanese activities.[34]

Wedemeyer, fearful of SACO's overt involvement in civil conflict, further ordered Miles not to permit any SACO American military operations in Communist areas. Unable to oppose Wedemeyer directly, Miles then relied on subterfuge to mobilize SACO strength against the Communists. As late as August 16, 1945, he ordered Americans in SACO to assist Tai Li.[35] He and Tai even collaborated with Japanese and puppet forces to regain control of Shanghai and to facilitate Nationalist recapture of coastal cities by arming a fleet of junks and seizing the harbor areas.[36]

By this time Wedemeyer believed that Miles was power hungry

and out of touch with reality at least as far as his own position in China was concerned. The commanding general recommended that American personnel not be permitted to work with Tai Li and urged the War Department to curtail most SACO activities in China. In September, Miles called a press conference in Shanghai at which he planned to announce that he did not recognize Wedemeyer's authority in the theater and to "blow the lid off," but before he could do so, the navy medical staff hustled him back to Washington. After his departure, SACO's role in China quickly diminished.[37]

Miles's superiors opposed much of what the errant admiral did but only because they found it crude and premature. He had aided the Kuomintang's preparation for civil war before it was official American policy to do so, but by summer 1945, Wedemeyer was beginning to make similar plans independently.[38] Nevertheless, Miles was much more interested in furthering Chiang's aims than in waging war against the Japanese. He was, therefore, violently anti-Communist and completely against the largely OSS Dixie Mission. He accused Barrett of misrepresenting the purpose of the Mission to the Nationalist government and charged that the men assigned to Dixie sympathized blindly with the Communists. The Communists, he said, actively supported the Japanese and vice versa.[39] Ironically, Miles himself did little against the Japanese, although he did a lot for Tai Li, who did nothing whatever for the United States.[40]

Those who knew Miles have described his personality as strange. He flaunted a pennant that he had designed himself. It displayed three question marks, three exclamation points, and three asterisks in a line (???!!!***). He reveled in barking "SACO!" and boasted to John Davies in 1942 that his agents had poisoned several Japanese naval officers in Hankow with aspirin. He asked Stilwell for 10,000 daggers with which to arm SACO agents assigned to stab Japanese in Indochina.[41]

Miles was hard to deal with, however, mainly because he was under orders from Admiral Ernest J. King to lay the groundwork for the future of the American navy in Asia. King believed that after the war Chiang Kai-shek would be one of the world's great leaders, a man destined to make China into one of the more important powers. From King's point of view, a close liaison between the Generalissimo and the U.S. Navy would give America a great voice in postwar Chinese naval matters. Conceivably, the United States could then use the Chinese navy as the British had used the Portuguese navy in earlier times, as an adjunct to help control the Pacific.[42] In retrospect it may be kindest to view Miles as a nineteenth-century adventurer, the kind of man who would go to a foreign land espousing noble motives but with the real purpose of carving out an empire of his own.

SACO's "Happy Valley" headquarters were set against the hills about twelve miles north of Chungking. "Valley" is a somewhat misleading term for this spot, which was enclosed, hotter and sultrier than the city, and relieved by few breezes. Chinese farmers had sculpted the valley into terraced fields, but it was subject to occasional small landslips as the fields slumped downward in wet weather. There was a small creek at the bottom, running amid rocks and mud slides, carrying water that was soapy at times from the washing of clothes.

The navy had taken over buildings high against the hills on the left bank of the valley. Their structures were scattered all along and over the upper slopes. The OSS facilities were lower down on the right side of the valley. More mud slides occurred lower down, and once a mud flow came through its rear wall and damaged Morale Operations. Of OSS's six small buildings, the largest was the general office/enlisted men's barracks. Another unit, located few feet higher, had a living room, two bedrooms and two baths, and a third unit had three bedrooms. About a hundred feet away and a bit higher than the general office unit sat a long unit containing a shower room, a kitchen, and a mess hall. The soapy mud creek ran between the three units and the structure with the shower and mess hall. Until the mud slide, MO was behind the mess hall. Two units of servants' quarters were located above and behind the three unit blocks, across Soap Creek.

If one walked about a hundred yards up a winding path through patches of kaoliang (a type of grain) and squash, one came to two long units, one belonging to the navy and the other to Research and Analysis. The latter had one long room for an office and quarters at the other end for the Chinese staff. Only a steel trunk protected R&A's small amount of classified material of outside origin, which was mostly correspondence.

Besides MO and R&A, the Secret Intelligence and Special Operations branches were also represented in Happy Valley. The men assigned to these branches were almost completely isolated. Transportation was scarce, and so it was hard to go into town, and no one except those with business came to the site. OSS people spoke only occasionally to the navy people, and official contacts between the two groups were distant and formal. Even though they shared the moving picture facilities, personal relations were casual and were kept to a minimum.[43]

How did OSS, an organization proud of its freewheeling style, manage to have its China operation placed under virtual house arrest? OSS had originated as part of the Office of the Coordinator of Information (COI), which had been established in the summer of 1941. Six months after Pearl Harbor, the propaganda division was severed from COI and was made into part of the new Office of War Information. The part left under Donovan was renamed the "Office of Strategic Services" and was given the job of planning and directing such special services as the U.S. Joint Chiefs of Staff might direct.

The creation of SACO was supposed to end the conflict between American and Chinese intelligence. For a while Donovan made Miles his coordinator for OSS in the Far East, but the OSS mission became disillusioned about the navy man's ability to work out any relationship with Tai Li that would be useful to the United States. In April 1943, Miles went to Washington to attend the SACO meetings. Donovan invited him to dinner at his home and drew him out about his attitudes and plans. What he heard destroyed his little remaining confidence in Miles, and Donovan decided to send Richard Heppner, a partner in the Donovan law firm, to China, ostensibly as Miles's assistant but actually to replace him.[44]

John Davies thought Heppner was a logical choice to head OSS China. He was very much a Donovan man and politically well informed. Both the diplomatic and the military staff in New Delhi liked him.[45] Heppner and Miles did not get along, however, and Tai Li obstructed both of them. By late 1943, OSS agents had proof that Tai Li was withholding most intelligence of value while contributing virtually nothing of importance to SACO.[46] Donovan confronted Miles, who responded by repeating his charges that OSS regularly violated the SACO agreement. "I don't agree with writing one thing and doing another. I quit," roared Miles. "You can't quit, you're fired!" Donovan rejoined.

Miles continued to head Naval Group, China, and to serve as Deputy Director of SACO, but on December 5, 1943, Donovan officially removed him from his OSS post. Lieutenant Colonel John G. Coughlin, who had been with OSS Detachment 101 in Burma, replaced him.[47]

John Davies wrote that OSS was a "pungent collection of thugs, post debutantes, millionaires, professors, corporation lawyers, professional military, and misfits, all operating under high tension and in whispers." Davies found them a diverting contrast to Cordell Hull's stupefying State Department.[48] Others found the OSS crew sometimes unprofessional and given to playing games. The group that was connected with Chennault's Fourteenth Air Force headquarters in Kweilin and operated under the cover of AGFRTS once received a substantial shipment of matériel from the OSS office in Kunming. Stenciled on the outside of the supposedly secret crate was "AGFRTS (OSS)."[49] AGFRTS was a joint OSS–Fourteenth Air Force unit formed in April 1944 under cover of Chennault's command. OSS gave it the unwieldy name of the 5329th Air and Ground Forces Resources and Technical Staff, but its moniker was "Agfighters" or "Agfarts."

During the first months of 1944, Coughlin tried to build an effective intelligence-gathering organization in China under OSS leadership. He planned for OSS to train at least twenty-five young, energetic Chinese, fluent in English and with some knowledge of radio, as intelligence operators.[50] Coughlin also sent Tai Li a directive requesting that secret intelligence be obtained surreptitiously from China, Manchuria, and Korea.[51]

Coughlin's demands led to a series of frustrating meetings with the Chinese, who refused to relinquish to the Americans command over training and control of agents. Furthermore, the Chinese saw no reason to establish the intermediate station that OSS wanted to relay messages from the advanced bases to SACO headquarters. The Chinese tried to convey the impression that operations would be more effective if messages could be dispatched directly to SACO headquarters, but the Americans did not believe that the Chinese portable radio sets could operate effectively over more than 500 miles. The Chinese thought that objections to an advance base reflected mistrust and the belief that all messages would be censored.

OSS had the impression that it could not move anywhere in China without a "hujao," or travel permit, from Tai Li. When OSS asked the Chinese to suggest a place suitable for an advanced base, the Chinese suggested Ningkwo, forty miles southwest of Wuhu, which was under Japanese control. The Chinese had picked Ningkwo precisely because it *was* unsuitable. Trying to locate in any area close to the Yangtze River, particularly one with as high a concentration of Japanese as Wuhu, would have been suicide for the Americans.

By using the SACO agreement to create obstacles, the Chinese were thus able to sabotage most of the OSS efforts. They made every possible excuse to prevent the American operators from operating the agent sets, including the invention of regulations and rules pertaining to the ownership and transportation of American radios.

Nor did the Chinese like too many Americans to go on reconnaissance trips. The objection voiced was that they aroused suspicion among the natives. OSS felt that American army personnel commanded greater respect from the Chinese than did the Chinese officers and soldiers, who plundered, looted, and raped their own people. What the Chinese wanted was to make the operations that OSS had proposed a completely Chinese show and for OSS to be "the sucker who paid the bills." They continually responded to American suggestions by stating that minor points needed to be worked out, but it became increasingly obvious that regardless of what adjustments were made, there would always be new obstructions and continual delays.[52]

Chinese objections did not paralyze OSS totally, however. Frequently, OSS field teams merely neglected to inform both the Chinese and the OSS leadership responsible for whatever area they were in.[53] The Chinese did not want OSS to "interfere" outside SACO. The Chinese wanted to control all messages from the time they were dispatched in occupied areas until they were received at SACO headquarters and were translated by "dilatory" translators. When and if the information reached the Americans, it was stale.[54]

The school for training operators did not prove to be very successful either, as the Chinese ignored American attempts at enforcing discipline. One example was the OSS attempt to enforce security regulations, which included requiring students to remain within the confines of the camp for the duration of the course. Within a week several Chinese students had gone to a nearby village for haircuts, thereby violating this rule. A few days later, on a day when classes were scheduled, all of the students were taken to hear a lecture observing the anniversary of General Tai Li's organization. Two days afterward, they were all taken to Chungking for religious services. No one notified the American instructors beforehand of any of these events. Any time the Chinese wanted to talk to individual students, they summoned them without regard for class schedules. Captain D. M. Hykes, the commandant of the school, wrote Coughlin that the situation prevented him from maintaining discipline and said he had completely lost face. The Chinese, he said, did not appreciate the time and effort the American instructors put into the school.[55]

Not only did SACO and Miles do nothing to help the OSS training efforts, but Miles's men even "infiltrated" and sent aggressive young men to take the classes. When OSS thought it had identified "Miles' men," it assigned them to a city and told them to wait for a contact. The contact never came, because OSS never trusted an agent it believed to be working for Miles and Tai Li.[56]

Indeed, reports filed by the unhappy group stuck in Happy Valley well illustrate their lack of accomplishment and the depth of their frustration.[57] They had been expecting action and were, among other things, willing to contact Mao and assist the Communists in sabotaging and harassing the Japanese to get it. Coughlin, who had been one of the original group that formed OSS, wanted to go to Yenan himself. He had a hard time understanding how self-serving empire builders like Tai Li and Chiang Kai-shek could hem in an organization that had a virtually unlimited budget and did not hesitate to bypass the rules. Neither Miles nor Tai Li would share any information with him. Once a week Tai would have dinner with the Americans, sitting at the head of the table, with Miles and Coughlin on either side. The rest of the diners were Chinese. A black-skinned chicken with its head on would be placed in a bowl on the table. Tai Li would pick it apart with chopsticks, placing some in Miles's dish and some in Coughlin's. Nothing of importance was ever discussed at these meals. When Coughlin told Miles he wanted a three-way talk, Miles said Tai Li was unwilling to have one.[58]

Dissatisfied with reports on how things were going, Donovan went to China to see for himself. To celebrate his visit, Tai Li hosted a banquet far more elaborate than the usual weekly dinners. Much wine was drunk, but according to eyewitnesses, Donovan remained sober. He bluntly told Tai Li that OSS had a mission to perform, and if it could not be performed with Tai Li's cooperation, then OSS would operate separately. Tai Li snarled, "If OSS tries to operate outside of SACO I will kill your agents." Donovan answered, "For every one of our agents you kill, we will kill one of your generals," pounding his fist on the table. "You can't talk to me like that," shouted Tai. "I *am* talking to you like that," said Donovan. Then they both calmed down and smiled.[59]

Stalemated in its attempts to initiate intelligence procurement through SACO, blocked at every turn by Tai Li and Naval Group, China, OSS found another means to begin achieving independent status in China. In December 1943, Donovan and Dr. William Langer of R&A conferred in Chungking with Chennault of the Fourteenth Air Force. The only American combat command operating throughout China, the Fourteenth badly needed a widespread tactical intelligence service to pinpoint enemy targets such as troop concentrations and supply dumps.[60]

Prior to establishing a relationship with OSS, Fourteenth Air Force had operated with surprisingly minimal intelligence-gathering capability. In late December 1942, General Bissell appointed Major Jesse Williams as Chennault's intelligence chief and Colonel Wilfred Smith as the deputy chief. Chennault assigned John Birch, his current intelligence officer, to Smith. They organized a war room and did what they could to augment the outdated intelligence that the navy gave the Fourteenth Air Force about Japanese shipping. Smith sent Birch to the China coast, where he organized the fisherfolk into two-man teams and taught them how to manipulate hand-cranked radios. Once trained, they ran a series of stations along the east China coast that relayed the messages that were sent to Kweilin. Chennault then sent B-25s or P-40s to attack, sometimes having his men sling 500-pound bombs under the P-40s to use them as bombers. Smith, Birch, and the Chinese with whom

The Yenan Observer Group in the fall of 1945. Front row, left to right: Chang (weather director), Tseng (liaison), Doc Ma, Ariyoshi, Young, Yeaton, Cook, John Roderick, Hsieh Sheng (compound manager), Ling Ching (liaison), and Shen (assistant weather director). Second row: two unidentified weather men, Breland, Brooks, Hansen, Lemon, Davis, Finley, Griffith, Otredosky, Robinson, and three unidentified weather men. Courtesy of Clifford F. Young.

they worked also acquired hydrographic charts and set up teams to watch shipping on the Yangtze River and the railroads.

In late 1943, while on leave in Washington, Smith got a call from Donovan. The general told him that Wedemeyer would be going to China and that he wanted all intelligence activities in the theater to be coordinated by OSS. Donovan wanted to know whether Smith had any objections, to which Smith replied that he was a soldier and would follow orders. Donovan then asked Smith to accompany him to China, which he did, touring the European Theater on the way.

When Smith arrived back at Chennault's command, he learned that word of the OSS takeover had preceded him and that he was terribly unpopular. For his part, Smith did not feel that he had sold out. As he saw it, Wedemeyer had issued an order, and Donovan had been gracious enough to ask his opinion.

The intelligence of the Fourteenth Air Force was thus transferred to OSS for administrative purposes, and personnel representing the major OSS branches were attached to it. Chennault still had the same services as before, but the general's prestige was so great that neither Tai Li nor Miles could keep the unit from undertaking its own intelligence operations. Only John Birch balked at becoming part of OSS. He sent Smith a message saying that he would rather be a buck private in the Fourteenth Air Force than a full colonel in OSS. He never transferred to OSS officially, although he continued to work, unwillingly, with the OSS teams in the field.[61]

Soon afterward, Coughlin moved his own headquarters from Chungking to Chennault's command in Kunming, several hundred miles to the southwest, although he left several dozen OSS men under nominal SACO control.[62] Donovan had tried to free OSS from Tai Li's clutches, but the SACO agreement made doing so difficult. On March 16, 1944, Donovan sent Coughlin a coded message confirming that although OSS was still in SACO, its command was to be separate from that of the navy. While Coughlin would continue to report to Tai Li directly, his activities would henceforth be coordinated by the theater commander. Donovan ordered OSS to transfer its headquarters out of Happy Valley as soon as possible. If it could not arrange to do so, the Chinese would be asked to set up separate headquarters for OSS in their present Valley accommodations.

In this communication, Donovan stressed continued OSS membership in SACO and seemed to acknowledge navy predominance.[63] Later communications, however, show how difficult it was to continue an impotent program within SACO under the eyes of Miles. As late as October 1944, the consensus was that although OSS might have been unwise to participate in the original SACO agreement, more would be lost by withdrawing from it than by staying in. OSS therefore continued to contribute minimum funds and personnel to SACO while independently expanding its own operations, in the form of AGFRTS, in cooperation with the theater command.[64] After Wedemeyer had transferred from Mountbatten's staff in Ceylon to command of the China Theater, Donovan sent a memorandum to the White House reviewing the past difficulties that OSS had encountered in China. He suggested that it was "a good time to make OSS in China directly responsible to the United States Commanding General and to serve him and his subordinates, as well as General MacArthur and Admiral Nimitz."[65]

Wedemeyer did not oppose having OSS in the theater. To Heppner's surprise he agreed to let the Special Operations branch as well as the Secret Intelligence branch operate there. In conversation, he also told Heppner that he would probably let OSS take over the Dixie Mission, but he was extremely concerned about the group's personnel. He did not want persons in the Mission who were subject to political influence and were likely to dabble in movements.[66]

One of Wedemeyer's first decisions was to relieve Miles of command and to place both OSS and the Naval Group under the theater commander. Heppner became strategic services chief in China and as such was invited to attend the weekly meetings of Wedemeyer's committee that formulated theater policy. As a result, for the first time OSS was authorized to organize resistance activities, conduct intelligence and sabotage, and equip and direct special commando groups in support of the Chinese armies.[67] The change in the relationship between SACO and OSS is evident in the minutes of Heppner's July 11, 1945, staff meeting. He directed the branch chiefs not to treat SACO as a stepchild and said that SACO was to be considered a major OSS operation. They were to advise their field teams to avoid placing OSS-SACO personnel in the field, however, since it was known that agents of Tai Li watched them closely.[68]

When Stilwell had been theater commander, he had opposed the idea of having OSS operate in the theater. Even after Carl Eifler persuaded him to change his mind, he told John Davies and F. MacCracken Fisher that he was afraid the organization would make awful mistakes.[69] Wedemeyer tried to coordinate all the intelligence agencies in China, including the British, with his headquarters. British intelligence activities also concerned him, because he believed the British had several thousand agents in China whose primary goal was to gather intelligence on the Chinese rather than on the enemy.

To many Americans, the primary British interests appeared to be preparation for the postwar period and protection of the British stakes in China, such as Hong Kong. Americans received excellent target and shipping data from the British but little more. Wedemeyer wanted to bring them under his jurisdiction, along with all the American agencies concerned with intelligence gathering. On January 2, 1945, he warned Hurley that the intelligence situation was confused and potentially dangerous and needed to be integrated and improved. After the war, General Robert McClure, Wedemeyer's chief of staff, said he doubted whether much unification of intelligence agencies had taken place. He had seen evidence that separate agencies purchased the same information from the same sources.[70]

After the war, many of those who had participated in intelligence gathering and had seen the multiple agencies operating at cross-purposes analyzed the weaknesses of the system. Some thought that during World War II anyone with a bright idea and access to someone on top could get himself a little empire. In wartime, it was easy to get money; and if one knew the ropes, one could get people. Little thought went into planning. Rather, money was spent loosely in hopes of improving military efficiency. In part, this resulted from the agencies' understanding that the public would not care about saving $10 million if doing so meant losing a battle. Also, the military recognized that if money was saved, its next budget would be cut.[71]

OSS's loose operating style made the traditional military intelligence agencies suspicious. Yet OSS saw itself not as competing but rather as better prepared to do certain kinds of jobs. Each branch within the organization had its specialty. R&A collected documents and assessed their value; X-2 dealt with counterespionage tried to catch spies. Morale Operations tried to use propaganda in new ways to disturb the enemy's confidence. Once MO found something to spray on Japanese officers to make them smell bad so that they would lose face.

OSS did some things well, like demolition training and organizing the natives to fight in places where they could be moved around in small airplanes. There was, however, burdening the organization, a conglomeration of people who honestly wanted to contribute to the war effort but did not know how. Coughlin saw this situation as an example of Donovan's style and noted that he personally often behaved in harum-scarum fashion. Donovan and Carl Eifler, for example, who had originally convinced Stilwell that OSS could make a major contribution to the war in his theater, went joy riding in a Piper Cub over Japanese-held territory in Burma. The two men, with a combined weight of more than 400 pounds, flew in a plane never meant to carry more than 250 pounds. Afterward, Donovan told Coughlin that he made the flight, which violated all rules of security, so that Eifler would not think him a coward.[72]

Some historians have concluded that the activities of Naval Group, China, pushed China far along the road to civil war and contributed to direct American involvement in the internal Chinese struggle.[73] Others believed that Roosevelt's penchant for the navy gave Miles the edge— that if Truman had been president, Chiang could have been coerced into allowing OSS to operate freely and without Tai Li's oversight.[74] Some of these people and others are convinced that if OSS had penetrated Manchuria, the weakness of the Japanese Kwantung Army in that location might have been revealed. As it was, Stalin claimed Russian troops held it in check, which he used as a bargaining point at the Yalta Conference of February 1945.[75]

And so the various intelligence groups continually competed with one another. Even OWI resented other agencies doing work that it considered within its domain, as the following episode illustrates.

OSS began dropping leaflets on target cities, warning the citizens to get out before bombing commenced. Colonel Smith ran an art contest in the University at Kunming, offering fifty dollars for the best leaflet design, twenty-five dollars for the next best, and ten dollars for the third best. He wanted Chinese students to do the designs because he knew they would be attuned culturally to the most effective motifs. The winner was printed on a leaflet made of cheap rice paper. It showed a fat sow and, over the sow, a butcher's knife. Up in the right-hand corner were birds. The implication was that if you were a fat sow you would feel the knife, but if you were smart you would fly away, like the birds. Other pictures showed airplanes with U.S. insignia and, in Chinese characters, "The American Air Force is coming." Supply planes carried these brochures and tossed them out to flutter down over the cities. When OWI found out that OSS was dropping them, they told Smith that he was stupid and unpatriotic, because leaflets on cheap rice paper were unprofessional and not worthy of a first rate power. OWI pamphlets, on the other hand, were designed in Washington and used good paper stock. OWI then got theater to order OSS to stop dropping its pig and bird leaflets.[76]

Such discord, and the inefficiency created by overlapping intelligence operations, may have the effect of making the Dixie Mission appear more viable than it really was. Apart from the operation run by Miles and Tai Li, the members of the Mission came from competing intelligence agencies, yet for the most part their rivalries did not seem to prevent them from functioning. Men representing different disciplines would put together lectures for the Communists on demolition weapons and techniques and on the ordnance suitable for guerrilla warfare.[77]

The basic reason that there *was* a Mission, however, was that Davies had talked with Spencer and Stelle, who were interested in setting it up, not only because it could aid the war effort, but also because it would provide a "tremendous opportunity for OSS to come out nicely."[78] Once the Mission was in place, reports from it seemed to validate their enthusiasm. David Barrett, for example, added the following comment to Ray Cromley's July 30 report on Yenan as the major order of battle China base of operations: "In my opinion the possibilities of an Order of Battle Office in Yenan are limited only by the amount of trained personnel which can be assigned to it."[79] Stelle's and Colling's confidence, illustrated by their report to Colonel R. B. Hall and Lieutenant Colonel William Ray Peers on August 7, 1944, echoes this optimism and states that it "will be possible to secure thorough cooperation from the Chinese Communists for OSS operations . . . [including] an independent communications and agent net . . . and provid[ing] Chinese personnel for training in our methods."[80]

Yet the problems resulting from the interagency competition were also mirrored in the Mission: efforts overlapped, and there was backbiting among the men. These problems are illustrated in the exchange of letters between Dickey in Chungking and Barrett in Yenan over reports Ray Cromley had tried to send directly to Washington without going through Barrett or G-2 headquarters. "Cromley seems to take a lot upon himself in these reports," Dickey wrote, "especially in recommending people for decorations and promotions (including himself)."[81] In this case Cromley had had the audacity to request that all sorts of equipment, a radio operator, and a stenographer named La Donna Anderson be sent to help him. "I must have her here," Cromley wrote. "She knows the ropes."[82] Barrett described Cromley as a troublemaker, an officer who did not understand the principles of command and was childish in his desire to build up an OSS "cell."[83] Coughlin resolved the problem by transferring Cromley to G-2. He reminded Cromley that he would be responsible to Dickey and Barrett simultaneously, since he still was attached to the Dixie Mission, and that all communications should be channeled through the head of the Mission. Tactfully, Coughlin praised Cromley's order-of-battle work while reminding him that he neither headed a mission nor had personnel assigned to him.[84]

Cromley was not the only member of the Mission whom Barrett criticized. The colonel saw Colling as a "very low-powered officer but at least willing to work to the best of his limited abilities"—unlike Stelle, who had "plenty of ability but was lazy."[85] Shortly after he received this assessment, Dickey reported to Stilwell that he had gone to Yenan for a brief visit and that his headquarters was maintaining very close contact with Dixie.[86]

To some extent the problems between Dixie and the various intelligence agencies it was created to serve lasted as long as the Mission. Sometimes there was ambivalence toward the group of a sort that Stelle expressed in an October 27, 1944, memorandum to Spencer:

> My assignment had been that of "target analyst," presumably representing the 14th Air Force. . . . .G-2 at Chungking had originally asked the 14th to send either Barnett or Schultheis on the Dixie trip. Either because of the indispensability of Bob and Fred at Kunming, which is the reason the 14th gave or because the 14th didn't want to incur the onus of taking part in a mission to the Communists and didn't like participating in something run by AMMISCA [American Military Mission to China], which are the reasons Theater suspected, the 14th was slow to name anybody and finally suggested somebody who was unacceptable to Dickey.
>
> Colonel Dickey decided to send me . . . and because of my AGFRTS connection chose to regard me as the 14th representative. The detachment from AGFRTS to the mission was cleared

with Colonel Smith, then CO AGFRTS, but not with 14th HQ. The 14th, which is habitually disgruntled with Theater, didn't like the idea of being represented in spite of itself. . . . Nevertheless the 14th was naturally eager to get the results of the Mission.

My actual position has been something like this: G-2 and Colonel Barrett have considered me to be a representative of the 14th specializing in target work. The 14th states that it has no representative in Yenan . . . [but] considers me the officer most nearly connected with it and whenever it is annoyed at the delays occasioned by the channeling of intelligence through G-2—and given the predisposition of the 14th to be annoyed with Theater and the limitations staff at G-2 this will probably be fairly frequently—the 14th will to a certain degree be inclined to hold me responsible.[87]

Part of the problem, Stelle complained, was that G-2 did a poor job of distributing the reports and the intelligence that OSS provided. Sometimes, in the small compound, it was possible to obtain information informally, but the "community style of living we enjoy at Yenan isn't too conducive to doing things unbeknownst to the powers that be."[88] The informality had other consequences as well. The Communists thought highly of Madame Sun Yat-sen and actively corresponded with her in Chungking. They sent letters to her in the pouch from Yenan. Smith took the letters to the embassy, which then passed them on to Madame Sun as a courtesy without knowing who had written them. Smith, born and raised of missionary parents and fluent in Chinese, looked at a couple of them out of curiosity and noted that the salutation read "Dear Elder Sister."[89]

OSS teams operating in North China sometimes found themselves in trouble with the Communists. On such occasions, Dixie was usually the go-between. In early June 1945, Peterkin reported to Dickey that four Americans and a Chinese interpreter had been arrested and disarmed after an exchange of shots in the Chin-Cha-Chi area. No one had been hurt, but the attitude of the Americans was very bad, according to the Chinese.[90] Eventually the Chinese were informed that the primary object of this mission had been to contact puppet troops to determine their mood and to see what could be expected of them if and when military operations reached their area. The Chinese man who had been arrested with the team was not an interpreter but had been taken along as a contact because he allegedly had intimate knowledge of the local people and the area.[91]

This team, known as "Spaniel," had been dropped near Fouping on May 28. The drop appeared to be successful, but the group made no radio contact, and there was no news about it until Yenan reported that the team was in a Communist jail. In spite of attempts to secure its release, including a letter from the theater commander to Mao Tse-tung, the men remained in jail until the end of the war.[92] The Communists had captured Spaniel after the team had opened fire on regular Communist troops. The Communists also objected that they had not been notified that the team was going in, and they issued instructions that henceforth all unidentified bands would be treated in similar fashion.[93] At about this time, the Communists learned that the OSS planned to drop arms and equipment to a couple of puppets just north of the Yellow River. They objected to this idea, too, noting that these puppets fought Communists, not the Japanese.[94]

Even as the war drew to a close, OSS hoped to upgrade the Dixie Mission in order to implement the radio net and asked theater to allow the Mission more personnel.[95] Wedemeyer did not assent to this request, however, and suggested that OSS study ways of curtailing activities that were not of the utmost importance.[96]

By mid-August 1945, when they tried to carry out their orders to occupy and seize the records in the cities that the Japanese had surrendered, all OSS field teams faced conflict with Communists. Major Gustav Krause, head of OSS in North China at that time, informed Heppner that he did not feel the teams should risk their lives.[97] It became evident on August 24 that his fear was far from groundless when a party consisting of John Birch, three Americans, seven or eight Chinese, and two Koreans set out by train from Kweiteh, Anwei, bound for Communist territory. On the twenty-fifth they encountered a Communist detachment. Birch spoke to them and gave them some watermelon, and they permitted the OSS group to pass. Birch's men noted that his manner toward the Communists was "rather severe," but when they told him it was dangerous to act that way, Birch replied, "Never mind. I want to see how the Communists treat Americans. I don't mind if they kill me, for then America will stop the Communist movement with atomic bombs." When the team subsequently encountered two other groups of soldiers destroying the track and telephone lines, he did agree to let the Chinese soldier accompanying them, First Lieutenant Tung Chin-sheng, do the talking.

Tung went to some soldiers in the station and asked to see the officer in charge. Although they were belligerent, they took him to an officer. Tung told this man that he and the rest of Birch's team were with the Fourteenth Air Force but that they had been ordered to go to Suchow. Tung overheard men whispering, "Here come more spies—

we had better disarm them first—wait till we find out the truth before we give them back their guns; otherwise kill them all."[98]

The Communists then took Tung back to Birch, whom he told in a low voice about what he had heard. With his hands on his hips Birch faced the Communist officer and spoke in an insulting, provocative manner. He grabbed one of the soldiers by the back of the collar, whereupon the Communists shot Birch and Tung and threw them into a ditch. Birch was dead, but farmers rescued Tung. Japanese soldiers passing through took him to a Japanese war hospital for treatment and wired the Chinese general in Hauchow about the whole affair. Later, they moved Tung to a general hospital in Hauchow.[99]

The Communists took the rest of Birch's party prisoner.[100] On August 30, Wedemeyer met in Ambassador Hurley's home with Mao Tse-tung and Chou En-lai, then in Chungking. He emphasized the seriousness of the incident, requested a report about it from the Communists, and demanded the release of the Americans being held. He also pressed for the release of "Spaniel." Details of this meeting and a directive from Mao to investigate the incident were transmitted to the Yenan Observer Group for delivery to Chu Teh.[101] As a consequence, Yeaton, then the commanding officer of Dixie, was soon able to advise AGAS that the three Spaniel members would be taken to Varoff Field and evacuated to Sian.[102]

Afterward, Tung blamed Birch for the shooting, noting that if the man had stayed calm, there probably would not have been an incident.[103] The officers who had commanded Birch tend to confirm Tung's assessment. They described him as an overzealous fanatic inclined toward martyrdom. During the war, he had perceived the Japanese as the "anti-Christ," an honor he transferred to the Communists at the time of Japan's defeat.[104] Nevertheless, the Birch incident may have helped prolong the Dixie Mission's life, because, with increasingly hostile relations between the Communists and the field teams, the group was the China Theater's only source of intelligence and political information from inside the Communist-held area. It also formed the only direct, ongoing liaison with the Communist leaders and was therefore a tool for maintaining at least some goodwill. It did so through personal contact, by supervising local Chinese weather stations and by occasionally transporting supplies that had been specially authorized, such as medicines.[105]

It can be seen that although not allowed to grow the way some had hoped, the Dixie Mission performed a variety of functions even after the defeat of Japan. It was not a perfect organization. To some extent it reflected the jealousies and rivalries of its constituent service groups. The Communists noticed its lack of proper military bearing and its internal discord.[106] They also knew that the Dixie Mission was an exception to the theater prohibition on dealing with Communists, upon which they had originally sought to capitalize. SACO never missed an opportunity to demean and vilify Donovan's officers for "working with the Communists," and since many of those involved with the Mission wrote reports advocating more extensive dealings with the Communists, the propaganda mill operated by Miles and Tai Li was well fueled.[107] The Communists remained polite while becoming increasingly discouraged by American unwillingness to support their role in China's future. And while the United States unsuccessfully tried to avoid becoming involved in the postwar upheaval that would rock China, Chinese politics were destined to influence American political thinking for many years after the war.

8

The Marshall Mission
and the End of Dixie

Patrick Hurley's resignation as ambassador to China, when it came
on November 27, 1945, caught everyone by surprise, as did the
extent of his freely expressed anger. In a letter to Truman the man from
Oklahoma attacked "the wide discrepancy between our *announced* policies and our *conduct* of international policies." He complained because
the career men whom he had asked to have removed (George Atcheson,
Jr., and John S. Service) had been transferred to the staff of the supreme commander in Asia (MacArthur). According to Hurley, they
continued to side with the Communists and to undermine American
foreign policy.[1] Hurley's outbursts triggered responses from the White
House. Attending a cabinet meeting after learning that Hurley had been
venting his rage in a public statement, Truman yelled, "See what a son-
of-a-bitch did to me!" The president thought Hurley duplicitous because he had resigned in a manner that would ensure a congressional
inquiry and would increase partisan political debate over the crisis in
China. In an effort to stem this political backlash, Truman appointed
General George C. Marshall special emissary to China.

The president's cabinet had recommended Marshall as Hurley's
replacement. Many others also thought him a good choice. He was a
hero unconnected to partisan politics, he was a man who could be trusted
not to involve the United States in a foolish war, and he was someone
one who would probably not be accused of betraying China.[2] The press
speculated that Marshall might recommend some alterations in American policy toward China and guessed that he was earmarked to succeed
James F. Byrnes as secretary of state.

Some people, like Congressman Ellis Paterson, denounced the
selection of Marshall, however, on grounds that the man knew nothing
about China and was a soldier, not a diplomat.[3] But Paterson's criticism
showed that he knew little about Marshall's background. The general

had been stationed in China in the 1920s. During this tour of duty he studied Chinese culture and became fluent enough in the Chinese language to deliver a short speech.[4]

Paterson was not alone in criticizing Marshall. Other critics felt that while Marshall might be the right man for the job, he might be wise to avoid it. When John Coughlin, former head of OSS in China, heard from General Donovan about the appointment, he reacted by saying, "I'm so sorry. Marshall has had such a successful career, but he can't succeed with this."[5]

When General Wedemeyer learned that Marshall would be coming to China, he expressed some jealousy. He wrote his friend Ivan Yeaton, who had assumed command of the Dixie Mission in July 1945, that during his thirteen months in China he had worked hard to avoid being drawn into political conflict. Unlike Miles and SACO, he had not taken sides in the civil war, but now he could see that if things worked well, the career diplomats would take credit, while if things failed, he would be blamed.[6]

Later, Wedemeyer was to become even more upset. He went back to the United States in May 1946, expecting to be appointed ambassador to China. He had not wanted the post, but Marshall had asked him to take it, so he agreed to serve for one year. Wedemeyer assumed that Marshall had chosen him because Marshall was going to be appointed secretary of state and wanted an ambassador to China whom he knew and trusted. Wedemeyer had bought his striped pants when Marshall abruptly decided that Dr. Leighton Stuart, former president of Yenching University, should get the post.[7] Wedemeyer was subsequently told that the Communists had found him unacceptable, which confirmed his belief that Mao was dictating who would be ambassador.[8] Indeed, Yeaton noted that the Communists were pleasantly surprised at Stuart's appointment. They did not care for Wedemeyer and regarded Stuart as an old, possibly sympathetic friend.[9]

Truman instructed Marshall to try to unify China peaceably and democratically and to end the civil war that had by this time broken out. He was to speak frankly with Chiang and use Chiang's desire for economic and military assistance as leverage. He was to persuade Chiang to call a conference that representatives from all the major political elements, including the Communists, would attend. These instructions did not contradict Chiang's publicly stated pledges regarding a peaceful settlement of the Communist problem. Nor did they conflict with the accord the two sides had reached in October 1945, when they had agreed to convene a conference to discuss the creation of a constitutional government.[10]

OSS in China informed the OSS office in Washington about the Chinese reaction to Marshall's new duty. They wrote that all groups in China had been genuinely surprised at Hurley's resignation and Marshall's appointment. Each group had reassured its constituency that Marshall was acceptable, yet privately each group harbored uncertainties about him. The government press reacted politely, but inside sources said the Kuomintang feared that the United States might halt its unequivocal support and unquestioning acceptance of Kuomintang propaganda. The Communists appeared optimistic, thinking that no one could be more antagonistic toward them than Hurley had been. They hoped Marshall would restore the policies of Roosevelt, Stilwell, and Gauss. General Yeh Chien-ying, their chief of staff, said he admired Marshall and would welcome a visit to Yenan from him as a professional comrade. Other groups in China also responded favorably, and some planned to bombard Marshall's headquarters with letters and petitions lamenting the absence of democracy in Chiang's government.[11]

American mediation of the Chinese situation seemed to please even the Russians, who had recalled their three representatives from Yenan. Nevertheless, relations between the two Communist powers were

Chou En-lai, Mao Tse-tung, and Chu Teh. Courtesy of Col. Wilbur J. Peterkin.

not as friendly during the period immediately following Japanese surrender as cold war rhetoric would have made people believe.[12]

Marshall arrived in Chungking on December 23, 1945. On December 31, the National Government announced that the Generalissimo had decided that the Political Consultative Conference (PCC) for
which the October agreement provided would convene on January 10,
1946. The government also suggested a cease-fire. General Chang Chun,
representing the national government, and General Chou En-lai, the
Communists' spokesman, announced on January 10 that hostilities
would cease immediately and that an executive headquarters would be
established in Peking to oversee it. When the PCC convened, it was
composed of one representative from the Nationalist government, one
Communist representative, and one American. It was an organization
without precedent, a pioneering attempt to substitute negotiation for
warfare as an instrument of national policy.

Originally, executive headquarters consisted of approximately 150
officers and men, including six field teams that could rush to points of
conflict. An American army officer chaired each team. National government, Chinese Communist Party members, one American soldier
to act as sergeant major, one neutral Chinese interpreter, and a radio
operator made up the rest of each team. Each had at its disposal a three-
quarter-ton closed vehicle, a jeep, and a quarter-ton trailer for transporting signal equipment and emergency rations. Within a month, it
was decided that six teams were not enough, and plans were made to
form an additional eleven.

At all levels the Americans acted as chairmen. They found that their
greatest task was to overcome the suspicion that existed between the two
Chinese factions, because neither side wanted to put itself at a disadvantage by introducing a proposal the other side could reject. The Americans therefore often found themselves initiating not just solutions but
also constructive proposals for solving problems in mediation.[13]

One of the men on Marshall's staff during the time of the Marshall
Mission was S. Herbert Hitch, one of the original members of the Dixie
Mission. Hitch had not been allowed to return to China after he had
delivered Mao's message to the Joint Chiefs of Staff in late 1944, but in
1946 he was back in Peking as assistant naval attaché on the staff of
Walter S. Robertson, the American minister to China. Hitch thought it
very strange that none of the American members of the three-man teams
spoke Chinese, had studied Chinese history, or associated with the
Chinese. The rationale was that ignorance permitted more impartial
observation, but the lack of the language actually meant that the observers had to rely on secondhand information.[14]

At this time many people believed that the United States might be able to make a new beginning in China. Even Ivan Yeaton, an extremely harsh critic of the Communists, felt optimistic.[15] As soon as word of the Marshall Mission reached Yenan, Chou sought out Yeaton. With hardly a word of greeting he said, "How do I handle Marshall?" From his personal experience Yeaton believed Marshall could become arrogant when he was crossed by persons he considered less powerful than himself. Yeaton was willing to share this insight with Chou, but he wanted to get something in return. "Do you have a war room?" Yeaton asked. Chou did not understand the expression, so Yeaton explained that a war, or map, room was a place where important military decisions were made with a map. Chou shook his head, whereupon Yeaton stated that without one, Marshall would think he was dealing with a bunch of farmers. Without a war room there would be no visible sign that Yenan was the military headquarters of a million-man army. He also pointed out that there was a world of difference between farmer-soldiers and soldier-farmers.

Yeaton had brought from Chungking all the necessary paraphernalia for setting up a map room of his own, but the war had ended, and there was no wall in his compound large enough to hang the map. It stood in a corner, so when Chou said he did not have the necessary material, Yeaton offered his. Chou accepted, and Yeaton, hoping to get the Communist order of battle in return, began organizing the war room. As for handling Marshall, Yeaton told Chou that the general was an austere, no-nonsense soldier with little or no sense of humor; that he would be determined to accomplish his mission in the shortest possible time; and that there must be no hint of failure. Chou, on the other hand, was naturally charming, witty, and tactful, and he therefore needed no coaching in how to approach the general. "Just do what comes naturally and you will have no trouble," Yeaton advised.

On January 9, after Chou and his wife had left with their team for the meeting in Chungking, Marshall sent a C-47 to Yenan to pick up Yeaton.[16] The American aircraft sat on the Yenan airfield next to two Soviet transport planes that had arrived in Yenan earlier, shrouded in secrecy. Clifford Young, at that time Yeaton's executive officer, wanted to take pictures of them and their pilots, who were bedecked with beautiful medals, but was refused permission to do so. Young speculated that the Soviet planes might have flown to Yenan empty so that they could return with a load that included Mao and Chu Teh. If this conjecture were true, he surmised that the Communists would have no further use for the Yenan location, as their center of operations would have shifted to Kalgan. Young had trouble reconciling this possibility

Chu Teh and Yeaton. Courtesy of Clifford F. Young.

with the fact that Chu Teh had told Yeaton he wanted Dixie to remain in place for at least two or three months. The Americans had concluded from this remark that the Communists regarded the observers as serving a purpose even if negotiations broke down.[17]

Yeaton had barely arrived in Chungking when Marshall summoned him. He was shown into the bedroom where the general was dressing for dinner. Marshall pointed to a chair and said, "Sit down, Yeaton. Tell me about the Communists." Yeaton had expected to answer questions. Instead, he delivered a short speech about how the Communism of the Chinese in Yenan was pure Marx, Lenin, and Mao. Until a few months earlier they had been in touch with Moscow via Vladivostok by way of Soviet radio, he said. The Communists' only hope for obtaining military hardware was to recover surrendered Japanese arms with Soviet connivance. On VJ- Day they had only a few small arms but they were having some success getting heavier weapons for their army of nearly one million well-fed, well-trained guerrilla fighters. Yeaton concluded by warning that the United States should not underestimate their high morale and their military potential. Then he stopped talking and waited for questions that never came. If Marshall had heard a word, he did not show it. He finished tying his bow tie, said, "Thank you," and showed Yeaton the door.

After this meeting Yeaton took a week's leave in Shanghai and then returned to Chungking. Without seeing Marshall again, he flew back to Yenan on the twenty-fourth, accompanied by Koji Ariyoshi.[18] In his absence Alfred Harding of the Mission and the Communists had completed the map room and were keeping it up to date. Yeaton sent Harding to Peking for reassignment, so that there would be no leak about the war room.[19] Each day a fine-looking Chinese battalion wearing new uniforms went through daily drills and honor guard formations in anticipation of General Marshall's visit.[20] Yeaton promoted Young, who had filled in for him, and told him that Marshall had said the Yenan Observer Group was most essential and would continue to exist.[21]

Early in March, the Committee of Three (General Chang Chih-chung, General Chou En-lai, and General Marshall) visited the Peking executive headquarters. They then made an extended tour, visiting most of the field teams[22] and Yenan. The Communists treated their visit to Yenan as an honor. On the morning of March 3, the day before the general's scheduled arrival, the Communists began gathering at the airfield, coming from all directions in well-organized groups. One battalion's honor guard marched around the field, training. At 11:00 A.M. on the fourth a C-46 arrived with extra fuel for Marshall's plane. By 2:00 P.M. everyone important had gathered at the airfield. Mao appeared in his finest rust-colored wool suit. Chu Teh wore a military uniform but no insignia. Madame Mao wore a vivid blue jacket and slacks. Over her shoulder was draped a beautiful man's military overcoat.

About 3:10 a C-46 came over the field, followed by a C-54. The C-46 landed first and unloaded a group of people, including photographers and journalists. A few minutes later the four-engine C-54 eased itself down on the dirt runway and slowly proceeded to its parking berth, with Sergeant Roland Brooks and Major Young directing it. The door opened and a chrome-plated ladder descended. First General Chou En-lai stepped off the plane, then a few seconds later Marshall started down the ladder, wearing a smart tan trench coat with a beaver skin collar. Five stars flashed on his shoulders. He was greeted by Mao Tse-tung. A period of handshaking followed, with photographers snapping away. Marshall and Chou inspected the honor guard, then got into the vehicles that were to transport them to the compound. Marshall led the parade in a weapons carrier driven by Colonel Yeaton. A homemade

Gen. George C. Marshall's arrival in Yenan in March 1946. Photo by the Chinese Communists, courtesy of Clifford F. Young.

five-star general's flag (red background and five yellow stars) flew on a pole on the left fender and an American flag flew on the right fender. The other two trucks flew flags with three triangles, the insignia of a full general in the Chinese army on the left fender and Chinese flags on the right. General Chang Chih-chung, covered by an ankle-length cape with three triangles on the collar, got into the second truck, which Clifford Young drove. General Chou En-lai, whom Young had never seen wearing a uniform with insignia, also wore three triangles on his collar and rode in the third truck, driven by Koji Ariyoshi.

Slowly the procession moved from the airfield through the shouting crowd of 6,000 that lined the streets. When Marshall stood up in his seat, Generals Chang and Chou did the same.[23] Upon reaching the compound, the visitors were billeted in caves, with Marshall in Young's cave. As a courtesy, the Communists provided day and night personal guards, a service that was quite unnecessary in Yenan.

The Communists had erected a temporary bridge over the river so that Yeaton could transport Marshall and the others to the conference scheduled at Communist headquarters that night. Constructing this bridge required ingenuity, because in Yenan no nails were available, and bamboo or wood of any kind was scarce. It was scaffoldlike, with two narrow wheel treads. As they approached the bridge that evening,

Left to right: Gen. Marshall, Mao Tse-tung, Chu Teh (with back to camera), and Walter Robertson from the American Embassy (in center background). Courtesy of Clifford F. Young.

Maj. Clifford F. Young's cave, at far right, which was used by Marshall while in Yenan. Courtesy of Clifford F. Young.

Marshall stiffened and asked Yeaton if it was safe. Yeaton told him that his hosts would never endanger his life by putting him in a position where he was forced to cross an unsafe bridge, but as soon as they rolled onto the bridge Marshall yelled, "Stop this car!" Yeaton did not want to stop, since under the circumstances rolling weight was safer than dead weight, however he did so as smoothly as he could. Marshall clambered gingerly down. Then, as soon as he felt safe, he got back in and ordered Yeaton, "Drive on."

According to Yeaton, when Marshall and he arrived at the door of the conference hall, Marshall got out and told him to wait outside. Two hours later the president's emissary returned to the truck, and Yeaton drove him back to the Dixie compound. For the entire evening the general had treated the Dixie Mission's commanding officer as nothing more than a chauffeur. Marshall had once again expressed no interest in Yeaton's views or the contributions that he might have been able to make to the discussions. Nor did he question Yeaton, who counted himself an expert on the Soviet Union, about Russian involvement, interest, or concern with Chinese Communist or American activities in Yenan.[24]

Marshall had decided that Mao held the key to solving the problems in the North, but the Chinese Communist leader evidently expected little from the negotiations. Yeaton thought he seemed detached, moving automatically through the discourse. He promised to abide by the terms of the various agreements, and said he hoped that the cease-fire would extend to Manchuria and that field teams would be sent there. When Marshall wrote Truman about this meeting, he said that he had been extremely frank and that Mao had not shown resentment.

That night General Chu Teh and Mao hosted a banquet honoring the American visitor. Mao toasted the "durable cooperation between America and China and between Nationalists and Communists."[25] The guests drank other toasts to China and the Chinese people, and to America and the American people. After dinner, General Chu, General Marshall, and General Chiang each gave a speech, to loud audience applause. Marshall spoke through his interpreter. In Young's opinion he made no mistakes about the China situation, nor did he mince his words. After dinner, everyone went to another hall for a program of speeches and music. It opened with a "drum" song and closed with a mass chorus singing the "Yellow River Grand Chorus."

The next morning Marshall left, taking with him Sergeant Brooks, who was scheduled to return to the States.[26] At the airfield he asked Mao when he would be prepared to go to Chungking to talk with Chiang again. "I shall go whenever Chiang asks me," Mao replied, as distant as a

Front row, with backs to camera: Mao Tse-tung and Mrs. Chu Teh. Back row, left to right: an unidentified American, Chou En-lai, Gen. Marshall, Gen. Gillem, Young, and Sgt. Robinson. Courtesy of Clifford F. Young.

mountain.[27] Marshall then asked for the five-star flag that the Communist women had made for him, told his aide to have Yeaton sign it, folded it over his arm, and said his good-byes.[28] He returned to the United States and assumed the duties of secretary of state on January 21.

Russell Buhite has observed that the termination of this mission placed American policymakers in a dilemma: Chiang Kai-shek's regime seemed corrupt, inefficient, dictatorial, and bent on self-destruction, yet American officials were reluctant to withdraw aid completely because of concern about the Soviet Union. At any rate, for many reasons they were not about to support the Chinese Communists. For one thing, they assumed them to be cooperating with the Soviets.[29]

In a more recent assessment, Luo Rongqu wrote that the failure of the Marshall Mission brought a very brief period of hesitation and indecision in Washington, a wait-and-see policy that continued until mid-1947. In July of that year, Wedemeyer was sent as a special envoy to China on a fact-finding mission. In his report to Truman he concluded that the military situation in China was grave.[30] This assessment would have surprised Yeaton, who wrote in his memoirs that Marshall asked questions about only the ancient history of Yenan during his visit.[31] Young believed that the general left Yenan happy, thinking things had worked out smoothly.[32] It had been, after all, primarily a goodwill tour, with little political discussion planned.[33] Unlike historians of the future, none of the Dixie participants interviewed for this book appear to have regarded the Marshall Mission as part of a greater chapter in American-Soviet relations or 1947 as a turning point in American policy in East Asia.

The contrast in the two men's responses to Marshall's visit probably reflected their differing political views as much as their opposed perspectives on the general himself. Young did not find Marshall, who thanked him for the use of his room, austere and commented on the historical significance of the general's visit in a letter to his wife.[34] Yeaton, on the other hand, considered himself an authority on Communism and more knowledgeable on Marx than either Mao or Chou.[35] His was the bitterness of a senior colonel in the U.S. Army who had expected his assignment in Yenan to bring him a star or at least recognition for his political insights. Instead, he felt that Marshall had slighted him and that after Marshall's departure his usefulness as an observer had ended. The majority of his crew soon left, and the Communists proceeded to run the weather station by themselves. On April 1 Yeaton started to take inventory of American property in Yenan. On April 11 he flew off to Shanghai and a new assignment.[36]

The Marshall Mission was an important historical event. It was also a milestone in the history of the Yenan Observer Group. For one thing, it made more people aware of the Dixie Mission's existence. Also, Marshall's visit affected individuals in the group, some positively, others negatively. For Brooks, Young, and those directly involved in the preparations, Marshall's visit provided a diversion and an exciting experience. Young helped choose the menu for the general's dinner, which could not include any shellfish, to which Marshall was allergic. He had to make sure that the vehicle in which the general rode in and the routes taken were acceptable.[37] During Marshall's stay in China, the men of the Dixie Mission maintained continuous radio contact with Chungking so that the president's emissary could have direct communication with headquarters at any time. They also provided the Air Corps with navigational and weather data for the plane trips made between Chungking and Yenan.[38]

Marshall's attempts to create a basis for ongoing cooperation between the two sides made it desirable to continue the existence of the Dixie Mission. Chou En-lai's comments to Marshall indicate that the Communists were comfortable dealing with the Mission. He said that they were content to submit lists related to their troops to Colonel Yeaton but were not at all content to submit them to a subcommittee that might pass them to the Nationalist government while hostilities

Left to right: Lt. Lee (Yeaton's personal interpreter), Gen. Ch'en, Yeaton, Chu Teh, Ariyoshi, and Peterkin in July 1945. Courtesy of Col. Wilbur J. Peterkin.

were still in progress.[39] It is important to remember that the Yenan Liaison Group, as it was called by this time, was *not* one of the field teams responsible to the Peking executive headquarters: it was an ongoing liaison group.

Having secured agreements on many important points and believing that the sincerity of both Chinese factions would ensure that these agreements were implemented, General Marshall left Chungking for Washington[40] to make a personal report to the president on the situation in China. He was particularly anxious to take up the question of the transfer of surplus property and shipping and the problem of loans to China.[41] No sooner did he leave China, however, than the situation there began to deteriorate. Field commanders ignored the orders of the field teams, and the teams' Chinese members began regarding themselves as representatives of their local commanders and subordinate to them rather than to executive headquarters.[42]

On March 16, with Lieutenant General Alvan C. Gillem acting for General Marshall, the Committee of Three issued a memorandum calling for the integration of the Communist forces into the national army under the supervision of executive headquarters.[43] In the meantime, following the evacuation of the Russian army, the Chinese Communists maneuvered themselves into a logistical position that allowed them to move into Manchuria ahead of the national government. They proceeded to do so, resisting national government occupation of that territory, to which they had previously agreed.[44] By the time Marshall returned to China on April 18, the impasse was complete except that the Chinese Communists were willing to include future military dispositions and local political reorganization in negotiations if and when the fighting ended.[45]

In short, although Marshall may have enjoyed some initial success in reducing the level of fighting in China, he was no more able to bring the two sides together than Hurley had been. Marshall knew that he was the target of both sides and that both sides had double-crossed him, although he told David Barrett that he believed the Communists had committed more violations. Chiang Kai-shek treated him shabbily, too, however. In the heat of the summer, the Generalissimo went to his cool mountain retreat in Kuling. Anytime Marshall wanted to see him, he had to risk his life flying into a little airfield on the river and be carried up the mountain in a sedan chair.

At times, Marshall appeared almost overwhelmed by the enormity of the task he had undertaken. Wedemeyer reported that Marshall said to him, "I'm going to solve this damn thing and you are going to help me and I don't want to hear what you have to say." Barrett was acting military attaché during the Marshall Mission. One of his duties was to brief Marshall, a job that Barrett likened to teaching a bald eagle to fly. Every Monday morning he would stand in front of a map and a chart and would brief Marshall on the military situation. The general would sit immobile, with no expression on his face, never smiling. If Barrett made an error, Marshall would point it out politely but ruthlessly.

We can conclude, therefore, that Marshall's lack of success in bringing the two sides together was not due to a lack of information, as he was completely aware of each side's strengths and weaknesses. While he never sat down with Chiang and Mao at the same time, he did not feel dependent on the assessment of some man up at Yenan or in Washington for his information. Barrett believed that Marshall had bent over backward to give the Communists a break because he was trying to do the best possible job of mediation.[46] It was a task that could not be accomplished. G-2 assumed that the Nationalists could be handled because the United States had the power to cut off their transportation and supply,[47] but reactionaries dominated the Kuomintang and rendered all Marshall's efforts to work for a coalition impossible.[48]

For their part, the Communists paid lip service by accepting the field teams without letting them see anything important. Meanwhile, they moved all their troops and materiel into strategic positions for attacks on the Nationalists. The older Communists wanted to produce economic chaos and bring down the government. Their deliberate misrepresentations and violently anti-American propaganda made Marshall particularly caustic.[49] He had enjoyed some initial success in reducing the level of fighting in China, and he strove to be evenhanded within the limits of his own prejudices. He opposed any policy of siding with the Communists against Chiang, but neither he nor Truman could escape the ideological and political fallout of the emerging cold war. Congress increased military and economic aid for Chiang at the insistence of the China Lobby, even though Truman pointed out that thieves headed the regime.[50]

Chou En-lai's return to Yenan on November 19 in an American army plane marked the end of negotiations and discussion. On January 7, 1947, President Truman announced Marshall's nomination as secretary of state.[51] Marshall then issued a frank statement to the press complaining that "sincere efforts to achieve settlement have been frustrated time and again by extremist elements of both sides." The "salvation of the situation," as he saw it, was the assumption of leadership by the "splendid groups of liberals of all parties" working under Generalissimo Chiang Kai-shek in carrying out practical steps leading to the enforcement of China's newly adopted democratic constitution. "The greatest obstacle to peace in China was the almost overwhelming suspicion between the Chinese Communist Party and the Kuomintang."[52]

Termination of the mediation effort did not change the traditional attitude of the United States toward China. Marshall believed that China should be viewed sympathetically. He also favored taking any action short of direct intervention in internal Chinese affairs to assist China in realizing aims that represented the hopes and aspirations of the Chinese people and of the United States.[53] There probably was no American solution for China, of course, and in the end China went its own way as if the Americans had never come.[54]

Shortly after Marshall's departure, the United States decided to end its connection with the Committee of Three and to close down the Peking executive headquarters.[55] The Yenan Observer Group was officially ended on April 11 and was almost immediately redesignated the Yenan Liaison Group. The radio station was closed, but two days later it opened again and maintained regular schedules with theater headquarters in Shanghai and executive headquarters in Peking. Chinese Communist personnel who had been trained in American army radio procedure operated the radios, as they had since September 1945. The departure of American army personnel from Yenan therefore does not appear to have seriously hampered the group's efficiency.[56] Major Clifford

F. Young became the group's commanding officer on April 20, 1946. For awhile he and Corporal Johnson D. Robinson were the only Americans left on the post.[57]

The Shanghai *Evening Post and Mercury* reported that the group went out of existence in the natural course of deactivating the China Theater, which had been scheduled for May 1. According to the article, General Chu Teh made a formal inspection of the Observer Group compound on March 29 and the following day hosted a farewell dinner for the departing Americans at the Communist Army headquarters. Seven vehicles, expensive radio equipment, clothing, and the buildings that the Americans had built were turned over to the Communists, but they received no arms, ammunition, or photographic equipment.[58]

Since Young had virtually no personnel, the Communists sent him a detachment of soldiers and told him to continue commanding the post. At that point Young was, in a sense, an American in command of a Chinese Communist group. The Chinese soldiers ran the weather station and functioned as radio operators and motor mechanics. Young insisted, however, that they not touch the American flag.[59]

The Dixie Mission, called the Yenan Liaison Group after June 24, was placed under the administrative and operational control of the Army Reorganization Group of the Peking executive headquarters. It had regular radio contact with the Peking headquarters at 6:30 A.M. and 2:30 P.M. every day. The courier plane that flew in every ten days, weather permitting, provided the post's only other contact with the outside world.[60]

As Communist expectations of American support or recognition dwindled, relations between the Communists and the Dixie Mission grew more tense. Beginning in May 1946 Communist anti-American propaganda increased significantly. Personal relations continued to be friendly, however, and hunting expeditions and conversation, particularly nonpolitical discourse, continued much as they always had.

The two groups were also continuing to cooperate in the face of increasing Nationalist military activity in the area. An example of the interaction is illustrated in the following account of a plane crash in April 1946. An American C-47 had left Chungking for Yenan on April 8, but thirty minutes' flying time north of Sian, the pilot was advised that conditions at Yenan were unfavorable for landing. The plane's radio operator acknowledged the message, but the plane continued toward Yenan. At about 1200 hours he asked for a homing signal on 1550 kilocycles, and that was the last Yenan heard from him. A search involving three planes began the following day. The Communists dispatched cavalry units to all the isolated outposts in the mountainous regions of Shensi and Shansi Provinces.[61]

Two days later Young received a report from Eighteenth Group Army headquarters stating that the wreckage of the missing plane had been found about 150 miles northeast of Yenan. There were no survivors.[62] Since there was an emergency landing strip approximately ten miles from the scene, on April 17 air evacuation of the bodies to Yenan began. The bodies of the four American airmen who had been on board were mangled beyond recognition and could not be identified.

Several important Communists were also killed in this crash, including Wang Jo-fei, Chou En-lai's assistant; General Yeh Ting, former commander of the New Fourth Army; Feng Fa; and Chin Peng-hsien, editor of the *New China News Agency*. Immediately after retrieving the last victim, the Communists held an elaborate funeral and reserved a special place of honor, separate from the Chinese, for the American bodies. Then the Americans were placed on two C-47s that departed for Chungking in the midst of the impressive ceremony, circling over the heads of the 10,000 people who attended the funeral services.

National government air activity over Yenan continued to increase throughout the spring of 1946, mostly in the form of reconnaissance and photographic sorties. On June 26 a B-24 Liberator bomber with national government markings manned by five Chinese Air Force crew members and six ground crew men circled over Yenan and landed on the airfield. The American-educated and trained pilot explained to the Communists that he had voluntarily taken refuge in Yenan because he opposed the civil war. The Communists then took the plane to a nearby valley and concealed it. They told Young that it would remain in Yenan but that they would not use it. When the Americans later inspected the plane, they found that the radio equipment, gasoline, and all other detachable interior equipment had been removed.[63]

A couple of days later two Nationalist P-40s reconnoitered Yenan. Then, on August 2, seven Kuomintang P-47 fighters and one B-25 appeared. The fighters strafed the airfield and also found the B-24, which they destroyed. The B-25 made three runs over the city, dropping eleven bombs about a half mile from the Communist headquarters on the third run.[64] The Communists claimed that the city and their headquarters had been the targets of the bombing raid, but according to Major Young and Major James L. Butler, who joined the Yenan Observer Group on August 1, it resulted from erratic bombing.[65]

A few days later national government troops attacked Communist forces in the vicinity of Anping. Before the month ended, several field teams had to be withdrawn, and efforts to effect a lasting truce had reached a stalemate. The Communists then began withdrawing from the field teams, further minimizing the chances of achieving peace. The

Nationalists withdrew from some of the field teams too, which left the Americans functioning primarily as powerless observers.[66]

Walter Robertson, the American Commissioner, lodged official protests with the Nationalist government about violations of the truce. In his July 23 protest to national government commissioner General Cheng Kai-min, Robertson noted that the strafing, bombing, and reconnaissance had been directed against both military and civilian populations. Unless these acts stopped, Robertson feared that in the future a plane used to supply field teams might be shot down.[67] This possibility concerned the Americans in Yenan, and so did the need to have proper air raid warnings. They knew the Communists were not qualified to distinguish a bomber from a transport plane and requested that Peking headquarters send a field manual and photographs on how to identify aircraft so that they could be taught.[68]

During the month of January 1947, almost all activity in executive headquarters ceased. On February 6 the headquarters was deactivated, and the operating sections were renamed the "Sino Liaison Office." The field teams in Manchuria and China proper were recalled to Peking. Preparations were made for the immediate evacuation of all American personnel.[69] As one of its final services to the Communists, the headquarters presented the Yenan library with samples of the official papers used to identify members of the executive headquarters field teams.[70] Peking headquarters also continued to receive copies of Communist propaganda literature collected by the Americans in Yenan.[71]

Even while the Mission was in the process of shutting down, a variety of press correspondents continued to visit Yenan. They always consulted with any Americans who were there. Anna Louise Strong of Associated Press, Freda Utley representing *Reader's Digest*, John Roderick, on assignment for Associated Press, F. Tillman Durdin of the *New York Times*, Jules Joelson, of the French News Agency, and Louis Rosinger, from the Institute of Pacific Relations, were some of the correspondents who made the trip during this period.[72] Anna Louise Strong happened to be in Yenan when the Nationalists destroyed the B-24. She wrote an eyewitness article describing everything she "heard" and "saw." In fact, she had neither seen the attack nor heard the bombs but had been filled in afterward by Clifford Young, who had witnessed and photographed the incident from the weather tower.[73]

The English writer Robert Payne visited in June 1946. He went to see Yenan University. On the way back his driver ran their jeep over a cliff and down an embankment. The jeep landed squarely on its nose. If it had fallen to the bottom, Payne and the driver would have been killed or seriously injured, but halfway down the steep incline, the jeep ran into a pigpen. The jeep killed two pigs, and the vehicle was badly damaged, but Payne and the driver sustained only scratches.[74] Another time a truck turned over. The drivers' lack of experience in handling army vehicles caused both accidents and created a critical shortage of transportation even though trucks, radios, and generators had been given to the Communists when the majority of the Observer Group had pulled out in April 1946.

After this incident, General Chu Teh asked Young whether he could have a truck for his personal use. Young did not object, but he cautioned the Chinese not to scatter the vehicles all over the countryside just to please an individual. He recommended that they create a central motor pool and provide for regular maintenance. He told them that if they did not, within six months the vehicles would all be junk.[75]

Young was reassigned in September 1946, and command passed first to Butler and then to Lieutenant Colonel John L. Lake. Lake and Butler continued to hold periodic conferences with the Communist general staff officers and to obtain reports on both Nationalist and Communist troop disposition. On November 1 Colonel John Sells took over as commanding officer. The ever-dwindling group continued to assist aircraft dispatched to Yenan from either Nanking or Peking and tried to promote goodwill with the increasingly recalcitrant Communists.[76] Social meetings still took place, but sometimes they were difficult as they had not been in earlier days. Once Young viewed a performance staged by the Communists. Two girls and two boys performed the opening number, which was filled with anti-American propaganda. At one point the four unexpectedly sang in chorus, "Oppose American aid to China, withdraw American troops from China!" Young laughed and wagged his finger at the stage so that his hosts would know he did not like being subjected to a diatribe. Nevertheless, his ears grew hot, and he felt uncomfortable being the only American in the midst of Communist zealots.

Irregular supply and mail service plagued Dixie during the last year of its existence. Young repeatedly complained that the army had forgotten him and his few remaining men. Once he sent a scorching telegram notifying headquarters at Peking that because they had sent him automobile gasoline instead of diesel fuel he was within forty-eight hours of having to close down the radio station. Since the post's major purpose continued to be its communications line, headquarters responded to his warning by flying a special plane to Yenan with the precious fuel.[77]

Another time Young could not make headquarters replace a broken-down generator. He flew to Peking on the courier plane and told the pilot of his plight. The pilot said he planned to spend two days in Peking, after which he would fly Young to Shanghai, where he could easily pick up a generator. Young believed that this idea would solve his problem, but when General Henry A. Byroade, the commanding general of the Peking headquarters, found out he was in Peking without orders, he summoned Young to his office and sharply reprimanded him.[78] Young suspected that executive headquarters worried that he was storing up supplies for future use or so that he could later sell them at a profit.[79] He also noticed that Kuomintang secret police followed him in Peking, probably, he thought, because he was from the Communist center.[80]

Young also suffered from the monotony of being stationed at a post with so few personnel and so little to do. For a while he was the only American at Yenan. When heavy rains caused weeds to sprout all over the compound, he worried that the post looked ugly and assigned men to dig them out. He raised some leghorn chicks that he turned over to the young boys in the Communists' experimental farm, much to their delight. He had so much time on his hands that he asked his wife to send model airplane kits he could assemble and use to amuse the children who hung around the post. He started to write a history of the Communists' 1936 Long March and was in the midst of interviewing some of those who had participated in it when he was reassigned in September 1946.[81]

On the personal level, relations between the Communists and the Americans stationed in Yenan always remained amiable, especially for Young, who spoke Chinese fluently. Nevertheless, the Americans knew how tense relations were between their country and those who were determined to become the leaders of the new China. During the first two weeks of October 1946, the Communists brought to a head what the Americans called their "Americans Get the Hell Out of China Crusade," posting "bloodcurdling and gruesome" posters of the alleged misbehaviors of Americans in China. This campaign, which had begun in July, escalated for the rest of year.

Yet in spite of the worsening relations, there were social contacts, entertainment of various kinds, and dinners until the last man left Dixie. These included a Thanksgiving dinner given by the group and attended by several important Chinese and by the American correspondents. As late as Christmas 1946 the Americans and Chinese held a party and dinner honoring members of the Chinese Communist Party and other foreigners currently in the Yenan area. The Maos and the Chus and other important Communists attended and reciprocated with a dinner on New Year's Day.[82]

Several times Young played bridge with the Communists, whom he described as enthusiastic beginners,[83] and he asked his wife to send toys and dolls for the small Communist children who frequented the post.[84] Other men in the group gave toys to the Communist children too. In a letter to his wife, Young observed that Lina, Mao's little daughter, was very intelligent and not spoiled. One night Lina watched a movie from Major Young's lap, eating watermelon and dripping juice all the while. When Lina's hair turned brown from playing in the sun, her mother shaved her head, explaining that she wanted Lina to have black hair.[85]

As long as Dixie continued to function, its members hung tenaciously to whatever threads of goodwill existed between them and the Communists. When executive headquarters officially closed on February 5, 1947, the Americans assisted in evacuating Communist personnel from Peking and Nanking to Yenan.[86] Planes continued to supply the post. Journalists and other people came and went. Among others, the chief liaison officer from Peking visited the post, had lunch with the Chinese leaders, and toured the city of Yenan.

On March 1 the remaining members of Dixie went bird hunting with the Chinese, who held a dinner and entertainment in their honor that night. Although the party had been intended as a farewell entertainment for the group, immediately afterward they received a message from Peking headquarters ordering them to stay until all Communist Party personnel in the Nationalist-controlled areas had been airlifted to Yenan. Over the next several days planes arrived with Communists, journalists, thousands of pounds of Communist Party cargo, medical supplies, and a doctor from the United Nations Relief and Works Agency (UNRWA). Generally these planes left Yenan the day they arrived, but if they did not, their crews stayed overnight in the Dixie compound.

On March 8, 1947, all the correspondents and the UNRWA doctor left. Two days later, because a Nationalist attack threatened the Shen-Kan-Ning border region, General Chu Teh decided to place the area in a state of complete emergency. He informed the Americans that the Yenan airfield was scheduled to be destroyed on March 11 and suggested that the communications plane depart early that day. Since that plane served as the Liaison Group's only connection with the outside world, Colonel Sells decided the time had come to move the group to Nanking. As a last responsibility he arranged for the Communists to broadcast the date when Major Rigg and Captain Collins, assistant military attachés captured by the Communists in Manchuria, arrived in Harbin. General Yeh Chien-ying issued the appropriate orders informing Ambassador Stuart that these two officers were to be immediately released when they reached Harbin.

At 8:00 A.M. on March 11, 1947, the few remaining members of the Yenan Liaison Group took off for Nanking. Their departure concluded the longest-lasting direct connection between the United States and the Chinese Communists during World War II. As they circled the Yenan airstrip, they looked down at the ground from the plane windows. As prophesied, they could see the Communists blowing up the airfield.[87]

9

The Dixie Mission in Retrospect

E ven before World War II ended, people began expressing opinions about the merit of the Dixie Mission. Some evaluations came from the military or OSS participants in the Mission itself or from the Foreign Service officers who had helped create it. Others originated with army, navy, and diplomatic personnel not assigned to Dixie but with direct Dixie experience, such as General Albert C. Wedemeyer and former ambassador Patrick J. Hurley. Policymakers in Washington, bureaucrats in the China Theater headquarters, politicians who considered themselves experts on China, journalists, the Chinese Communists, and, of course, historians have all had their say as to whether Dixie was vital, could have been important, or was merely a historical incident.

To determine the Dixie Mission's place in history, we must ask whose interests it best served and how well it performed its assigned tasks. We must also consider its military appropriateness and ascertain whether its existence had significant impact on short- and long-term diplomatic relations between America and China. In doing so, historians must concern themselves with the following questions: did the Mission meet its military and intelligence obligations? Were its goals realistic, given that the shooting war was drawing to a close and the cold war was intensifying? Were the right men selected to serve in Dixie and to lead it? At what point did the Dixie Mission complete its work? Did the Dixie Mission function primarily as an OSS adventure and an attempt at empire building? Finally, was it inevitable that the U.S. government would maintain a hostile position toward the Communists regardless of the Dixie Mission, or would the United States have taken an even less flexible position without it?

Some testimony comes from those who served with the Mission, offered from a fifty-year perspective; other judgments have been made by people who did not serve in the Mission but otherwise had direct contact with it. Recent developments in China may unquestionably affect perceptions of these earlier appraisals, but it is important to consider what participants and observers of the Mission thought about it, since many of them have contributed their impressions to the written body of knowledge on the war in Asia.

Ongoing contact with the Chinese Communists caused the men of the Dixie Mission to develop a sensitivity toward their "hosts." Visitors, either military personnel or journalists, were not attuned to the Communists in the same way. Men like Clifford Young even noticed when someone prominent, like Chou En-lai, was tired from overwork. In March 1946 Young wrote his wife that the Communists worked unceasingly,[1] an observation that he repeated many years later when an interviewer asked what he thought the Dixie Mission had accomplished. In that interview Young noted that the Mission had been created to establish and maintain close liaison and communication among China Theater headquarters, Peking executive headquarters, the Marshall Mission, and the Chinese Communists' military headquarters. It also made air transportation to and from Chungking, Shanghai, and Peking available to the Communist military and Party members; hosted United States military personnel and the various correspondents and writers who visited Yenan; maintained a friendly and diplomatic posture with the Chinese Communists; and generally observed and collected available intelligence data. In the sense that it performed these duties, Young believed the Dixie Mission accomplished its goals.[2]

Young's appraisal harmonizes with the "official" Peking headquarters history of the "Yenan Liaison Team," which noted that the Yenan Observer Group processed a great deal of information regarding Japanese order of battle in North China and captured Japanese documents. The author of this work alleged that more than 100 American fliers downed in North China were rescued and were moved to safety through Dixie. The report went on to note that the group had collected facts about weather and navigation and had operated a receiving and transmitting station, which it had trained Chinese personnel to use.

Evaluations made by participants in Dixie are inconsistent and must be used cautiously by historians studying Dixie's role in the war. Either they mightily praise the men, the Mission, and its accomplishments, or they are highly critical of the unit, its personnel, or both. The opinions do not appear to correlate with the rank of the man doing the judging, as positive and negative opinions are held by both those who served and those who led. Also, there appears to be no correlation with the timing of participation, that is, with whether the participant was a part of the original group or was there at a later time.

We have seen that the Mission had four regular commanding officers: Colonel David D. Barrett, Lieutenant Colonel Wilbur J. Peterkin, Colonel Ivan D. Yeaton, and Major Clifford F. Young. It was also noted that Colonel Morris DePass served as commanding officer for a brief time but was removed when the Communists complained that he had an affiliation with Tai Li, the head of Chiang's secret police. The final commander, Colonel John Sells, flew out on the last plane just as the Communists blew up the airstrip. Three of the commanding officers believed that the Mission was necessary and that it did its job well. One believed that it was ill conceived and improperly staffed. No information is available as to the feelings that DePass or Sells had about the Mission, although Sells's memos are strongly anti-Communist in tone.

Barrett—perhaps predictably, since he was linked to the Mission's creation—took an exceedingly positive attitude during the war about the Mission, its goals, and its accomplishments. Afterward, however, in an interview with Forrest Pogue, General Marshall's biographer, he indicated that Communist "sweet talk" might have taken him in.[3] When the Mission had been in existence only a little over a month, he stated in a memo that its preliminary work had been accomplished and that the men were busy gathering and studying background information, order of battle, target, and bombing results intelligence. He went on to say that the Chinese had cooperated most enthusiastically, and had shown a willingness to construct landing fields, without asking anything in return, although they *had* indicated that they would be able to contribute more if their forces were better armed. Barrett believed that the Communists had assumed that the Observer Group's presence would in time bring greater assistance from the United States. He thought such aid was a good idea, not for the Communists' sake, but because the Communists could contribute significantly to the war effort. Furthermore, he considered it unreasonable to expect them to continue rendering aid to the section without any hope of receiving help in return. Like many Dixie Mission members, Barrett expected the Communists to win the inevitable civil war and believed that unilateral sponsorship of the Chiang regime would destroy any chance of American influence in the new China.[4]

Barrett's mea culpa to Forrest Pogue reflected the cold war atmosphere that prevailed at the time of their interview. Formulation of the Mission and his direction of it formed the apex of Barrett's career, which would no doubt have ended on a happier note for him if his suggestions to tighten relations with the Chinese Communists had been followed.

The second commanding officer, Lieutenant Colonel Wilbur J. Peterkin, led the Dixie Mission from January to July 1945. He told me that in retrospect he thought the Mission would really have come into its own if the United States had found it necessary to invade the Japanese home islands. In Peterkin's opinion, a successful American invasion launched from China would have required the Communists' help. The dropping of two atomic bombs obviated any such need, however, so that Peterkin's theory is hard to prove.[5]

Peterkin and others had wanted top-level officials to visit the Mission and meet with the Communists. Peterkin believed that such meetings would have lent prestige to the Mission and would have given its observations greater credibility. Peterkin also believed that certain respected men deemed to possess greater than average insight into the China situation should have been made members of the Mission, particularly Evans Carlson, the major in the U.S. Marines who had been the only American military man to have been in the Communist areas prior to the Dixie Mission. As it was, the Americans acquired battle order and weather information but mounted no real intelligence-gathering operation because there was no possibility that the Communists would be used to help fight the Japanese.[6]

Ivan D. Yeaton replaced Peterkin as commanding officer of the Yenan Observer Group in July 1945. His friendship with General Albert C. Wedemeyer and their shared political conservatism may have played a part in his selection. Like Barrett, Yeaton mistakenly thought the appointment might lead to a promotion while he was on active duty.

When I asked Yeaton to evaluate the Dixie Mission, he did not need to think twice. He claimed to be the first person to report the facts about it accurately and the only commanding officer who had gone to Yenan with previous training in intelligence. According to Yeaton, the others wrongly believed a Chinese Communist to be just another Chinese. Yeaton considered Koji Ariyoshi the most important man in the Dixie Mission, because the Communists trusted him and gave him free access to their compound. Yeaton trusted Ariyoshi too and used him extensively. Otherwise, he regarded the Dixie Mission as "a great big farce" that people noticed only because Hurley and Marshall had traveled to Yenan. The Communists did not fight the Japanese at all, Yeaton said, but saved their men for the inevitable civil war. The town of Yenan appeared silent, cowed by their oppressive presence.[7] According to Yeaton, a stalwart critic of the Mission and of Barrett, he would have been most disapproving if he had known of Barrett's failure to report that the Chinese Communists illegally maintained a large number of troops that were not part of the regular armed forces of the national government.[8]

Clearly, during the time the Dixie Mission existed, both the Chinese Communists and the Kuomintang were making preparations for a postwar showdown. Yeaton did not fool himself that it would be a struggle between good guys and bad guys. He knew that Chiang's government was corrupt, but he thought it was unrealistic to expect or demand that any government, even a corrupt one, change its ways overnight. Furthermore, he doubted that the Communists sincerely wanted to be part of a coalition, for he saw that all of their maneuvers were aimed at stalling until they were strong enough to take over.[9] Yeaton would have agreed with James Reardon-Anderson that the Communist leaders in Yenan were unwilling to forgo opportunities for wartime military expansion even at the risk of lessening chances for American support.[10]

Years later, Yeaton observed that relations between the Chinese Communists and the United States, including the Dixie Mission, began wearing thin in 1944 and 1945, after Hurley failed to bring the Communists and the Kuomintang together. At the time, he thought the Mission was partly to blame for this failure. He wrote Wedemeyer that "since 'Hurley Day' the Mission ha[s] done everything wrong." He attributed much of what was wrong to Peterkin's poor leadership and bad judgment. For example, "some organizations *told* the Chinese what they were going to do, instead of asking, and one CO had left without saying goodbye" [DePass].[11]

In a personal letter dated September 18, 1945, Hurley complimented Yeaton: "You have handled yourself well in a trying situation. I wish you'd been in Yenan a year ago. If you had been, I feel the results of our efforts [at conciliation] would have been more successful." Yeaton considered Hurley's words kind but incorrect; even if he rather than Peterkin had replaced Barrett, the Dixie Mission would still have accomplished little. When Hurley asked Yeaton what he thought he, Hurley, might accomplish, Yeaton recalled his own experience telling Harry Hopkins what he had not wanted to hear about Russia. Yeaton suggested to Hurley that he might be able to put something together on a temporary basis. He knew that Hurley had taken on an impossible task[12] that the Mission's errors, broken promises, and snubs toward the Chinese did not make easier. Meanwhile, the Chinese behaved like perfect hosts, even paying for the Mission's food.[13]

Unlike the other commanding officers of the Dixie Mission, Yeaton contended that Moscow provided clandestine aid to the Chinese Communists. This conviction affected his relations with the Communists as well as his perception of events. On April 15, 1946, for instance, he wrote a report to Wedemeyer stating that until three months earlier the Russians had maintained a three-man "TASS" agency in Yenan, not to report the news, but to provide political and military advice. He also assumed that messages were transmitted through the Yenan radio into the Soviet net. Through "personal observations and circumstantial evidence" he reached the conclusion that the Soviets continued to guide the destiny of the Chinese, as they had in the past.[14]

Yeaton's report containing these observations differed greatly from one he had written the previous year. At that time, he saw no evidence to confirm rumors that the Communists had received or were receiving Russian supplies, either directly into Yenan by air or from nearby but hard-to-detect airfields that the Communists had built for covert deliveries.[15] Pilots who flew into Yenan regularly and knew the terrain well confirmed that the rumors were false. According to these pilots, Yeaton said, stories that large amounts of Russian supplies were being delivered to secret Communist airfields around Yenan were fabrications. No plane could fly into Yenan without everyone's knowing about it, including the Americans, and any dealings the Russians might have had with the Chinese Communists took place elsewhere. Any activity of this sort that took place during the time of Dixie would necessarily have been handled with great finesse.

During the spring and summer of 1945, the Communists started evacuating Yenan and moving to Kalgan in preparation for the coming showdown with the Nationalists. By October, only Colonel Yeaton and Lieutenant Ariyoshi were still doing intelligence work for the Dixie Mission. The Mission primarily serviced itself and did some liaison work, with OSS maintaining one motor mechanic. Leonard Meeker of the OSS office in Chungking found this situation discouraging, given the Mission's potential value. Yeaton agreed and seemed anxious to remain with the Communist leaders, even if doing so meant moving to Kalgan.[16]

Major Clifford F. Young, who succeeded Yeaton as commanding officer after having served as his executive officer, had neither Barrett's enthusiasm for the Communists nor Yeaton's political conservatism. Young, who commanded the Mission from April to November 1946, told me that the Communists were "fond" of some of the Americans. When he first arrived in Yenan, they had looked upon him with suspicion, but after a few months they accepted him. They always took great care when making friends with strangers, because many Kuomintang spies operated in the area.

The Communists wanted Young to move with them to Kalgan.

Looking back, he thought it might have been an interesting assignment. General Chu Teh also spoke to him about the possibility that
overseas Chinese might bring their capital and skills to China to help
with the development of the "liberated" areas. He told Young that he
considered American military officers superior to the Chinese. In general, although they called him a "petit bourgeoisie," Young found his
Chinese hosts congenial and regarded his tour of duty in Yenan as his
best military experience.[17]

How accurate were the assessments of these commanding officers? Did their positions of command enable them to make more accurate judgments of those with whom they interfaced than the Foreign
Service Officers, Hurley, or theater headquarters? Yeaton, determinedly
anti-Communist, thought it unrealistic for the United States ever to
expect to do business with Mao's people. He steadfastly held that the
Dixie Mission proved this theory because it accomplished nothing.[18]
Yeaton, who was highly critical of Barrett's closeness with the Chinese,
his personal behavior, and the looseness of the Mission under his command, nevertheless found his predecessor's reports on the Chinese
Communist leadership excellent and acknowledged that they formed
the basis for future estimates of Chinese potential.[19] Yet while Yeaton
did not have high regard for Barrett (they had served together as young
officers), he did not believe that someone other than Barrett could
have made the Mission more successful.[20] And even Barrett, for all his
strong belief in the Mission and its purpose, recognized its low priority
with China Theater headquarters. About once a month he flew to
Chungking or Kunming, and each time he made "a pitiful little plea for
some crumbs from the rich man's table."[21]

Although Peterkin and Yeaton did not care for each other, they
both believed that the Dixie Mission accomplished little. Unlike Yeaton,
however, Peterkin attributed the Mission's weakness to theater's refusal to allow the Communists to be directly involved in fighting the
Japanese. As a result, he said, the Mission did nothing but get order-of-
battle and weather data,[22] which were secondary to its real purpose of
trying to make the Kuomintang and the Communists stop fighting each
other.[23] If theater had allowed the Mission to provide equipment and
some training, the Communists could have tied up the Japanese quickly.
As it was, Colling's demolition demonstrations were like taking a kid
into a candy store and letting him look but not touch.[24]

Young and Barrett held more liberal opinions on the proper role
of the Dixie Mission. As it turned out, these men were accurate in their
predictions about the future control of China. Peterkin and Yeaton both
began as staunch anti-Communists, but by the time Peterkin left the

Mission, he had changed his opinion and saw the Communists' peasant base as a force that might benefit China. Yeaton, on the other hand, always maintained that, regardless of any short-term benefits which Mao's regime might bring to China, in the end one Communist regime was as bad as another.

In addition to the commanding officers, the men who served in the Dixie Mission offered interesting insights into its importance. Virtually all of them understood that they were participating in a historically important event. For some, it was to be the high point in their lives; for others it meant severe career repercussions. They represented an educational, economic, and ethnic cross section of America. Most were Caucasian, but a few were Nisei or Chinese-American. The following comments are representative of their views.[25]

Arnold Dadian believed that although Dixie did not accomplish much, at least it afforded a point of contact with the Communists—at a minimum it contributed to America's meager knowledge about North China and Manchuria. Yet Dadian confessed to me that he had trouble defining the Mission's value. He remembered that it was run loosely, that he felt unprepared, and that he did not know what he was after.[26] S. Herbert Hitch expanded on this point, noting that the Mission gave the Chinese leaders, most of whom had never known any American, a chance to know men who were by and large average Americans. Hitch thought the Communist leadership saw the Dixie men as pretty good, dependable people. He thought that this statement was true even after the Hurley fiasco, since the Chinese were smart enough to recognize that the president's emissary was an exception.[27] The two groups mostly got together to eat and drink, and although the Communists sometimes spouted dogma or performed plays laden with political rhetoric, they never held political discussions or debates with the Americans. Even after Hurley's disastrous visit, relations remained cordial.[28]

Dr. Melvin A. Casberg, the first medic assigned to the group, believed that John Service's discussions with Mao and Chou En-lai were Dixie's most valuable contribution even though they produced nothing at the time. Looking back, Casberg thought that the negative American response given to Service's reports should be remembered as an excellent illustration of the fate of an acute and alert State Department field officer who reports news that the department does not want to hear. In Casberg's opinion, Service was brighter than Barrett and a worthy, nonmilitary addition to the Mission. Casberg's own trip behind the Japanese lines further validated the information that the Communists had been giving Barrett and Service about their activities. Apart from Service's reports and his own reorganization of the Communists' medical setup, however, Casberg thought the Mission accomplished very little. He likened the work of the Dixie Mission to an incomplete diagnosis of an illness; all the facts were there, but no one put them together.

Casberg returned to Washington on Christmas Eve, 1945, and went directly to OSS headquarters, where he made three statements. He told his audience that civil war between the Communists and the Nationalists was unavoidable, and he predicted that the Communists would win. He also predicted that after the Communists took over, China would not maintain close ties with the Soviet Union. Third, he offered the opinion that in the long term Chou En-lai and those who wore his mantle would have the greatest influence on China. Although events have borne out his analysis, those to whom Casberg spoke in

Left to right: An unidentified man, John Roderick, Chu Teh, Yeaton, Young, and Ariyoshi. The Yenan pagoda is visible in the background. Associated Press photo courtesy of Clifford F. Young.

1945 laughed, probably thinking him merely a medical man, not qualified to predict military outcomes.[29]

Hitch perceived the Mission as viable in the beginning but not
later. In his opinion things fell apart after the original group departed.[30]
Others, like Gustav Krause of OSS China, thought that Barrett *was* the
Dixie Mission, that the Mission lost its punch when he left.[31] John Service believed that Yalta marked the end of Dixie's significance, because
that and Roosevelt's decision to split the theater and pull Stilwell out
demonstrated that Europe had highest priority.[32] Ludden also felt that
Stilwell's removal ended the usefulness of the Mission, but he added
that Ambassador Clarence E. Gauss's resignation weakened its purpose
too. These events took place when Ludden, Peterkin, and others were
behind the Japanese lines and learned the news from a little Chinese
newspaper put out for the troops. At the time, Ludden said to Peterkin,
"Hell, we might as well start walking back," meaning that he did not
believe any support would be forthcoming from a successor to Stilwell.
From his point of view, Dixie had been an intelligence operation in the
best sense until that time. Many of its personnel had associated with the
Chinese Communists in Chungking, knew a great deal about them,
and looked for and evaluated information skillfully.[33]

Captain Paul Domke and Sergeant (later Lieutenant) Anton
Remenih, the OSS men responsible for establishing and operating the
Mission's radio, differed as to whether the Mission succeeded or failed.
Domke reasoned that the Mission existed primarily to collect data from
the Chinese that would be fed to higher headquarters in Chungking.
Since this process continued throughout the Mission's lifetime, Domke
considered the undertaking a success.[34] Remenih, on the other hand,
thought that even though much of the information gathered and transmitted probably had value, the real reason for creating the Dixie Mission had been to make the Kuomintang and the Communists stop fighting each other and concentrate their forces on the Japanese. Since that
goal was not accomplished, to him the Mission failed even though it
became involved in other useful activities, such as saving the lives of
airmen. He liked the concept of the Mission and believed that it might
have succeeded if higher-ups in theater and Washington had listened to
Barrett, Service, Davies, and Ludden rather than to Hurley.[35]

Alfred Harding, who served with the Mission as an enlisted man
from January 1945 to January 1946 and was later a Fulbright scholar,
thought that the Dixie Mission had earned its way by bringing out
downed fliers and collecting intelligence. He believed that the group
would have played a larger role if the war had lasted longer. Its primary
weakness, as he saw it, was its lack of control over the use of the informa-

tion it gathered. Furthermore, the facts it assembled were often improperly interpreted. He criticized some of the men for not taking advantage of the opportunities that duty in Dixie offered. Barrett encouraged the enlisted personnel to study Chinese, for example, and arranged for private teachers to instruct the officers. Ling Ch'ing started a class for the enlisted men, but after a time Harding was his only student.[36]

Jack Klein saw the Chinese as having been oppressed for so many centuries that Mao's brand of communism had the best chance to work as a form of government. To Klein, the average Chinese appeared uneducated and ignorant, and the United States was ignorant too, at least as far as the motives and capabilities of the Communist Chinese were concerned. The Mission offered a chance to correct this ignorance, and Washington's failure to take advantage of it was stupid.[37]

Hitch, like Klein, faulted the American government for its lack of foresight and for ignoring the truth about China when it formulated its postwar strategy.[38] Hitch thought his experience in Yenan gave him a much greater freedom of choice and broadened his view of the world; the simple Chinese lifestyle showed him that money was not everything. Hitch, who was himself the son of a missionary, noted that the Chinese Communist leadership had been educated at the Christian missionary schools. He also recognized that playing at least a small part in the events that shook China in the 1940s made him more than just another naval officer. By serving in Dixie he was able to distinguish himself, so that he was offered a good post in Korea during the Korean War. He thought he might have had a superior career in the State Department if he had chosen to follow that path.[39]

Not all of the men who participated in Dixie felt as positive about the assignment as Klein and Hitch. One unnamed soldier told the OSS Chili team that Yenan was hell compared with Chungking, since men in Yenan could take no whores to take to their quarters.[40] Also, as noted earlier, personality issues surfaced. Because he was sensitive to such matters, Coughlin wrote Stelle a letter admonishing him to enhance OSS's position with the Mission by making Barrett feel that he was the kingpin. "Don't be too obvious in any compliments you pay Barrett," Coughlin advised, "but never make any complaints that would reflect on him. . . . Make him feel you are trying to get that star for him."[41]

Apart from those who served in Dixie, the most important persons associated with the Mission were the theater commanders. Stilwell, of course, favored and furthered liaison with the Communists, while Wedemeyer relied heavily on Yeaton's reports and felt obliged to follow Hurley's lead. Wedemeyer therefore distanced himself from Dixie and discounted its warnings about the future control of China.[42] He appears to have been determined to maintain an objective intelligence view regardless of overall policy restraints imposed from Washington. By recognizing this attitude OSS was able to keep his confidence and to maintain its connection with the Dixie Mission.[43]

Hurley, on the other hand, did not try to be objective, because he believed that American policy obligated Americans in China to support the national government without reservation. He claimed that he had been making progress toward reconciling the Communists and the Nationalists until, without his knowledge, Barrett and General Robert McClure entered the Red areas with their scheme for American forces to cooperate with the Eighth Route Army. According to Hurley, when the Communist leaders in Yenan learned about this plan, they immediately assumed that they could get American support without complying with the terms of the agreement that Hurley was in the process of negotiating. They promptly dropped Hurley and the Nationalists, raised their demands, and turned hopefully toward the Americans in Dixie.[44] These events led Hurley to turn his wrath on those associated with the Mission, who he believed had betrayed him.

Hurley overlooked what recent historians have noted: that by the time he got to China to try to patch things up, and certainly by 1945, the shining image of Generalissimo and Madame Chiang Kai-shek was badly tarnished. During the ensuing civil war, only the American right wing persisted in regarding Chiang as a great leader, although he reemerged after the "loss of China" as an anti-Communist elder statesman.[45]

Kenneth Lau served as G-2 on General George C. Marshall's staff in Peking and spent a few weeks in Yenan in the fall of 1945, when the American military was transporting Chou En-lai's staff from Chungking to Yenan. Lau believed that the reports sent from Yenan impressed most of those who read them, if only because they gave information on a situation about which little was known. The office handled a large volume of reports, however, and Lau never knew how or whether they were acted upon.[46] In contrast, General Thomas Van Natta was convinced, as he told me, that G-2 got no important information from Yenan and that whatever it did get was provided at the Communists' discretion.[47]

What about outside military units either represented in or serviced by the Dixie Mission? In its official history the Twentieth Bomber Command acknowledged that one of the reasons for the group's creation was to assist the Communists' rescue of B-29 airmen forced down in parts of China occupied by Japan. Of four Twentieth Bomber Command crews that went down in or near the Communist-controlled areas, a total of forty-six men, twenty-eight were returned with the aid of the Communists. Four others were presumed captured and the rest killed with their ships. This was a high percentage of returns from an area that the command had considered totally unprepared to aid evaders prior to the establishment of Dixie.

With Dixie's help, the Communists had also supplied information about targets, weather, and airfields. The target data was almost faultless in its detail. When asked for particulars about weather and airfields, General Yeh formed an elaborate organization for receiving and processing air intelligence that stretched from individual villages to the leadership at Yenan. The bomber command did not use the target information as much as it had anticipated doing so, however, primarily because little of its campaign was directed against North China.[48]

Foreign correspondents posted to China found eager readership in America, even after some of them began to show themselves partial to Yenan rather than to Chungking.[49] Sometimes the lack of evenhandedness reflected the fast pace of events and disparities in what they saw. F. Tillman Durdin was the most objective, according to Israel Epstein of the *New York Times*.

Epstein, who had lived in China since the age of two, thought the American presence in Yenan benefited both the Americans and the Chinese. By stationing men there, the United States had positioned itself to receive information about the activities of both the Japanese and the Communists, and the Chinese were able to use the Mission to spread the word about their contributions to the war effort. According to Epstein, relations between the two groups were quite casual. Once, he said, he had seen Raymond Ludden, John Service, and some of the Chinese, including Yeh Chien-ying, sitting together with their feet in a single tub of water after they had crossed the muddy river. The Chinese soldiers who came in contact with Dixie unanimously expressed positive feelings about it, and only once that he knew of did they refuse an American request. Early in the Mission the Americans had wanted to give Mao a birthday gift. The Chinese had refused to permit the gift, saying they felt responsible for the Americans' poor living conditions.[50]

John Roderick, the Associated Press man in Yenan for six months in 1945, described his Yenan experiences in his memoirs. Yeaton was "tight-lipped, humorless, and suspicious, . . . embittered when he, like David Barrett, was not promoted to Brigadier General." The trouble with Yeaton, according to Roderick, was that he considered Yenan a comedown and failed to recognize that the men with whom he was dealing might one day rule China.[51] Mao struck him as the coldest and most calculating of the Communists he met in Yenan. Roderick saw warmth in Chou En-lai and worthy personal characteristics in many of the others, but Mao was a thinker and a doer, a complex, rebellious, driven individual possessed of a peasant's shrewdness and cunning, by turns kind and cruel, passionate and cold, romantic and hardheaded. It was no surprise to Roderick that as he aged, Mao's negative character-istics became stronger, while the positive ones withered. "Pride, envy, and an insane jealousy took over. Flattered by those around him, he allowed himself to be raised to the status of a god. . . . He no longer was the confident, ebullient, rational human I had known in Yenan."[52]

Like the men of the Dixie Mission, the journalists saw that the Chinese Communists were no happy band of brothers, that they put up a front for outsiders.[53] Nor did all of them believe the Dixie Mission benefited the United States. Father Cormac Shanahan, editor of the *Catholic Monthly* and *China Correspondent* and correspondent for the *Sign,* disapproved of it highly. Although the people of Yenan were well fed and the spirit of the Communist troops was good, he wrote, there was no freedom in Yenan. The people were regimented and subdued so strictly that a complete cleavage existed between them and their Commu-nist rulers. Most of what is known about the citizens of Yenan does not bear out these statements, however, and Shanahan contradicted some of his own words in later interviews with a State Department official.[54]

Theodore White was less critical. He was impressed by the Com-munists' quick reaction times in battle, their easy camaraderie with and acceptance of the Dixie Mission, and their gallant handling of Hurley and his crass behavior. White's opinions brought him into sharp con-flict with Henry Luce, his employer, who fired him.[55]

In a scholarly paper delivered at a meeting of historians in 1990, Stephen R. MacKinnon explored the relationship between the Chinese and American men of the press during this period. In it, he noted that Chiang Kai-shek's chief censor and sometime minister of information through much of the 1930s and 1940s was Hollinton Tong, a Univer-sity of Missouri graduate "who prided himself on his American approach to journalism." He had worked closely on Shanghai English language publications with American journalists Harold Isaacs, F. Tillman Durdin, and Edgar Snow. He understood the importance of image making and frustrated or irritated American reporters whom he censored during the war years.

Another individual played a similar role but with respect to cover-age of the Chinese Communists. This person, Liu Zunqi, was adept at using American techniques to improve the image of the Chinese Com-munists. Joseph Esherick examined archives that revealed careful man-agement of the 1944 visits by American journalists. There were staged visits to villages, the burying of evidence of the 1943-1944 Chengfeng party propaganda rectification campaigns, and concealment of the fact that units of the Eighth Route Army grew opium for profit. As a result, the Western press corps usually reported as positively about what the Communists were doing as did those reporters who covered Chungking under Tong's guidance.[56]

The American military often regarded Dixie with disdain. Some of their regular intelligence outfits, like the one that serviced Chennault's Fourteenth Air Force, disliked it because OSS participated in it, because it associated with the Communists, and because Stilwell touted it. General Alvan C. Gillem, who considered Stilwell an excellent field soldier but one of the world's worst diplomats, believed that by the end of the war, Stilwell was so filled with memories of the "Stilwell Mission" that he went overboard praising the fighting qualities of the Communist troops. In a 1971 interview Gillem recollected Stilwell's enthusiasm about his good friend General Chu Teh, whom he considered a fine and reliable man. Gillem took into account what he had learned from the Nationalists, including Chiang Kai-shek: the Communists had fought tenaciously during the Stilwell period so that they could maintain control over the areas they cleared of Japanese.[57]

Raymond Ludden agreed with Gillem. In Ludden's view, Stilwell was primarily interested in firing at the enemy, and he would support any group able to help him achieve this goal. Ludden told me that Davies had known the Chinese Communists in Chungking, and Stilwell trusted Davies's appraisal of them. The relationship helped get Dixie started, as did the B-29 raids out of Chengtu that began about a week after D-Day. Ludden believed that the Mission had died when Barrett left, because that was when the idea of supplying and equipping the Communists was scuttled. Had the United States increased its interests in North China, Dixie would have expanded. As it was, the group grew in numbers but not in function. Washington would not accept the inevitability of a Communist victory, and the Foreign Service officers who predicted one found their careers in trouble.[58]

Ludden wrote to Mrs. Peterkin in 1945 that it looked as if they had wasted their time and effort, because many people were afraid to acknowledge and act on the truths they had observed. He warned that Peterkin—whom he considered to be ideal for the Mission because he was conservative politically yet willing to learn—might be removed. Ludden closed this letter by commenting that regardless of the final effect, whatever it might be, the men of the Mission had experienced intimate contact with a group of people who felt strongly that certain things were worth fighting for.[59]

Dole believed that the Mission could have been pulled out after

Stilwell was relieved but that Wedemeyer had allowed it to continue because it was already in Yenan. He may have doubted the efficacy of the Mission, but he could see that stationing men in Yenan would not necessarily help the Communists and might help the United States work against them.[60] Wedemeyer, who was candid about his lack of information about developments in Yenan, worried about the Mission because it dealt with the Communists, whom he did not trust. He braved criticism in the American press when, with Chiang Kai-shek's knowledge and Hurley's approval, he sent eleven tons of medical supplies to Yenan to relieve a meningitis epidemic there.[61]

Wedemeyer's fears about dealing with the Communists may have been exaggerated, but some of the Foreign Service officers' analyses of the Chinese situation also lacked realism. Davies, more cautious than Service in evaluating the Communists as "democrats" and more circumspect in his comments about their relationship with the Soviet Union, thought the United States should assume a *realpolitik* orientation toward them while nominally continuing to support Chiang. On the other hand, Service's reports emphasized his disillusionment with the Kuomintang, which may have increased his admiration for the Chinese Communists. He was less concerned with the reality than was Davies, who viewed the Communists as opportunists truly interested in gradualism and willing to alter their ideology to fit the Chinese experience. Service believed the Communists' widespread support in the region they controlled meant that they were "democrats." He was not alone in shying away from the fact that they were genuine Communists. In several reports, Hurley spoke of them as "so-called Communists."[62]

The U.S. Navy as a whole may not have had a position regarding the worthiness of Dixie, but at least one of its high-ranking officers was extremely negative toward it. Vice Admiral Milton Miles's criticism expressed the same tone of OSS/SACO rivalry that had led John Coughlin in 1944 to recommend to Donovan that OSS leave SACO. Coughlin wrote Dickey in October of that year, "In China to date, it doesn't seem as though we have convinced anybody that we are even working."[63] In his autobiography *A Different Kind of War,* Miles incorrectly described the Mission, the length of its stay, and the number of people attached to it. He alleged that the Communists had made a deal with the Japanese in spring 1944. He accused Barrett of being less than candid with the Nationalist government regarding the Mission's purpose and of being dazzled by everything the Communists presented. According to Miles, the Dixie Mission never went into the field yet managed to give the Communists a big boost toward enlarging their hold on North China.[64]

Aside from whether the American government erred in snubbing the Communists' overtures, it is certain that participation in the Dixie Mission negatively affected the careers of Barrett and the Foreign Service officers.

John Service was the first of the Dixie Foreign Service officers to be penalized for his involvement with Dixie. He was arrested in June 1945 and was charged with leaking State Department documents to *Amerasia,* a publication reputedly sympathetic to communism. Cleared by a federal grand jury, he returned to work at the State Department, first as part of its advisory staff to General MacArthur in Tokyo, then as deputy chief of mission in Wellington, New Zealand. On March 14, 1950, Senator Joseph McCarthy made charges against Service in the Senate. A year and a half later, despite a congressional investigation clearing him, the State Department fired him. Service fought for years and ultimately brought his case before the Supreme Court. In June 1957 the Court voted unanimously in his favor. He then returned to active duty in the State Department, where he worked until his retirement in 1962.[65]

At the time of Service's arrest in 1945, Ludden was in Washington. He did not want to go to China under Hurley's ambassadorship, so he arranged to be assigned to the Army-Navy War College, where he remained for about a year. He called it his "fox hole," where FBI interrogators could not reach him. He then developed pulmonary tuberculosis, which required the removal of part of a lung and hospitalization. He returned to the American embassy in China in 1946 and was made consul general in Canton in 1948, a post he occupied until the State Department pulled out representation following the Communist takeover.[66]

John K. Emmerson, whom Wedemeyer rated the most studious of the four Foreign Service officers associated with Dixie,[67] foresaw that his stay in Yenan and his association with Okano might engender suspicions that he was pro-Communist. His reports expressed his conviction that the United States should end the war quickly and prepare the Japanese psychologically for the occupation of their country. Hurley considered Emmerson's words dangerous and cited him as one of those who had sabotaged his own attempts to negotiate between Mao and Chiang.[68]

Emmerson returned to Washington in 1945 and continued to be active in Japanese affairs until the war's end. He then served in the U.S. political adviser's office in occupied Tokyo and later in Moscow, the United Nations General Assembly, the National War College, and a variety of places from Pakistan to Africa. He returned to Tokyo in 1962, where he worked until his retirement. The McCarthyites accused him of sponsoring the Japanese Communist leaders whom he had interrogated, of advocating policies that led to the "loss" of Asia, and of being a Communist or a "fellow traveler." While Emmerson's dispatches and memoranda exerted no demonstrable effect on Allied policy, his prescience, his way of promoting ideas, and his perspicacity about the workings of the Japanese mind during those critical times were conspicuous in his political reporting.[69]

John Davies, the strongest character among the Foreign Service officers[70] and the one closest to Stilwell, was transferred to Moscow when he fell into Hurley's bad graces. He remained there until 1947, when he was transferred to the State Department as a policy planner. McCarthy accused him and others of contributing to the American "loss" of China, but Davies refused to resign, so in 1954 Secretary of State John Foster Dulles fired him as a security risk. The State Department reexamined his case in 1969 and granted him a security clearance.[71] At the time, he was manufacturing furniture in Peru.[72]

Others besides the Foreign Service officers suffered for having offered advice that no one wanted to hear. At the end of 1944 David Barrett was reassigned to what he thought was a more important post, that of chief of staff of the China Combat Command, under General Robert McClure. Throughout 1946 he served as acting military attaché, and during the Marshall Mission his duties included briefing General Marshall on the military situation in China. He later went to Hanoi in connection with the hunt for missing Americans. There Ho Chi Minh approached him, saying, "We Vietnamese are in a bad situation and we have a conflict of interest with the French. We don't want to get rid of the French, whom we need commercially and in the field of foreign relations, but we would like to have a fair deal. We'd like to have the United States of America on our side. Here's a letter I wish you to present to President Truman and to General MacArthur."[73]

Barrett replied that he had no authority to present letters to anyone except Wedemeyer. Ho Chi Minh said, "Fine, take these and give them to him," which Barrett did. In the course of their conversation, Barrett asked Ho if he were a Communist. Ho replied, "If I told you I was not a Communist you wouldn't believe me. I have been associated with Communists all my life." Barrett delivered Ho's missive to Wedemeyer but heard nothing further about it.[74]

In the end, the Chinese also turned against Barrett. The Communists refused to let him move back to China after he retired from the army, and the Nationalists denied his request to settle in Taiwan, where they had retreated in 1949. He returned to his home state of Colorado to teach at the University of Colorado in Boulder. He always believed

Left to right: Dolan, Service, Chu Teh, and Mao. Courtesy of Col. Wilbur J. Peterkin.

that the Dixie Mission, while not of great importance to the war effort as a whole, had been well worth its small cost in dollars. He thought that Dixie credibly covered most of the subjects listed in its directive, that the Air Force and navy benefited from the weather reporting, and that AGAS increased the efficiency of its operations because of the Mission.[75]

Although Barrett's retirement without the star he coveted seems to have brought a career of dedicated service to a sad conclusion, General Ray Peers's evaluation of him should not be overlooked either. Peers believed that the Nationalist Chinese respected Barrett's intelligence work but that as he got older, Barrett grew somewhat careless. He talked too much and became overly involved politically with various Chinese groups. Peers did not blame Barrett for the failure of American policy in China, however, which he attributed directly to General Marshall and the men who went with him to China as part of the Marshall Mission. To Peers, those people had spent most of the war Stateside and knew nothing about how to run a mission or advise the Chinese. This weak advisory group encouraged Marshall to continue trying to bring the two sides together rather than to back the Nationalists fully.[76]

We have seen that one of Dixie's tasks involved witnessing what the Chinese Communists were doing for the war effort and gathering evidence to help predict whether China would wind up in their hands or in those of the Nationalists. In determining how accurately Dixie carried out the latter assignment it is helpful to compare its assessments of the Communist effort with those made by other groups of Americans sent into North China with more or less the same task. We have seen that OSS, mostly through the Catholic church, quietly set up intelligence units all through China without the knowledge of either Marshall or Dixie. OSS did not usually inform Dixie about these undertakings, probably to prevent the Mission from losing face.[77] One OSS team did make contact, however. In August and September 1945, this team, code named Chili, spent six weeks traveling over 800 miles in north Shensi and north Shansi Provinces. Major Leonard Clark headed the team, which included a Chinese-American who read and wrote Chinese. The Communists treated the men as hostile observers, especially for the first two weeks, and so at the end of each day the Americans had to recall what they had seen and secretly write it in notebooks. These Americans had no radio contact with their headquarters, nor did they associate with any high-level leaders. All of their information came from rank-and-file army men, villagers, farmers, teachers, and low-level commissars and officers.

Like the men of Dixie, the Chili team noted the Communists' optimism regarding China's ability to match Western and American living standards. They reported that the Chinese expected to achieve a comparable quality of life in ten to twenty years. The Communists' energy and self-confidence, as well as their literacy rates, impressed the observers. The observers never considered the possibility that the public library at Suiteh, about 130 miles north of Yenan, and the spectacle of low-level officers reading or discussing politics with the men might have been faked for their benefit. Education in Yenan and the surrounding area was compulsory for all children starting at age six, however, and books by Russian authors were plentiful, although there were works by writers of other nationalities too. Some Chinese spoke Russian, which they learned at the English-Russian Language School in Yenan.

Chili perceived that the Communists regarded Stilwell and the Dixie Mission as friends and that they disliked both Hurley and Wedemeyer. They particularly resented Hurley's April 1945 statement, in which he called them an armed party within a state. In its report of October 5, 1945, the Chili team maintained that while writers like Edgar Snow had been overly enthusiastic about the changes brought about by the Communists, the Communists seemed really to want to work with Chungking and to avoid civil war. Like the Dixie Mission, this OSS team considered its conclusions objective and accurate, since they reflected firsthand observations.[78]

By comparing different opinions about the Dixie Mission, we can see both the strong and the weak points of the operation. As with the blind men describing an elephant, each view reveals a part of the whole. What is significant, therefore, is not whether the Mission fulfilled its assignment—it did—but how it was perceived, its part in the overall American plan for China, and its role as a player in international affairs.

The Mission was proof that Donovan could sell an idea to FDR. It also shows that OSS planned its own aggrandizement. It attracted greatest attention as one of the elements responsible for the U.S. loss of China, but it also contradicted at least in part the theory of Professor Ray C. Cline, a former OSS man, that in general the story of American intelligence efforts in China during World War II was a sorry one, with agencies working at cross purposes and with objective reporting on China mired in the bitter political controversies that raged between the partisans of Chiang Kai-shek and his critics.[79]

In a sense, creation of the Dixie Mission signaled a redirection of American foreign policy, temporary though it might have been. In those days many people did not consider it so bad to be friendly with the Communists if that meant that one was opposed to Chiang Kai-shek. From afar, the Dixie people and their activities appeared to be support for Mao less than they were a means of getting people to Yenan to learn whether the Communists were doing anything constructive to end the war.[80] The question of whether they were *real* Communists or not seems to have little bearing on the matter.

The Chinese Communists *were* real Communists, of course, and democracy in the American sense of the word did not exist in Yenan. In 1944, however, appearances were deceiving and the problem more complex. Some but not all observers undoubtedly reached the erroneous conclusion that they were not Communists (in the totalitarian sense of the word) because their mass support prompted a few of these outsid-

ers to believe that they were democratic.[81] In the wake of the Marshall
Mission's failure, when both sides were blaming the United States for
not constructing a peace, Young wrote letters to his wife describing the
Communists' propaganda as childish.[82] Still, the Communists continued to want an American liaison officer, and as late as February 24,
1947, they communicated with General Gillem on this subject. They
hoped that all arrangements could be made before headquarters closed
on March 5 and that supplies for the American personnel would be
provided. They wanted to know whether the Americans would maintain their own radio station or would continue to use the Communists'
facilities.[83]

If one or two officers could have fulfilled this function in 1947,
we may conclude that it was probably unnecessary for an entire mission
to have been stationed in Yenan for almost three years. One or two
skillful persons, such as Barrett and Service, could have informed themselves regarding the Communists' work and reported back.

We may wonder about this point in light of Service's evaluation of
Dixie. According to John Garver, Mao minimized his Soviet connection to Service. Vladimirov, the TASS man in Yenan, claimed in his
diaries that Service was kept ignorant of the extent of the Soviet presence in Yenan, that the Soviets operated a radio from their caves, and
that Vladimirov himself was a liaison officer posted to the Chinese Communists.[84] Service never quit believing that things might have been more
harmonious between the United States and the Chinese Communists if
Barrett had remained in Yenan or if someone like Barrett had replaced
him, and he thought that the basic issue remained the Communists'
disappointment at being turned down by the United States. But it was
preposterous to think that the young Foreign Service officers influenced Stilwell as much as the China Lobby led the American public to
believe.[85]

Yet while the Foreign Service did the best reporting because it
had good people in the field,[86] by the late 1940s, the State Department
was "a quivering mass," fearful of cold war reprisals. According to
Carlton Swift, an OSS operative in Indochina who later went into the
State Department, the attitude at State was the reason why so much
covert activity was ultimately placed in the hands of the CIA.[87]

The San Francisco conference of 1945 that created the United
Nations triggered one of the first postwar diplomatic showdowns between the Communists and the Nationalists. For the Communists, the
meeting presented an opportunity to gain recognition from the world
community. They wanted Chou En-lai to head a prestigious delegation
and made the question of their representation at the conference a ma-

jor issue. The Kuomintang did not want any important Communists in the Chinese delegation, but after stalling and refusing, the Nationalists suddenly announced that *they* would pick a Communist to be part of the Chinese delegation. They chose Tung Pi-wu, who was important enough in Communist circles that the followers of Mao could not protest his choice. Tung spoke very little English, however, and was not as smooth a politician as many of the Kuomintang men.

Major Joseph Spencer, head of R&A, China, noted the political shrewdness of the Nationalists' move when he informed Langer that the immediate international reaction favored the Kuomintang for tolerating Communist representation. The gesture seemed to have proved to the world that China was united and that the Kuomintang were sincerely interested in cooperation. In reality, Chiang had prevented the Communists from having eloquent and able international representation. The Communists made the best of a bad situation by providing Tung with a "staff," including Ch'en Chia-k'ang, Chou En-lai's secretary.[88]

During these events, the Dixie Mission continued to function, but by January 1946, Major Young expected it to close down soon. The few men who remained on duty in Yenan did not even have an interpreter. Yet when Yeaton returned from meeting with Marshall in Chungking, he told Young that the general considered it essential for the group to continue.[89] Definite plans to discontinue it were not made even when the United States withdrew from participation in the Committee of Three and the Peking executive headquarters. Since the transporting of the Communists to Yenan on American planes was to continue even after withdrawal, Dixie remained in place with the stipulation that it would receive no further equipment except what its commanding officer deemed essential.[90]

February 18, 1947, was set as the deadline for the pullout. On February 28, however, General Yeh Chien-ying asked Colonel John Sells, Young's replacement, to ask Peking to delay departure, because the Kuomintang had ordered the Communist offices in Chungking and Nanking closed and had demanded that all personnel be withdrawn without guaranteeing their safety.[91] As they discussed this matter, General Yeh and Colonel Sells also talked about continuing to maintain a liaison officer in Yenan.[92] Helping to shift Communist personnel to Yenan, then, was the Dixie Mission's final chore.

By documenting the Dixie Mission from the inside out, we can make a distinctive contribution to our knowledge about the war in that part of the world. What made the Dixie Mission stand out was its spirit of collective enterprise. This spirit had figured in the idea of jointly constructing an airstrip and then executing the plan. The unit was not a training team, although John Colling gave demolition demonstrations, nor was it strictly an army unit, since it combined many services.[93] Most of its personnel were officers, but they did not hesitate to do manual labor. They were good observers and believed that they knew why such a large part of the population supported the Chinese Communists rather than the Kuomintang.[94] They should probably have been selected with greater care. Perhaps they should all have been trained public relations experts.

At any rate, the political insights provided by the Foreign Service staff might have been invaluable in predicting the future of China if the policymakers in Washington had regarded them as worthy of attention. They could have provided ample information that the American government might have used in making realistic policy decisions. At the very least, as far as Chiang Kai-shek was concerned, the Mission had a somewhat sinister aspect that might have been exploited more fully to elicit his cooperation.

Even before the Mission's inception, there was concern about those who would serve in it. In a memo dated February 2, 1944, Harry Hopkins cautioned FDR about the importance of getting the right people for the U.S. Army Observer Group,[95] and an OSS report of October 30, 1945, warned that unless OSS associates were careful not to be seen cooperating with the Japanese in China or with Chinese puppets, it would be difficult to maintain the goodwill of Chinese liberals and educated groups who neither wholeheartedly supported the Kuomintang nor were willing to cooperate fully with the Communists.[96]

Furthermore, some of the Mission's strongest advocates questioned the unit's accomplishments. They believed that its work was finished after the completion of the four-month trip behind the Japanese lines between October 1944 and January 1945 and the report about what had been seen on that trip. After all, the original plan had been for the group to go there for six months, with no communication except by radio. Regular flights did not begin until after they had built an airstrip.

The Dixie experience suggests that goals for a group of this type must always be planned long range, even when the operation comes to life in an emergency situation such as war. If the frame of reference had been long term, perhaps the reports would have been more restrained.

The members of Dixie formed a positive impression of the Communists partly because they practiced the closest thing to democracy that the Americans had seen in China. Service and some of the others optimistically believed that with American influence the Communists could be converted to American-style democracy. They were a sharp contrast to what some of the Mission members had seen with respect to the Kuomintang.[97] Jack Klein, for example, had served in Kunming before he went to Dixie, and one of his responsibilities had been to run inspections. In the process, he found many caves filled with new airplanes, rifles, and artillery that the Kuomintang were storing for the coming revolution. Intelligence officers told him that in South Chinese cities supposedly retaken by Chiang's troops they had found no Japanese within fifty miles. The Kuomintang reported that a Japanese group had taken a particular city so that the United States would send in the Fourteenth Air Force to do heavy bombing. The Kuomintang would then take the city easily.[98]

In the beginning the Chinese distrusted the Dixie Mission because it was made up principally of OSS men and because it included a representative from Naval Intelligence, which the Chinese associated with Admiral Miles's Navy Group, China.

As time went on, the Chinese remained unhappy about the Mission's composition, although they liked the idea of having the Mission in Yenan. This was the case even after it became clear that the Communists would benefit little from it.[99] Personal pleasantries continued as long as the Mission was in Yenan, but by the summer of 1945 the deterioration of American-Chinese relations and growing suspicion regarding Soviet designs in Europe and Asia were shaping the Truman administration's policy toward China.[100] The group's morale began declining, and from time to time the Chinese expressed animosity. At one party, General Yeh became angry and shook his finger at the Americans, saying, "You are foolish if you think we won't be fighting the Kuomintang." Stelle had been drinking heavily at this gathering and may have provoked the exchange.[101] Later, pheasant hunting was suspended because the Americans were not supposed to lend guns to the Chinese. Previously, the Chinese who accompanied the Americans on hunting expeditions had been allowed to shoot the carbines, which they enjoyed, but after the directive about the guns, everyone just stayed in the compound.[102]

During the 1950s, when the Communist-run government embarked upon a "hate America" reeducation campaign, they falsely told the Chinese people that although there had been some official contact between the United States and the Communists in Yenan starting in 1944, it had been instigated by the United States merely to placate Chinese sensibilities.[103] Nevertheless, at the time the Dixie Mission existed the kind of direct, informal interaction at which the Mission excelled helped each group learn to understand the other.[104] Those who were part of the operation believed that they were making an important contribution to the theater's war effort.[105] The following brief example illustrates the kind of easy interchange that frequently took place, even on subjects that carried tense undertones. In the course of a conversation with Huang Hua at Hitch's house in Peking in 1945 or 1946, Hitch asked, "Why do you believe that with only captured weapons you, a second rate military power, can defeat an army [the Kuomintang] the United States is going to give its best?" Hua replied, "Yes, but you're relying on weapons. We don't rely on weapons, we rely on people."[106]

In the final analysis the Dixie Mission was neither the failure that policymakers of the time generally considered it nor the "firm step on the right road" that many of the participants believed. It would have played a more vital role had the United States attacked Japan from China. It was unfortunate for American understanding of the Chinese situation that its observations were not taken into account. The men of the Mission may have been flawed, but often they were first-rate, first-hand observers in a good position to offset the image of Yenan as a sort of a Shangri-la from which only a few starry-eyed visitors had emerged. Rightly or wrongly, those who did associate with the Communists usually pushed relentlessly for the United States to assume a more flexible posture rather than blindly backing Chiang.[107]

The presence of the U.S. Army Observer Group gave the Communists an opportunity to let the world know that their men were better fed and that the people living in the areas under their control were more supportive than those living under the Nationalists. For a variety of reasons, each Mission man came away from the experience feeling that although they might not agree ideologically, he and his hosts shared some basic concerns about human rights.

Contrary to what the Yenan leadership intended, however, the Observer Group's reports became part of the fuel for the McCarthy era. These reports harmed most of the former observers, whose political thinking ranged from ultraconservative to socialist. Their positive attitudes must be evaluated within the context of the time in which the Mission functioned, even though the events and actions of Mao's regime after the Communists gained power led critics, including some of the participants, to believe that they had been oversold.[108]

By 1949, the Communists controlled the China mainland and the cold war gripped the United States. People formerly associated with the Dixie Mission, those who had written reports advising closer contact with or fuller recognition of the Communists, found themselves unemployed or with career problems. There was no longer ground for hope that the establishment of the Dixie Mission signaled a changed direction in foreign policy. The Dixie Mission's recommendations faded into the background.

Yet in the later years of that frigid period, attitudes toward the Mission and its historical significance began to change. At first many people in the State Department had treated the Dixie Mission as a joke,[109] but after the United Nations admitted the Chinese Communists to membership, after President Richard Nixon had visited China in 1972, after tourists had begun to include China in their itineraries, after Chinese scholars had started seeking American educations, and after Chinese goods had been introduced into the American marketplace, people began to stop considering the Chinese Communists merely the tools of Moscow. Revised views led to new interpretations of the roles that the Foreign Service officers had played in the entire saga of American-Chinese relations during World War II.

The United States failed to realize that the most effective way to deal with the Chinese Communists would probably have been to send a very few, very well qualified men to Yenan rather than an entire group. The next biggest policy error the United States made with respect to using the Mission to the fullest lay in its failure to send a really influential person to Yenan to see what the Communists were doing and to assess the relationship between the Communists and the Mission. This was the step that Ludden had urged Wedemeyer to take in February 1945. At the time, Wedemeyer did not appear hostile to the idea,[110] and many years later he told me that he thought such a trip would have been a good move. The general said that Mao and Chou En-lai liked him and appreciated his honesty. He admitted that he had erred by not going to Yenan in person and by not paying closer attention to the reports of the Foreign Service officers.[111]

Still, the Dixie Mission is far more important than one would expect, given the relatively small number of participants in its operations at any one time. It stands out as an exception to official American policy toward China.[112] In addition, it greatly affected the lives of the men assigned to it, of those otherwise directly associated with it, and of those who had less direct or even peripheral contact with it, such as Hurley and the journalists. It is doubtful that a more committed, more vigorously independent American policy accompanied by military cooperation with the Communists in the last few months of the war could have altered U.S. relations with China in the cold war. Luo Rongqu wrote in 1990 that although American involvement in Chinese domestic affairs was conditioned by the long-term objectives of its global strategy, it had the effect of accelerating the civil war at a crucial moment.

Chinese Communist Minister of Defense Yeh Chien-ying and Yeaton at a Saturday morning inspection at Yeaton's headquarters. Courtesy of Clifford F. Young.

John Service and some of the others, however, never stopped regarding the Dixie Mission as a foundation on which greater American influence could have been built. They thought such a course of action might have forestalled the civil war or might at least have made it shorter and far less destructive.[113] Mel Casberg most certainly would have wanted to see the legacy of the Dixie Mission in such terms. Of all the Field Service officers, intelligence officers, commanders, and theater professionals who believed in the promise and potential of the Dixie Mission, the group's first medical doctor predicted most accurately the course of history as it unfolded before all of the participants.

Appendix: Pinyin to Wade-Giles*

Pinyin	Wade-Giles	Pinyin	Wade-Giles
a	a	cen	ts'en
ai	ai	ceng	ts'eng
an	an	cha	ch'a
ang	ang	chai	ch'ai
ao	ao	chan	ch'an
		chang	ch'ang
ba	pa	chao	ch'ao
bai	pai	che	ch'e
ban	pan	cheng	ch'eng
bang	pang	chi	ch'ih
bao	pao	chong	ch'ung
bei	pei	chou	ch'ou
ben	pen	chu	ch'u
beng	peng	chua	ch'ua
bi	pi	chuai	ch'uai
bian	pien	chuan	ch'uan
biao	piao	chuan	ch'uang
bie	pieh	chui	ch'ui
bin	pin	chun	ch'un
bing	pinh	chuo	ch'o
bo	po	ci	tz'u
bou	pou	cong	ts'ung
bu	pu	cou	ts'ou
		cu	ts'uan
ca	ts'a	cui	ts'ui
cai	ts'ai	cun	ts'un
can	ts'an	cuo	ts'o
cang	ts'ang		
cao	ts'ao	da	ta
ce	ts'e	dai	tai

---

*From *People's Republic of China: Administrative Atlas* (Washington, D.C.: Central Intelligence Agency, 1975), 46-47.

Pinyin	Wade-Giles	Pinyin	Wade-Giles
dan	tan	gua	kua
dang	tang	guai	kuai
dao	tao	guan	kuan
de	te	guang	kuang
deng	teng	gui	kuei
di	ti	gun	kun
dian	tien	guo	kuo
diao	tiao		
die	tieh	ha	ha
ding	ting	hai	hai
diu	tiu	han	han
dong	tung	hang	hang
dou	tou	hao	hao
du	tu	he	ho
duan	tuan	hei	hei
dui	tui	hen	hen
dun	tun	heng	heng
duo	to	hong	hung
		hou	hou
e	o	hu	hu
en	en	hua	hua
er	erh	huai	huai
		huan	huan
fa	fa	huang	huang
fan	fan	hui	hui
fang	fang	hun	hun
fei	fei	huo	huo
fen	fen		
feng	feng	ji	chi
fo	fo	jia	chia
fou	fou	jian	chien
fu	fu	jiang	chiang
		jiao	chiao
ga	ka	jie	chieh
gai	kai	jin	chin
gan	kan	jing	ching
gang	kang	jiong	chiung
gao	kao	jiu	chui
ge	ko	ju	chü
gei	kei	juan	chüan
gen	ken	jue	chüeh
geng	keng	jun	chün
gong	kung		
gou	kou	ka	k'a
gu	ku	kai	k'ai

Pinyin	Wade-Giles	Pinyin	Wade-Giles
kan	k'an	mai	mai
kang	k'ang	man	man
kao	k'ao	mang	mang
ke	k'o	mao	mao
kei	k'ei	mei	nei
ken	k'en	men	men
keng	k'eng	meng	meng
kong	k'ung	mi	mi
kuo	k'ou	mian	mien
ku	k'u	miao	miao
kua	k'ua	mie	mieh
kuai	kuan	min	min
kuang	k'uang	ming	ming
kui	k'uei	miu	miu
kun	k'un	mo	mo
kuo	k'uo	mou	mou
		mu	mu
la	la		
lai	lai	na	na
lan	lan	nai	nai
lang	lang	nan	nan
lao	lao	nang	nang
le	le	nao	nao
lei	lei	nei	nei
leng	leng	nen	nen
li	li	neng	neng
lia	lia	ni	ni
lian	lien	nian	nien
liang	liang	niang	niang
liao	liao	niao	niao
lie	lieh	nie	nieh
lin	lin	nin	nin
ling	ling	ning	ning
liu	liu	niu	niu
long	lung	nong	nung
lou	lou	nou	nu
lu	lu	nü	nü
lü	lü	nuan	nuan
luan	luan	nue	nueh
lüan	lüan	nuo	no
lüe	lüeh		
lun	lun	ou	ou
luo	lo		
		pa	p'a
ma	ma	pai	p'ai

Pinyin	Wade-Giles	Pinyin	Wade-Giles
pan	p'an	sa	sa
pang	p'ang	sai	sai
pao	p'ao	san	san
pei	p'ei	sang	sang
pen	p'en	sao	sao
peng	p'eng	se	se
pi	p'i	sen	sen
pian	p'ien	seng	seng
piao	p'iao	sha	sha
pie	p'ieh	shai	shai
pin	p'in	shan	shan
ping	p'ing	shang	shang
po	p'o	shao	shao
pou	p'ou	she	she
pu	p'u	shen	shen
		sheng	sheng
qi	ch'i	shi	shih
qia	ch'ia	shou	shou
qian	ch'ien	shu	shu
qiang	ch'iang	shua	shua
qiao	ch'iao	shuai	shuai
qie	ch'ieh	shuan	shuan
qin	ch'in	shuang	shuang
qing	ch'ing	shui	shui
qiong	ch'iung	shun	shun
qiu	ch'iu	shuo	shuo
qu	ch'ü	si	ssu
quan	chüan	song	sung
que	ch'üeh	sou	sou
qun	ch'ün	su	su
		suan	suan
ran	jan	sui	sui
rang	jang	sun	sun
rao	jao	suo	so
re	je		
ren	jen	ta	t'a
reng	jeng	tai	t'ai
ri	jih	tan	t'an
rong	jung	tang	t'ang
rou	jou	tao	t'ao
ru	ju	te	t'e
ruan	juan	teng	t'eng
rui	jui	ti	t'i
run	jun	tian	t'ien
ruo	jo	tiao	t'iao

Pinyin	Wade-Giles	Pinyin	Wade-Giles
tie	t'ieh	za	tsa
ting	t'ing	zai	tsai
tong	t'ung	zan	tsan
tou	t'ou	zang	tsang
tu	t'u	zao	tsao
tuan	t'uan	ze	tse
tui	t'ui	zei	tsei
tun	t'un	zen	tsen
tuo	t'o	zeng	tseng
		zha	cha
xi	hsi	zhai	chai
xia	hsia	zhan	chan
xian	hsien	zhang	chang
xiang	hsiang	zhao	chao
xiao	hsiao	zhe	che
xie	hsieh	zhen	chen
xin	hsin	zheng	cheng
xing	hsing	zhi	chih
xiong	hsiung	zhong	chung
xiu	hsiu	zhou	chou
xu	hsu	zhu	chu
xuan	hsüan	zhua	chua
xue	hsüeh	zhuai	chuai
xun	hsün	zhuan	chuan
		zhuang	chuang
ya	ya	zhui	chui
yai	yai	zhun	chun
yan	yen	zhuo	cho
yang	yang	zi	tzu
yao	yao	zong	tsung
ye	yeh	zou	tsou
yi	i	zu	tsu
yin	yin	zuan	tsuan
ying	ying	zui	tsui
yong	yung	zun	tsun
you	yu	zuo	tso
yu	yü		
yuan	yüan		
yue	yüeh		
yun	yün		

Notes

Note: For complete bibliographic information on works cited, see the Bibliography.

Abbreviations

DS   General Records of the Department of State
FRUS   U.S. Department of State, Foreign Relations of the United States
NARA   National Archives and Records Administration
OSS   Records of the Office of Strategic Services
RG   Record Group
WD   Records of the War Department: General and Special Staffs

Introduction

1. Spence, *Search for Modern China*, 474-78.
2. Levine, "On the Brink of Disaster: China and the U.S. in 1945," in Harding and Ming, *Sino-American Relations*, 9.
3. Clubb, *Twentieth Century China*, 108-22.
4. Hull, *Memoirs*, 2:1073, 1077, 1081-82.
5. Stimson and Bundy, *On Active Service in Peace and War*, 528.
6. R.H. Smith, *OSS: The Secret History*, 254.
7. *FRUS*, 1943, 5:624-25.
8. Report, July 25, 1943, OSS, NARA, RG 226.
9. Memo, Tolstoy to Buxton, Jan. 20, 1944, DS, NARA, RG 59.
10. Donovan to Dunn, April 14, 1944, DS, NARA, RG 59.
11. Memo, Davies to Gauss, March 9, 1943, DS, NARA, RG 59.
12. Memo, Davies to Department of State, Jan. 10, 1944, DS, NARA, RG 59.
13. Memo, Davies to Gauss, March 9, 1943, DS, NARA, RG 59.
14. Memo, Davies to Gauss, Sept. 17, 1943, DS, NARA, RG 59.
15. Memo, Davies to Department of State, Feb. 19, 1944, DS, NARA, RG 59.
16. Memo, Davies to Gauss, Nov. 15, 1943, DS, NARA, RG 59.
17. Memo, Davies to Department of State, Feb. 19, 1944, DS, NARA RG 59.

18. Ibid.

19. Memo, Davies to Gauss, Dec. 31. 1943, DS, NARA, RG 59.

20. Memo, Davies to Department of State, Jan. 15, 1944, DS, NARA, RG 59.

21. Ibid.

22. Rongqu, "China and East Asia in America's Global Strategy," in Iriye and Cohen, *American, Chinese, and Japanese Perspectives*, 283.

23. Clubb, *Twentieth Century China*, 238.

24. Zhang Baijia, "Chinese Policies toward the United States, 1937—1945," in Harding and Ming, *Sino-American Relations*, 21.

25. Barrett, *Dixie Mission*, 22-23.

26. Head, *Yenan!* 159.

27. Ibid., 33.

28. Ibid., 43.

29. Ibid., 161.

30. Ivan D. Yeaton, *Memoirs*, pt. 3, chap. 2, "China Story," Ivan D. Yeaton Papers.

31. Clifford F. Young, interview by Lt. Col. Patrick H. Gorman, Boulder, Colo. (undated copy supplied to author by Young)

32. Clifford F. Young, unpublished letters to Mrs. Young, March 23, 1946 (in author's possession).

33. Raymond Ludden, interview by author, South Yarmouth, Mass., July 1978.

34. "Historical Summary of Yenan Liaison Team, Shensi Province, China," undated and unsigned, Records of the Adjutant General's Office, World War II Operations Reports, Asiatic Theater, Peking Headquarters, Sec. III—Operations B, Jan. 5-Feb. 5, 1947, NARA, RG 407.

35. Goldstein, "Sino-American Relations," in Harding and Ming, *Sino-American Relations*, 125.

Chapter 1

1. Barrett, *Dixie Mission*, 22-23.

2. Davies, *Dragon by the Tail*, 196.

3. Memo, Davies, Jan. 15, 1944, DS, NARA, RG 59.

4. Garver, *Chinese-Soviet Relations*, 252-53.

5. Memo, Spencer to Langer and Fahs, June 14, 1944, OSS, NARA, RG 226.

6. General Alfred Wedemeyer, interview by author, Boyds, Md., Aug. 1978.

7. Handy to McFarland, Aug. 10, 1944, OSS, NARA, RG 226.

8. Memo, Hopkins to FDR, Feb. 2, 1944, SD, NARA, RG 59.

9. Memo, FDR to Chiang Kai-shek, Feb. 9, 1944, SD, NARA, RG 59.

10. Memo, Marshall to Leahy, Feb. 28, 1944, WD, NARA, RG 165.

11. Stettinius to Stimson, Feb. 25, 1944, WD, NARA, RG 165.

12. Memo, Stimson to Stettinius, March 7, 1944, WD, NARA, RG 165.

13. Feis, *China Tangle*, 305-15.

14. Stilwell to War Department, April 4, 1944, WD, NARA, RG 165.

15. Feis, *China Tangle,* 159-60.

16. Ibid., 145-56.

17. Service, *Amerasia Papers: Some Problems,* 141-44.

18. Feis, *China Tangle,* 145-56.

19. Davies, *Dragon by the Tail,* 305-6.

20. Seagrave, *Soong Dynasty,* 399.

21. Davies, *Dragon by the Tail,* 306.

22. Service, *Amerasia Papers: Some Problems,* 99.

23. Davies, *Dragon by the Tail,* 307-8.

24. Barrett, *Dixie Mission,* 22-23.

25. Davies, *Dragon by the Tail,* 308.

26. Ibid., 250-58.

27. Ibid., 305-15.

28. Feis, *China Tangle,* 145-56.

29. Henry A. Wallace, letter to *U.S. News and World Report,* Jan. 9, 1953.

30. Feis, *China Tangle,* 145-56.

31. Ibid., 156 n 12.

32. Davies, *Dragon by the Tail,* 309.

33. Service, *Amerasia Papers: Some Problems,* 67-68.

34. Memo, Spencer to Langer and Fahs, June 4, 1944, OSS, NARA, RG 226.

35. Memo, Handy to McFarland, Aug. 10, 1944, OSS, NARA, RG 226.

36. Memo, Spencer to Langer and Fahs, July 8, 1944, OSS, NARA, RG 226.

37. Memo, Handy to McFarland, Aug. 10, 1944, OSS, NARA, RG 226.

38. Davies, *Dragon by the Tail,* 318.

39. Barrett, *Dixie Mission,* 25.

40. Nancy Stilwell Easterbrook, interview by author, Carmel, Calif., Jan. 1977.

41. Barrett, *Dixie Mission,* 25.

42. "China," unsigned memo for the record dated July 4, 1944, WD, NARA, RG 165.

43. David D. Barrett, interview by author, San Francisco, Calif., Oct. 1976.

44. Barrett, *Dixie Mission,* 26-27.

45. Report No. 7, July 22-27, 1944, Barrett to Stilwell, OSS, NARA, RG 226.

46. Barrett, *Dixie Mission,* 14.

47. Report No. 7, July 22-27, 1944, Barrett to Stilwell, OSS, NARA, RG 226.

48. Memo, Spencer to Langer and Fahs, Aug. 1, 1944, OSS, NARA, RG 226.

49. Report No. 10, July 28-Aug. 14, 1944, Barrett to Stilwell, OSS, NARA, RG 226.

50. Barrett, *Dixie Mission,* 13.

51. Memo, Spencer to Langer and Fahs, Aug. 1, 1944, OSS, NARA, RG 226.

52. Special orders: No. 137, July 18, 1944, signed by Maj.-Gen. T.G. Hearn, GSC, WD, NARA, RG 165.

53. Klehr and Radosh, *Amerasia Spy Case,* 12-15.

54. Davies, *Dragon by the Tail,* 318-19.

55. Raymond Ludden, interview by author, South Yarmouth, Mass., Aug. 1978.

56. Davies, *Dragon by the Tail,* 355.

57. R.H. Smith, *OSS: The Secret History,* 262-65.

58. Paul Domke, interview by author, Honolulu, Hi., Dec. 1976.

59. *Tacoma News Tribune,* Sept. 26, 1976, C-1.

60. Condensation of *Yankee Samurai* by Joseph D. Harrington (Detroit, 1979), *Pacific Citizen,* May 11, 1979, 9-10.

61. Domke, interview, Dec. 1976.

62. Anton H. Remenih, interview by author, North Hollywood, Calif., April 1980.

63. Charles Dole, interview by author, San Francisco, Calif., April 1980.

64. U.S. Senate, *Amerasia Papers: A Clue,* 2:1731.

65. Barrett, *Dixie Mission,* 81-82.

66. Spengler, "American Liaison Groups," 61.

67. David D. Barrett, interview by author, San Francisco, Oct. 1976.

68. Clifford F. Young, interview by author, Honolulu, Hi., July 1978.

69. Service, *Lost Chance in China,* 26.

70. Zhang Baijia, "Chinese Policies toward the United States, 1937-1945," in Harding and Ming, *Sino-American Relations,* 21.

Chapter 2

1. Clifford F. Young, interviews by author, Honolulu, Hi., Aug. 1977 and July 1978.

2. Barrett, *Dixie Mission,* 29.

3. Young, interviews, Aug. 1977 and July 1978.

4. Barrett, *Dixie Mission,* 29.

5. Dr. Melvin A. Casberg, interview by author, Santa Barbara, Calif., July 1979.

6. Young, interviews, Aug. 1977 and July 1978.

7. Davies, *Dragon by the Tail,* 346.

8. Young, interviews, Aug. 1977 and July 1978.

9. Barrett, *Dixie Mission,* 49-55.

10. Young, interviews, Aug. 1977 and July 1978.

11. Barrett, *Dixie Mission,* 49-55.

12. Peterkin to Dickey, June 13, 1945, OSS, NARA, RG 226.

13. Tuchman, *Stilwell and the American Experience,* 611.

14. Young, interviews, Aug. 1977 and July 1978.

15. Memo, Wedemeyer to Commanding Officer, Yenan Observer Group, July 28, 1945, OSS, NARA, RG 226.

16. Memo, Hector to Davis for Heppner, Aug. 12, 1945, OSS, NARA. RG 226.

17. Memo, Stevens to Heppner, Aug. 9, 1945, OSS, NARA, RG 226.

18. Barrett, *Dixie Mission,* 35, 52, 55; Young, interviews, Aug. 1977 and July 1978.

19. Alfred Harding, interview by author, Washington, D.C., Aug. 1980.

20. Young, interviews, Aug. 1977 and July 1978.

21. Peterkin to Dickey, April 11, 1945, OSS, NARA, RG 226.

22. "Historical Summary of Yenan Liaison Team, Shensi Province, China," undated and unsigned, Records of the Adjutant General's Office, NARA, RG 407.

23. Peterkin to Dickey, April 11, 1945, OSS, NARA, RG 226.

24. Young, interviews, Aug. 1977 and July 1978.

25. Charles Dole, interview by author, San Francisco, Calif., May 1978.

26. Barrett, *Dixie Mission,* 89.

27. Peterkin to Dickey, April 25, 1945, OSS, NARA, RG 226; Clifford F. Young, unpublished letters to Mrs. Young (cited hereafter as Young, letters).

28. Dole, interview, May 1978.

29. Young, interviews, Aug. 1977 and July 1978.

30. Casberg, interview, July 1979.

31. Peterkin diary and letters to Mrs. Peterkin, Peterkin Papers, Hoover Institution.

32. Report of speech given by W.J. Peterkin to Gyro Club of Tacoma, Wash., Jan. 1946 (clipping provided the author by Peterkin).

33. Radio interview of W.J. Peterkin, Sumner, Wash., Dec. 13, 1945; transcript in author's possession.

34. Ivan Yeaton, interview by author, Rancho Santa Fe, Calif., Aug. 1979.

35. Report, ALUM-Hsian Field Team (also known as Team Chili), Oct. 5, 1945, OSS, NARA, RG 226.

36. Peterkin, radio interview.

37. Peterkin diary and letters to Mrs. Peterkin.

38. Peterkin speech to Gyro Club; copy in author's possession.

39. Barrett, *Dixie Mission,* 40-41, 85-86.

40. Ibid., 84; Wilbur J. Peterkin, interview by author, Sumner, Wash., Aug. 1976; Young, interviews, Aug. 1977 and July 1978.

41. Davies, *Dragon by the Tail,* 359-60.

42. Harding, interview, Aug. 1980.

43. Young, interviews, Aug. 1977 and July 1978, and letters.

44. Peterkin, interview by author, Sumner, Wash., Aug. 1976; Peterkin to Dickey, June 10, 1945, OSS, NARA, RG 226.

45. Davies, *Dragon by the Tail,* 355.

46. Testimony of John K. Emmerson, March 23, 1957, U.S. Senate, *Amerasia Papers: A Clue,* Appendix A, 2:1760.

47. Barrett, *Dixie Mission,* 35, 52, 55.

48. Davies, *Dragon by the Tail,* 355-59.

49. Casberg, "Go Ahead—Ask Me."

50. Casberg, interview, July 1979.

51. Barrett, *Dixie Mission,* 44.

52. Casberg, interview, July 1979.

53. Peterkin to Dickey, April 11, 1945, OSS, NARA, RG 226.

54. Young, interviews, Aug. 1977 and July 1978.

55. Davies, *Dragon by the Tail,* 361; Casberg, interview, July 1979.

56. U.S. Senate, *Amerasia Papers: A Clue,* 2:1444-45.

57. Casberg, interview, July 1979.

58. Telephone conversation with John Service, July 1993; U.S. Senate, *Amerasia Papers: A Clue,* 2:1444-45.

59. Young, interviews, Aug. 1977 and July 1978.

60. Barrett, *Dixie Mission,* 81-82; Casberg, interview, July 1979.

61. Young, letters, May 3, 1946.

Chapter 3

1. Garver, *Chinese-Soviet Relations,* 252-53.

2. Barrett, *Dixie Mission,* 34-35.

3. Cromley to Barrett, enclosure to Report No. 19, U.S. Army Observer Section, Sept. 28, 1944, OSS, NARA, RG 226.

4. John K. Emmerson, interview by author, Stanford, Calif., July 1977.

5. Memo, Pomeranze to Surgeon General, May 25, 1945, OSS, NARA, RG 226.

6. Davies, *Dragon by the Tail,* 86, 344, 353-55.

7. Emmerson, *Japanese Thread,* 195.

8. Ibid., 196-97.

9. Davies, *Dragon by the Tail,* 354.

10. Barrett, *Dixie Mission,* 34-35.

11. Emmerson, *Japanese Thread,* 190-94.

12. Arnold Dadian, interview by author, Washington, D.C., Aug. 1978.

13. Emmerson, *Japanese Thread,* 200.

14. Report, Emmerson, Jan. 1, 1945, OSS, NARA, RG 226.

15. Diary, Emmerson, Dec. 14, 1944 (made available to author by Emmerson).

16. Report, Emmerson, Nov. 7, 1944, OSS, NARA, RG 226.

17. Emmerson, interview, July 1977.

18. Report, Colling to Commanding General, China Theater, Dec. 11, 1944; report, Hitch to Naval Attaché at Chungking, Dec. 16, 1944, OSS, NARA, RG 226.

19. Emmerson, *Japanese Thread,* 193-95.

20. Koji Ariyoshi, Chungking Outpost Report, U.S. Senate, *Amerasia Papers: A Clue,* Jan. 31, 1945, 2:1364-71.

21. Service, Report No. 12 to Commanding General, Forward Echelon, Aug. 16, 1944, OSS, NARA, RG 226.

22. Emmerson, *Japanese Thread,* 195-97; Emmerson, interview, July 1977.

23. Koji Ariyoshi, Yenan Report No. 33, Dec. 28, 1944, U.S. Senate, *Amerasia Papers: A Clue,* 2:1186-90.

24. Koji Ariyoshi, Chungking Outpost Report to China Division OWI, Jan. 31, 1945, *Amerasia Papers: A Clue,* 2:1364-68.

25. Ibid., 1364-71.

26. Memo, Brown to Peterkin, China Theater, March 27, 1945; Report, Stelle to Heppner, April 12, 1945, OSS, NARA, RG 226; Dadian, interview, Aug. 1978.

27. Coffey, *Iron Eagle,* 120-21.

28. Memo, Dickey to Stilwell, Sept. 5, 1944, OSS, NARA, RG 226.

29. Barrett, *Dixie Mission,* 36-37.

30. Memo, Whittlesey to Commanding Officer, AGAS-China, Sept. 12, 1944, OSS, NARA, RG 226.

31. Whittlesey to Commanding Officer, AGAS-China, Sept. 15, 1944, OSS, NARA, RG 226.

32. Peterkin, *Dixie Mission Memoirs,* 30.

33. Service, Report No. 23, Sept. 6, 1944, U.S. Senate, *Amerasia Papers: A Clue,* 1:842-44.

34. Report No. 18, Barrett to Commanding General, Forward Echelon, Sept. 20. 1944, OSS, NARA, RG 226.

35. Report, Barrett to Commanding General, Sept. 9, 1944, OSS, NARA, RG 226.

36. Service, Report No. 23, Sept. 6, 1944, U.S. Senate, *Amerasia Papers: A Clue,* 1:842-43; Report No. 45, Oct. 15, 1944, *Amerasia Papers: A Clue,* 2:1082-83.

37. Barrett to Commanding General, Forward Echelon, Report No. 18, Sept. 20, 1944, OSS, NARA, RG 226.

38. Memo, Whittlesey to Commanding Officer, AGAS-China, Oct. 3, 1944, OSS, NARA, RG 226.

39. Report, Stelle to Spencer, Oct. 27, 1944, OSS, NARA, RG 226.

40. Memo, Cromley to Gen. Yeh Chien-ying, Jan. 20, 1945, OSS, NARA, RG 226.

41. Wilbur J. Peterkin, interview by author, Sumner, Wash., Aug. 1976.

42. Memo, Cromley to Gen. Yeh Chien-ying, Jan. 20, 1945, OSS, NARA, RG 226.

43. Report, Eaton to Commanding Officer, AGAS-China, May 3, 1945, OSS, NARA, RG 226.

44. Report, Eaton to Commanding Officer, AGAS-China, April 12, 1945, OSS, NARA, RG 226.

45. Eaton to Commanding Officer, AGAS-China, May 3, 1945, OSS, NARA, RG 226.

46. Peterkin to Dickey, May 7, 1945, OSS, NARA, RG 226.

47. Peterkin to Dickey, April 28, 1945, OSS, NARA, RG 226.

48. Memo, Whittlesey to AGAS-China, Oct. 20, 1944, OSS, NARA, RG 226.

49. Peterkin to Dickey, June 10, 1945, OSS, NARA, RG 226.

50. Report, Eaton to Commanding Officer, AGAS-China, April 12, 1945, OSS, NARA, RG 226.

51. Eaton to Commanding Officer, AGAS-China, May 3, 1945, OSS, NARA, RG 226.

52. Yeh Chien-ying to Yeaton, Oct. 4, 1945, OSS, NARA, RG 226.

53. Yeaton to Tsai Rho-hung, Dean of Art, Yenan University, Oct. 8, 1945, OSS, NARA, RG 226.

54. Edwards to Dickey, Jan. 18, 1945, OSS, NARA, RG 226.

55. Cromley and Barrett to OSS Headquarters, Chungking, and Commanding General, China Theater, Nov. 8, 1944, OSS, NARA, RG 226.

56. "History of the Clandestine Branch, G-5 Headquarters, U.S. Forces, China Theater," prepared by Maj. Martin F. Sullivan, Nov. 15, 1945 (document in author's possession).

57. Jack Klein, interview by author, San Francisco, Calif., Aug. 1977.

58. Clifford F. Young, unpublished letters to Mrs. Young, Dec. 19, 1945 (cited hereafter as Young, letters; copies in author's possession).

59. Charles Dole, interview by author, San Francisco, Calif., April 1980.

60. Memo, Dickey to Stilwell, Sept. 5, 1944, OSS, NARA, RG 226.

61. Young, letters, Nov. 30, 1945.

62. Report No. 19, U.S. Army Observer Section to Commanding General, Forward Echelon, Sept. 28, 1944, OSS, NARA, RG 226.

63. Peterkin to Dickey, April 11, 1945, OSS, NARA, RG 226.

64. Dole, interview, April 1980.

65. Barrett, *Dixie Mission*, 91.

66. Davies, *Dragon by the Tail*, 290.

67. Memo, Barrett to Acting Chief of Staff, G-2, Dec. 30, 1944, OSS, NARA, RG 226.

68. Memo, Edwards to Dickey, Jan. 12, 1945, OSS, NARA, RG 226.

69. Memo, Eaton to Commanding Officer, AGAS-China, May 1, 1945, OSS, NARA, RG 226.

70. Dickey to Peterkin, June 24, 1945, OSS, NARA, RG 226.

71. Klein, interview, Aug. 1977.

72. Peterkin to Dickey, May 6 and May 15, 1945, OSS, NARA, RG 226.

73. Memo, Remenih to Peterkin, May 21, 1945, OSS, NARA, RG 226.

74. Peterkin to Dickey, May 21, 1945, OSS, NARA, RG 226.

75. Petrkin to Dickey, June 24, 1945.

76. Memo, Yeaton to Chief of Staff, 18th Group Army, Aug. 8, 1945, OSS, NARA, RG 226.

77. "Historical Summary of Yenan Liaison Team, Shensi Province, China," undated and unsigned, Records of the Adjutant General's Office, NARA, RG 407.

78. Young, letters, Nov. 30 and Dec. 19, 1945.

79. Barrett, *Dixie Mission*, 91.

80. Raymond Ludden, interview by author, South Yarmouth, Mass., July 1978.

Chapter 4

1. Paul Domke, interview by author, Honolulu, Hi., Aug. 1978.
2. Anton H. Remenih, interview by author, North Hollywood, Calif., Aug. 1977.
3. Domke, interview, Aug. 1978.
4. Remenih, interview, Aug. 1977.
5. Jack Klein, interview by author, San Francisco, Calif., Aug. 1977.
6. Remenih, interview, Aug. 1977.
7. Klein, interview, Aug. 1977.
8. Report No. 1, Barrett to Commanding General, July 24, 1944, OSS, NARA, RG 226.
9. Yenan Signal 2 (radio) (cited hereafter as Yensig): Report, Domke to Commanding General, Forward Echelon, Chungking, Aug. 1, 1944, OSS, NARA, RG 226.
10. Memo, Dickey to Stilwell, Sept. 5, 1944, OSS, NARA, RG 226.
11. Yensig 3: Domke to Commanding General, Forward Echelon, Chungking, Aug. 22, 1944.
12. Yensig 10: Domke to Commanding General, Forward Echelon, Chungking, Nov. 17, 1944, OSS, NARA, RG 226.
13. Yensig 3: Aug. 22, 1944, OSS, NARA, RG 226.
14. Yensig 10: Nov. 17, 1944, OSS, NARA, RG 226.
15. Yensig 4: Domke to Commanding General, Forward Echelon, Chungking, Sept. 6, 1944, OSS, NARA, RG 226.
16. Memo, Foss to Headquarters, XX Bomber Command, Sept. 12, 1944, OSS, NARA, RG 226.
17. Memo, Whittlesey to Commanding Officer, AGAS-China, Sept. 15, 1944, OSS, NARA, RG 226.
18. Report, Eaton to Commanding Officer, AGAS-China, April 12, 1945, OSS, NARA, RG 226.
19. Memo, Emmerson to OWI, Nov. 7, 1944, OSS, NARA, RG 226.
20. Memo, Barrett to Commanding General, Forward Echelon, Sept. 28, 1944, OSS, NARA, RG 226.
21. Memo, Cromley to Mayer, Jan. 10, 1945, OSS, NARA, RG 226.
22. Memo, Stelle to Spencer, OSS R&A, Headquarters 14th Air Force, Oct. 27, 1944, OSS, NARA, RG 226.
23. Memo, Stelle to Heppner, SSO OSS China, May 1, 1945, OSS, NARA, RG 226.
24. Memo, Stelle to Spencer, Oct. 27, 1944, OSS, NARA, RG 226.
25. Memo, Stelle to Heppner, April 12, 1945, OSS, NARA, RG 226.
26. Memo, Stelle to Heppner, May 1, 1945, OSS, NARA, RG 226.
27. Memo, Heppner to Donovan, April 19, 1945, OSS, NARA, RG 226.
28. Memo, Gross to Commanding Officer, OSS, China Theater, April 25, 1945, OSS, NARA, RG 226.
29. Memo, Bird to Heppner, April 28, 1945, OSS, NARA, RG 226.

30. Yensig 15: Domke to Commanding General, Forward Echelon, Chungking, Feb. 12, 1945, OSS, NARA, RG 226.

31. Peterkin to Dickey, May 7, 1945, OSS, NARA, RG 226.

32. Peterkin to Dickey, May 15, 1945, OSS, NARA, RG 226.

33. Report by Remenih, May 21, 1945, OSS, NARA, RG 226.

34. Memo, Peterkin, Swenson, and Stelle to Heppner and Whittaker, June 2, 1945, OSS, NARA, RG 226.

35. Memo, Peterkin to Dickey, June 4, 1945, OSS, NARA, RG 226.

36. Memo, Stelle to Heppner, June 6, 1945, OSS, NARA, RG 226.

37. Yensig 12: Domke to Commanding General, Forward Echelon, Chungking, Jan. 5, 1945; Yensig 12: Domke to Commanding General, Forward Echelon, Chungking, Oct. 25, 1944, OSS, NARA, RG 226.

38. Yensig 17: Domke to Commanding General, Forward Echelon, Chungking, Jan. 27, 1945, OSS, NARA, RG 226.

39. Yensig 20: Domke to Commanding General, Forward Echelon, Chungking, Feb.17, 1945, OSS, NARA, RG 226.

40. Yensig 19: Domke to Commanding General, Forward Echelon, Chungking, Feb. 15, 1944, OSS, NARA, RG 226.

41. Yensig 17: Jan. 27, 1945, OSS, NARA, RG 226.

42. Yensig 20: Feb. 17, 1945, OSS, NARA, RG 226.

43. Memo, Hitch to Jarrell, Dec. 16, 1944, OSS, NARA, RG 226.

44. George Nakamura, interview by Capt. Robert L. Bodell, Theater Historian, 1946; copy in author's possession.

45. Peterkin to Dickey, June 4, 1945, OSS, NARA, RG 226.

46. Memo, Yeaton for the Chief of Staff, 18th Group Army, Aug. 8, 1945, OSS, NARA, RG 226.

47. Memo, Crawford to Stidd, Oct. 6, 1945, OSS, NARA, RG 226.

48. Unsigned directive, Signal Corps., U.S. Army, Nov. 3, 1945; copy in author's possession.

49. Memo, Maloney to Young, June 10, 1946, OSS, NARA, RG 226.

50. Clifford F. Young, interview by Lt. Col. Patrick H. Gorman, Boulder, Colo. (undated copy supplied to author by Young).

Chapter 5

1. Feis, *China Tangle,* 172-77.

2. Schaller, *U.S. Crusade in China,* 167.

3. Feis, *China Tangle,* 172-73.

4. Buhite, *Patrick J. Hurley,* 94-95.

5. Feis, *China Tangle,* 178-79.

6. Denning, *Sino-American Alliance,* 248.

7. U.S. Department of State, *United States Relations with China with Special Reference to the Period 1944-1949.* Department of State Publication No. 3573 (cited hereafter as *China White Paper*), 71-72.

8. Memo, Chief of Staff to the President, Aug. 12, 1944, OSS, NARA, RG 226.

9. *China White Paper,* 71-72.

10. Feis, *China Tangle,* 81-82.

11. Schaller, *U.S. Crusade in China,* 167.

12. Service, *Lost Chance in China,* 329-33.

13. Davies, *Dragon by the Tail,* 327.

14. Memo, Gauss to Hull, Aug. 31, 1944, and memo, Hull to Gauss, Sept. 9, 1944, *China White Paper,* 561-63, 563-64.

15. Davies, *Dragon by the Tail,* 328-31.

16. Service, *Amerasia Papers: Some Problems,* 64-65.

17. Memo, Stilwell to Chiang-Kai-shek, Sept. 19, 1944, OSS, NARA, RG 226.

18. U.S. Congress, Joint Committee on the Military Situation in the Far East, Hearings, 82d Cong., 1st Sess., 1951, 2868.

19. Davies, *Dragon by the Tail,* 351.

20. Unpublished papers of Joseph W. Stilwell, diary entry of Sept. 19, 1944, Stilwell Papers, Hoover Institution.

21. Davies, *Dragon by the Tail,* 332.

22. Feis, *China Tangle,* 191-92.

23. Schaller, *United States and China,* 171.

24. *China White Paper,* 69.

25. Davies, *Dragon by the Tail,* 336-38.

26. General Ernest Easterbrook, interview by author, Carmel, Calif., June 1977.

27. Feis, *China Tangle,* 201.

28. General Alfred Wedemeyer, interview by author, Boyds, Md., Aug. 1978.

29. Feis, *China Tangle,* 201-2.

30. Service, *Amerasia Papers: Some Problems,* 64-66.

31. Davies, *Dragon by the Tail,* 338-39.

32. Feis, *China Tangle,* 200; Clubb, *Twentieth Century China,* 241-42.

33. Schaller, *United States and China,* 90.

34. White, *In Search of History,* 235-36.

35. Fairbank, *Chinabound,* 294.

36. Memo, Domke to Peterkin, May 22, 1945, OSS, NARA, RG 226.

37. *China White Paper,* 73.

38. Schaller, *U.S. Crusade in China,* 171, 191-93.

39. Davies, *Dragon by the Tail,* 352.

40. Barrett, *Dixie Mission,* 56-57.

41. White, *In Search of History,* 264-66.

42. Barrett, *Dixie Mission,* 57.

43. White, *In Search of History,* 263-65.

44. Anton H. Remenih, interview by author, North Hollywood, Calif., Aug. 1977.

45. White, *In Search of History,* 265.

46. Louis Jones, interview by author, New Orleans, La., 1982.

47. *FRUS,* 1944, 6:674-77.

48. Barrett, *Dixie Mission,* 58.

49. Ibid., 61-62.

50. *China White Paper,* 73-75.

51. Barrett, *Dixie Mission,* 63-65.

52. Davies, *Dragon by the Tail,* 368, 379-80.

53. John K. Emmerson, interview by author, Stanford, Calif., July 1977.

54. Davies, *Dragon by the Tail,* 368, 379-80.

55. Denning, *Sino-American Alliance,* 248.

56. *China White Paper,* 75.

57. Schaller, *U.S. Crusade in China,* 198.

58. Barrett, *Dixie Mission,* 69-70.

59. Barrett to Wedemeyer, Dec. 10, 1944, *FRUS,* 1944, 6:727-32.

60. Barrett, *Dixie Mission,* 75.

61. Hurley to Chou En-Lai, Dec. 11, 1944, *FRUS,* 1944, 6:732-33; Chou En-Lai to Hurley, Dec. 16, 1944, *FRUS,* 1944, 6:739-40.

62. Hurley to the President, Nov. 29, 1944, WD, NARA, RG 165.

63. Feis, *China Tangle,* 360-61.

64. Wedemeyer to Mao, Aug. 22, 23, 25, 1945, OSS, NARA, RG 226.

65. Feis, *China Tangle,* 360-62.

66. Davies, *Dragon by the Tail,* 386.

67. Ibid., 416-19.

68. Buhite, *Patrick J. Hurley,* 268-74.

69. S. Herbert Hitch, interview by author, Charlotte, N.C., Oct. 19, 1988.

70. Schaller, *U.S. Crusade in China,* 168.

71. Quoted in Schaller, *United States and China,* 89.

72. Wedemeyer, interview, Aug. 1978.

73. *China White Paper,* 581-84.

74. Davies, *Dragon by the Tail,* 384-86.

75. Wedemeyer, interview, Aug. 1978.

76. Raymond Ludden, interview by author, South Yarmouth, Mass., July 1978.

77. Wedemeyer, interview, Aug. 1978.

78. Ludden, interview, July 1978.

79. Wedemeyer, interview, Aug. 1978.

80. Ludden, interview, July 1978.

81. *China White Paper,* 575-76.

82. Ibid., 87-92.

83. Schaller, *U.S. Crusade in China,* 207.

84. Buhite, *Patrick J. Hurley,* 188-93.

85. Memo, Domke to Peterkin, May 22, 1945, OSS, NARA, RG 226.

86. Buhite, *Patrick J. Hurley,* 202.

87. Ibid., 179-80, 190.

88. Wedemeyer, interview, Aug. 1978.

89. Telephone conversation with Russell Buhite, Feb. 2, 1989.

90. Domke to Peterkin, June 17, 1945, OSS, NARA, RG 226.

91. Ludden, interview, July 1978.

92. John S. Service, interview by author, Berkeley, Calif., April 1977.

93. David D. Barrett, interview by Dr. Forrest C. Pogue, Washington, D.C., Dec. 17, 1959.; interview in the possession of Pogue.

94. *Stars and Stripes,* Dec. 3 and 7, 1945.

95. Nancy Stilwell Easterbrook, interview by author, Carmel, Calif., Jan. 1977

96. Emmerson, interview, July 1977.

97. S. Herbert Hitch, interview by author, Charlotte, N.C., Oct. 19, 1988.

98. Charles Dole, interview by author, San Francisco, Calif., April 1980.

99. John Colling, interview by author, Palo Alto, Calif., Sept. 1977.

100. Remenih, interview, Aug. 1977.

101. Hitch, interview, Oct. 19, 1988.

102. R.H. Smith, *OSS: The Secret History,* 272.

103. F. MacCracken Fisher, interview by author, Riva, Md., Aug. 1978.

104. Buhite, *Patrick J. Hurley,* 191-92, 317-21.

105. Barrett, interview by Pogue, Dec. 17, 1959.

106. Emmerson, interview, July 1977.

107. Schaller, *U.S. Crusade in China,* 221-22.

108. Denning, *Sino-American Alliance,* 260-62.

Chapter 6

1. Schaller, *U.S. Crusade in China,* 200-201.

2. S. Herbert Hitch, interview by author, Charlotte, N.C., Oct. 19, 1988.

3. Ibid.

4. Ibid.

5. Ibid.

6. Report, the Assistant Naval Attaché to Naval Ataché, Dec. 16, 1944, OSS, NARA, RG 226.

7. Hitch, interview, Oct. 19, 1988.

8. U.S. Department of State, memo of conversation of Nov. 8, 1944, *FRUS,* 1944, 6:756.

9. Hitch, interview, Oct. 19, 1988.

10. Romanus and Sutherland, *Time Runs Out,* 72-75.

11. Barrett to Wedemeyer, Nov. 30, 1944, OSS, NARA, RG 226.; McClure, memo for the record, cited in Romanus and Sutherland, *Time Runs Out,* 72.

12. Barrett, *Dixie Mission,* 76.

13. Hurley to Chou En-lai, Dec. 11, 1944, *FRUS,* 1944, 6:739-40.

14. Barrett, *Dixie Mission,* 76.

15. *FRUS,* 1944, 6:739-40.

16. Ibid., 721-23.

17. Romanus and Sutherland, *Time Runs Out,* 75.

18. Minutes of meeting between General Chen Cheng and General Robert B. McClure, Dec. 19, 1944, OSS, NARA, RG 226

19. Barrett, *Dixie Mission,* 77-79.

20. Romanus and Sunderland, *Time Runs Out,* 251.

21. Schaller, *U.S. Crusade in China,* 204.

22. Barrett, *Dixie Mission,* 76-80.

23. Wedemeyer to Marshall, Jan. 22, 1945; Marshall to Wedemeyer, Jan. 22, 1945; Wedemeyer to Marshall, Jan. 23, 1945, OSS, NARA, RG 226.

24. Wedemeyer, *Wedemeyer Reports!* 303-6.

25. Wedemeyer to Marshall, OSS, NARA, RG 226.

26. David D. Barrett, interview by Forrest C. Pogue, Washington, D.C., Dec. 17, 1959.

27. Barrett, *Dixie Mission,* 78; General Alfred Wedemeyer, interview by author, Boyds, Md., Aug. 1978.

28. Wedemeyer, interview, Aug. 1978.

29. John S. Service, interview by author, Washington, D.C., April 1977.

30. Raymond Ludden, interview by author, South Yarmouth, Mass., July 1978.

31. Romanus and Sunderland, *Time Runs Out,* 251.

32. Wedemeyer, interview, Aug. 1978.

33. Fahs to Langer, Jan. 16, 1945, OSS, NARA, RG 226.

34. R.H. Smith, *OSS: The Secret History,* 273.

35. Wedemeyer, interview, Aug. 1978.

36. Bird to Chief-of-Staff, U.S. Forces, China Theater (McClure), Jan. 14, 1945, OSS, NARA, RG 226.

37. Wedemeyer to Marshall, Jan. 27, 1945, OSS, NARA, RG 226.

38. Schaller, *U.S. Crusade in China,* 203.

39. Davies, memo, Dec. 27, 1944, *FRUS,* 1944, 6:753-54.

40. Evans to Wedemeyer for Dickey, Jan. 10, 1945, OSS, NARA, RG 226.

41. Tuchman, "If Mao Had Come to Washington," 44-64.

42. Patrick J. Hurley Collection, Western History Collection, University of Oklahoma Library, Jan. 14, 1945.

43. Hurley to FDR, Jan. 14, 1945, OSS, NARA, RG 226.

44. Buhite, *Patrick J. Hurley,* 180.

45. Chu Teh to General Donovan (translation), Jan. 23, 1945, OSS, NARA, RG 226.

46. Schaller, *U.S. Crusade in China,* 204-6.

47. Tuchman, "If Mao Had Come to Washington," 44-64.

48. Ibid., 45-46.

49. Arnold Dadian, interview by author, Washington, D.C., Aug. 1978.

50. Buhite, *Patrick J. Hurley,* 180.

51. Wedemeyer to Joint Chiefs-of-Staff, Dec. 29, 1944, cited in Schaller, *U.S. Crusade in China,* 205.

52. R.H. Smith, *OSS: The Secret History,* 274.

Chapter 7

1. F. MacCracken Fisher, interview by author, Riva, Md., Aug. 1978.

2. Ariyoshi, "Steps to Civil War," A-13.

3. Kahn, *China Hands*, 164-65.

4. Fisher, interview, Aug. 1978.

5. Memo, Dickey to Stilwell, Sept. 5, 1944, OSS, NARA, RG 226.

6. General Thomas Van Natta, interview by author, Santa Barbara, Calif., July 1979.

7. Dr. Alfred Burden, interview by author, Lahaina, Hi., Aug. 1977.

8. Wilbur J. Peterkin, interview by author, Sumner, Wash., Aug. 1976.

9. Burden, interview, Aug. 1977.

10. Van Natta, interview, July 1979.

11. Burden, interview, Aug. 1977.

12. Colonel Wilfred Smith, interview by author, Washington, D.C., July 1980.

13. Burden, interview, Aug. 1977.

14. Report, ALUM-Hsian Field Team (also known as Team Chili), Oct. 5, 1945, OSS, NARA, RG 226.

15. Dickey to Wedemeyer, Jan. 10, 1945, Patrick J. Hurley Collection, Western History Collection, University of Oklahoma Library.

16. Fairbank, *Chinabound*, 215-18.

17. Miles, *A Different Kind of War*, 116-19.

18. Romanus and Sunderland, *Time Runs Out*, 158-60.

19. General Alfred Wedemeyer, interview by author, Boyds, Md., Aug. 1978.

20. Miles, *A Different Kind of War*, 12-18.

21. Romanus and Sunderland, *Time Runs Out*, 158.

22. Schaller, *U.S. Crusade in China*, 246-47.

23. Fairbank, *Chinabound*, 219.

24. Schaller, *U.S. Crusade in China*, 235.

25. Herbert Little, interview, cited in R.H. Smith, *OSS: The Secret History*, 255-57.

26. Ibid., 257.

27. Fairbank, *Chinabound*, 221.

28. Memo, Wessels to Sultan, May 25, 1944; radio, Marshall to Stilwell, June 18, 1944, OSS, NARA, RG 226.

29. Schaller, *U.S. Crusade in China*, 239.

30. S. Herbert Hitch, interview by author, Charlotte, N.C., Oct. 19, 1988.

31. Schaller, *U.S. Crusade in China*, 240-42.

32. Wedemeyer, interview, Aug. 1978.

33. Smith, interview, July 1980.

34. Miles, *A Different Kind of War*, 344-45, 457-58.

35. Schaller, *U.S. Crusade in China*, 246-47.

36. Miles, *A Different Kind of War*, 492-95.

37. Schaller, *U.S. Crusade in China*, 248-49; Wedemeyer, interview, Aug. 1978.

38. Schaller, *U.S. Crusade in China*, 250.

39. Miles, *A Different Kind of War*, 343-44.

40. Seagrave, *Soong Dynasty*, 397.

41. Davies, *Dragon by the Tail*, 277-88.

42. Smith, interview, July 1980.

43. Memo, Spencer to Langer, attention Berni Hanson, July 12, 1944, OSS, NARA, RG 226.

44. Dunlop, *Donovan*, 426.

45. Davies, *Dragon by the Tail*, 286-87.

46. Dunlop, *Donovan*, 426.

47. Smith, interview, July 1980.

48. Davies, *Dragon by the Tail*, 287.

49. Smith, interview, July 1980.

50. Undated memo, Hykes to Hoffman, OSS, NARA, RG 226.

51. Memo, Coughlin to General Tai Li, Jan 7, 1944, OSS, NARA, RG 226.

52. Memo, Hykes, Feb. 24, 1944, OSS, NARA, RG 226.

53. Smith, interview, July 1980.

54. Memo, Hykes, March 22, 1944, OSS, NARA, RG 226.

55. Undated memo, Hykes to Coughlin, OSS, NARA, RG 226.

56. Smith, interview, July 1980.

57. Memo, Coughlin to Donovan, May 6, 1944, OSS, NARA, RG 226.

58. Colonel John G. Coughlin, interview by author, Sun City, Ariz, Dec. 1978.

59. Caldwell, *A Secret War*, 56-57.

60. Ford, *Donovan of OSS*, 168.

61. Smith, interview, July 1980.

62. R.H. Smith, *OSS: The Secret History*, 261.

63. Official Dispatch, Donovan to Coughlin, March 16, 1944, OSS, NARA, RG 226.

64. Memo, Buxton to Donovan, Oct. 25, 1944, OSS, NARA, RG 226.

65. Fisher, interview, Aug. 1978.

66. Ford, *Donovan of OSS*, 270.

67. Memo, Heppner to Donovan, April 20, 1945, OSS, NARA, RG 226.

68. Minutes of weekly staff meeting, OSS Headquarters, China Headquarters, July 11, 1945, OSS, NARA, RG 226.

69. Fisher, interview, Aug. 1978.

70. Romanus and Sunderland, *Time Runs Out*, 158-60.

71. Van Natta, interview, July 1979.

72. Coughlin, interview, Dec. 1978.

73. Schaller, *U.S. Crusade in China*, 232.

74. Coughlin, interview, Dec. 1978.

75. Ford, *Donovan of OSS*, 275.

76. Smith, interview, July 1980.

77. Memo, Colling to Theater Commander and Peers, Aug. 30, 1944, OSS, NARA, RG 226.

78. Memos, Spencer to Langer and Fahs, July 4 and 8, 1944, OSS, NARA, RG 226.

79. Barrett to Commanding General, Forward Echelon, Aug. 6, 1944, OSS, NARA, RG 226.

80. Memo, Stelle and Colling to Hall and Peers, Aug. 7, 1944, OSS, NARA, RG 226.

81. Dickey to Barrett, Aug. 19, 1944, OSS, NARA, RG 226.

82. Report, Cromley, July 31, 1944, OSS, NARA, RG 226.

83. Memo, Dickey to Stilwell, Sept. 5, 1944, OSS, NARA, RG 226.

84. Memo, Coughlin to Cromley, Sept. 12, 1944, OSS, NARA, RG 226.

85. Barrett to Dickey, Aug. 27, 1944, OSS, NARA, RG 226.

86. Memo, Dickey to Stilwell, Sept. 5, 1944, OSS, NARA, RG 226.

87. Memo, Stelle to Spencer, Oct. 27, 1944, OSS, NARA, RG 226.

88. Ibid.

89. Smith, interview, July 1980.

90. Peterkin to Dickey, June 4, 1945, OSS, NARA, RG 226.

91. Yeaton to Mao Tse-tung, Aug. 5, 1945, OSS, NARA, RG 226.

92. "History of Special Operations Branch, Oct. 1944-Aug. 1945" (made available to the author by Betty Heppner McIntosh).

93. Memo, Heppner to Opso and Wampler, June 11, 1945, OSS, NARA, RG 226.

94. Peterkin to Dickey, June 4, 1945, OSS, NARA, RG 226.

95. Memo, Davis to Commanding General, attention Assistant Chief-of-Staff, G-5, July 31, 1945, OSS, NARA, RG 226.

96. Memo, Theater Headquarters to OSS Chief, China Theater, Aug. 3, 1945, OSS, NARA, RG 336.

97. Memo, Krause to Heppner, Aug. 14, 1945, OSS, NARA, RG 226.

98. Statement of First Lt. Tung Chin-sheng, Oct. 3, 1945, OSS, NARA, RG 226.

99. Ibid.

100. Memo, Thomson to Krause, Sept. 14, 1945, OSS, NARA, RG 226.

101. "History of the Clandestine Branch, G-5 Section, Headquarters, United States Forces, China Theater," by Maj. Martin F. Sullivan, Nov. 15, 1945, OSS, NARA, RG 226.

102. Relay of NR 935 to Kunming from Hsian, Sept. 16, 1945, OSS, NARA, RG 226.

103. Statement of First Lt. Tung Chin-sheng, Oct. 3, 1945, OSS, NARA, RG 226.

104. Colonel Gustav Krause, interview by author, Los Angeles, Calif., Aug. 1979; Smith, interview, July 1980.

105. Letter for signature, Dickey to Commanding General, Army Air Force, China Theater, Dec. 6, 1945, OSS, NARA, RG 226.

106. Clifford Young, interviews by author, August 1977 and July 1978.

107. Smith, interview, July 1980.

Chapter 8

1. Hurley to Truman, Nov. 26, 1945.

2. Schaller, *U.S. Crusade in China,* 287-88.

3. *Stars and Stripes,* Dec. 3, 1945.

4. David D. Barrett, interview by Forrest C. Pogue, Washington, D.C., Dec. 17, 1959.

5. Colonel John G. Coughlin, interview by author, Sun City, Ariz., Dec. 1978.

6. Schaller; *U.S. Crusade in China,* 296; General Albert Wedemeyer, interview by author, Boyds, Md., Aug. 1978.

7. Wedemeyer, interview, Aug. 1978.

8. Barrett, interview by Pogue, Dec. 17, 1959.

9. Clifford F. Young, unpublished letters to Mrs. Young, July 10, 1945 (cited hereafter as Young, letters) (copies in author's posession).

10. U.S. Department of State, *United States Relations with China, with Special Reference to the Period 1944-1949.* Publication 3573 (cited hereafter as *China White Paper),* 135-36.

11. China cables, Nov. 1945-May 1946, Wilbur and Bloomfield to Langer, Dec. 9, 1945, OSS, NARA, RG 226.

12. Schaller, *U.S. Crusade in China,* 295-96.

13. History of the Executive Headquarters, Peiping, China (cited hereafter as "Headquarters History"); made available to the author by Cifford F. Young.

14. S. Herbert Hitch, interview by author, Charlotte, N.C., Oct. 19, 1988.

15. Ivan Yeaton, interview by author, Rancho Santa Fe, Calif., Aug. 1979.

16. Ivan Yeaton, Memoirs, 40-46, Yeaton Papers, Hoover Institution.

17. Young, letters, Jan. 8, 1946.

18. Yeaton, interview, Aug. 1979.

19. Alfred Harding, interview by author, Washington, D.C., Aug. 1980.

20. Yeaton, Memoirs, 43.

21. Young letters, Jan. 25, 1946.

22. *Headquarters History,* 14.

23. Young, letters, March 5, 1946.

24. Yeaton, Memoirs, 44-45.

25. Pogue, *George C. Marshall,* 101-2.

26. Young, letters, March 5, 1946.

27. Pogue, *George C. Marshall,* 102.

28. Yeaton, Memoirs, 45.

29. Buhite, *Soviet American Relations,* 55.

30. Rongqu, "China and East Asia in America's Global Strategy," in Iriye and Cohen, *Perspectives on Wartime China,* 286.

31. Yeaton, Memoirs, 45.

32. Young, letters, March 5, 1946.

33. "Historical Summary of Yenan Liaison Team, Shensi Province, China," undated and unsigned, World War II Operations Reports, Asiatic Theater, Peking Headquarters, Sec. III, Operations B, Jan.5-Feb. 5, 1947, 3, Records of the Adjutant General's Office, NARA, RG 407 (cited hereafter as "Historical Summary" AGO, NARA, RG 407).

34. Young, letters, March 5, 1946.

35. Yeaton, interview, Aug. 1979.

36. Yeaton, Memoirs, 46.

37. Clifford F. Young, interview by Lt. Col. Patrick H. Gorman, Boulder, Colo. (undated copy supplied to author by Young).

38. Clifford Young, interviews by author, Aug. 1977 and July 1978.

39. U.S. Department of State, minutes of meeting between Gen. Marshall and Gen. Chou En-lai, Nanking, June 27, 1946, *FRUS*, 1946, 9:1218-24.

40. *China White Paper*, 145.

41. *Headquarters History*, 14-16.

42. *China White Paper*, 626-27.

43. *Headquerters History*, 16.

45. *China White Paper*, 149.

46. Barrett, interview, Dec. 17, 1959.

46. General Thomas Van Natta, interview by author, Santa Barbara, Calif., July 1979.

47. Pogue, *George C. Marshall*, 142.

48. Van Natta, interview, July 1979.

49. Schaller, *U.S. Crusade in China*, 300-301.

50. Press release by Department of State, Jan. 29, 1947, *China White Paper*, 695.

51. *China White Paper*, 686.

52. Ibid., 219-20.

53. Tuchman, *Stilwell and the American Experience*, 68, 620-22.

54. Press release by the Department of State, Jan. 29, 1947, *China White Paper*, 695.

55. "Historical Summary," AGO, NARA, RG 407.

56. "Extract from the Second Quarter Report of the History of the Yenan Liaison Group," undated, AGO, NARA, RG 407 (cited hereafter as "Extract," AGO, NARA, RG 407).

57. "U.S. Observer Group Leaves Yenan," *Shanghai Evening Post and Mercury*, April 21, 1946.

58. Young, interview by Gorman, n.d.

59. "Extract," AGO, NARA, RG 407.

60. "Historical Summary," AGO, NARA, RG 407.

61. U.S. Department of the Army, "Record of Events, 1946-1947, Yenan Observer Group," Army Intelligence File, NARA, RG 319 (cited hereafter as "Record of Events," Army Intelligence, NARA, RG 319).

62. "Historical Summary," AGO, NARA, RG 407.

63. "Record of Events," Army Intelligence, NARA, RG 319.

64. "Historical Summary," AGO, NARA, RG 407.

65. *Headquarters History*, 20-24.

66. Memo, Robertson to Gen. Cheng Kai-min, July 23, 1946, OSS, NARA, RG 226.

67. Butler to Kaiser, Nov. 12, 1946, OSS, NARA, RG 226.

68. *Headquarters History*, 20-24.

69. Ward to Sells, Feb. 19, 1947, OSS, NARA, RG 226.

70. Lau to Sells, Feb. 3, 1947, and Sells to Lau, Feb. 18, 1947, OSS, NARA, RG 226.

71. "Historical Summary," AGO, NARA, RG 407.

72. Young, letters, Aug. 8, 1946.

73. Young, letters, June 12, 1946.

74. Young, letters, June 17, 1946.

75. "Historical Summary," AGO, NARA, RG 407.

76. Young, letters, June 12, 1946.

77. Young, interview by Gorman, n.d.

78. Young, letters, June 12, 1946.

79. Young, letters, July 17, 1946.

80. Young, letters, July 14, 1946.

81. Ibid.

82. "Record of Events," Army Intelligence, NARA, RG 319.

83. Young, letters, July 14, 1946.

84. Young, letters, May 14, 1946.

85. Young, letters, Aug. 20, 1946.

86. "Historical Summary," AGO, NARA, RG 407.

87. "Record of Events," Army Intelligence, NARA, RG 319.

Chapter 9

1. Clifford F. Young, unpublished letters to Mrs. Young (cited hereafter as Young, letters; copies in the author's possession), March 23, 1946.

2. Clifford F. Young, interview by Lt. Col Patrick H. Gorman, Boulder, Colo., n.d.

3. David D. Barrett, interview by Forrest C. Pogue, Washington, D.C., Dec. 17, 1959.

4. Memo, Barrett to Commanding General, U.S. Army Forces, China, Burma, and India, Aug. 27, 1944, OSS, NARA, RG 226.

5. Wilbur J. Peterkin, interview by author, Sumner, Wash., Aug. 1976.

6. Head, *Yenan!* 116-20.

7. Ivan Yeaton, interview by author, Rancho Santa Fe, Calif., Aug. 1979.

8. Barrett, interview by Pogue, Dec. 17, 1959.

9. Yeaton, interview, Aug. 1979.

10. James Reardon-Anderson, *Yenan and the Great Powers,* quoted in Levine, "On the Brink of Disaster: China and the U.S. in 1945," in Harding and Ming, *Sino-American Relations,* 9.

11. Morris De Pass served briefly after Barrett left. Colonel Ivan D. Yeaton probably wrote this personal, undated letter to General Alfred Wedemeyer shortly after he took command of the Dixie Mission in July 1945.

12. Yeaton, interview, Aug. 1979.

13. Personal, undated letter from Yeaton to Wedemeyer, OSS, NARA, RG 226.

14. Yeaton, interview, Aug. 1979; Report, Yeaton to Wedemeyer, April 15, 1946, OSS, NARA, RG 226.

15. Meeker and Greene to Helliwell and Spencer (radio), Sept. 13, 1945, OSS, NARA, RG 226.

16. Memo, Meeker to Chief, Research and Intelligence Service, China, Oct. 25, 1945, OSS, NARA, RG 226.

17. Young, letters, Feb. 16 and March 26, 1946.

18. Yeaton, interview, Aug. 1979.

19. Ibid.; Yeaton, Memoirs, 1987.

20. Yeaton, interview, Aug. 1979.

21. General Thomas Van Natta, interview by author, Santa Barbara, Calif., July 1979.

22. Wilbur J. Peterkin, interview, Aug. 1976.

23. Anton H. Remenih, interview by author, North Hollywood, Calif., Aug. 1977.

24. Raymond Ludden, interview by author, South Yarmouth, Mass., July 1978.

25. S. Herbert Hitch, interview by author, Charlotte, N.C., Oct. 19, 1988.

26. Arnold Dadian, interview by author, Washington, D.C., Aug. 1978.

27. Hitch, interview, Oct. 19, 1988.

28. Remenih, interview, Aug. 1977.

29. Dr. Melvin A. Casberg, interview by author, Santa Barbara, Calif., July 1979.

30. Hitch, interview, Oct. 19, 1988.

31. Colonel Gustav Krause, interview by author, Los Angeles, Calif., Aug. 1979.

32. John S. Service, interview by author, Berkeley, Calif., April 1977.

33. Ludden, interview, July 1978.

34. Paul Domke, interview by author, Honolulu, Ii., Aug. 1978.

35. Remenih, interview, Aug. 1977.

36. Alfred Harding, interview by author, Washington, D.C., Aug. 1980.

37. Jack Klein, interview by author, San Francisco, Calif., Aug. 1977.

38. Lu Zhengrong, quoted in "Mao's Plan to Support US Soldiers Disclosed," *Beijing Review,* Dec. 1990.

39. Hitch, interview, Oct. 19, 1988.

40. Report, ALUM-Hsian Field Team (also known as Team Chili), Oct. 5, 1945, OSS, NARA, RG 226.

41. Memo, Coughlin to Commanding Officer, OSS SU Det 627, Attn: Capt. Charles Stelle, Oct. 21, 1944, OSS, NARA, RG 226.

42. General Alfred Wedemeyer, interview by author, Boyds, Md., Aug. 1978.

43. Cline, *Secrets, Spies, and Scholars,* 75.

44. Memo, Quentin Roosevelt to Heppner, May 3, 1945, OSS, NARA, RG 226.

45. Levine, "On the Brink of Disaster," 8-9.

46. Kenneth Lau, interview by author, Honolulu, Hi., July 1979.

47. Van Natta, interview, July 1979.

48. U.S. Forces, *History of XX Bomber Command, Oct. 1944-March 1945,* vol. 3, Appendix IV.

49. Fairbank, *Chinabound,* 265, 293.

50. Israel Epstein, interview by author, Beijing, People's Republic of China, June 1991.

51. Roderick, *Covering China,* 30-31.

52. Ibid., 34-35.

53. Ludden, interview, July 1978.

54. Fr. Cormac Shanahan, "China's Communist Puzzle," 9-12.

55. White, *In Search of History,* 240-70 passim.

56. MacKinnon, "On Shooting the Messengers."

57. Gillem to Gibney, March 31, 1960, OSS, NARA, RG 226.

58. Ludden, interview, July 1978.

59. Ludden to Mrs. Wilbur J. Peterkin, April 23, 1945.

60. Charles Dole, interview by author, San Francisco, Calif., April 1980.

61. Wedemeyer, interview, Aug. 1978.

62. Buhite, *Patrick J. Hurley,* 194-200.

63. Coughlin to Dickey, Oct. 21, 1944, OSS, NARA, RG 226.

64. Miles, *A Different Kind of War,* 342-43.

65. Chalmers Johnson, Foreword, in Service, *Amerasia Papers: Some Problems,* 9.

66. Ludden, interview, July 1978.

67. Wedemeyer, interview, Aug. 1978.

68. John K. Emmerson, unpublished manuscript, "Yenan" (provided to the author, 1978).

69. Martin F. Herz, Foreword, in Emmerson, *A View from Yenan,* Institute for the Study of Diplomacy, Edmund A. Walsh School of Foreign Service, Georgetown University.

70. Wedemeyer, interview, Aug. 1978.

71. Davies, *Dragon by the Tail,* 10.

72. Gross, "John Paton Davies," 82.

73. David D. Barrett, interview by Forrest C. Pogue, Washington, D.C., Dec. 17, 1959.

74. Ibid.

75. Barrett, *Dixie Mission,* 91.

76. General William Ray Peers, interview by author, Larkspur, Calif., April 1979.

77. Krause, interview, Aug. 1979.

78. Report, ALUM-Hsian Field Team, Oct. 5, 1945, OSS, NARA, RG 226.

79. Cline, *Secrets, Spies, and Scholars,* 75.

80. Claude Buss, interview by author, Palo Alto, Calif., Jan. 1982.

81. Tozer, "Foreign Correspondents' Visit," 220-24.

82. Young, letters, Aug. 16, 1946.

83. Proposed radio message from Yeh Chi'ien-ying to Gillem, Feb. 24, 1947, OSS, NARA, RG 226.

84. Garver, *Chinese-Soviet Relations,* 254-55.

85. Service, interview, April 1977.

86. Ludden, interview, July 1978.

87. Carlton Swift, interview by author, Washington, D.C., Aug. 1978.

88. Memo, Spencer to Wilbur, attention William L. Langer, May 15, 1945, OSS, NARA, RG 226.

89. Young, interview by Gorman, n.d.

90. Stanton to Sells, Feb. 1, 1947; Stanton to Kaiser, Feb. 4, 1947, OSS, NARA, RG 226.

91. Yeh Chien-ying to Gillem, letter for transmittal, March 1, 1947, OSS, NARA, RG 226.

92. Sells to Yeh Ch'ien-ying, Feb. 24, 1947, OSS, NARA, RG 226.

93. Dole, interview, April 1980.

94. Klein, interview, Aug. 1977.

95. Memo, H.L.H. (Harry L. Hopkins) for the President, Feb. 2, 1944, OSS, NARA, RG 226.

96. Interim Report, Oct. 30, 1945, 12-13, 16, OSS, NARA, RG 226.

97. Dr. Alfred Burden, interview by author, Lahaina, Hi., Aug. 1977.

98. Klein, interview, Aug. 1977.

99. Young, interview by Gorman, n.d.

100. Schaller, *U.S. Crusade in China,* 228-29.

101. Dadian, interview, Aug. 1978.

102. Louis Jones, interview by author, New Orleans, La., Dec. 1988.

103. Hitch, interview, Oct. 19, 1988.

104. Jonesinterview, Dec. 1988.

105. Barrett, *Dixie Mission,* 89.

106. Hitch, interview, Oct. 19, 1988.

107. Iriye, *Across the Pacific,* 301.

108. Colonel Wilfred Smith, interview by author, Washington, D.C., July 1980.

109. Rhea C. Blue, interview by author, Walnut Creek, Calif., Aug. 1978.

110. Ludden, interview, July 1978.

111. Wedemeyer, interview, Aug. 1978.

112. Smith, interview, July 1980.

113. Rongqu, "China and East Asia in America's Global Strategy," in Iriye and Cohen, *American, Chinese, and Japanese Perspectives on Wartime Asia,* 283.

Bibliography

Interviews by the Author

Alsop, Joseph. Washington, D.C., July 1980.

Barrett, David D. San Francisco, Calif., Oct. 1976.

Blue, Rhea C. Walnut Creek, Calif., Aug. 1978.

Buhite, Russell D. telephone conversation, Feb. 2, 1989.

Burden, Alfred, M.D. Lahaina, Hi., Aug. 1977.

Buss, Claude. Palo Alto, Calif., Jan. 1982.

Casberg, Melvin A., M.D. Santa Barbara, Calif., July 1979.

Colling, John. Palo Alto, Calif., Sept. 1977.

Coughlin, John. Sun City, Ariz, Dec. 1978.

Dadian, Arnold. Washington, D.C., Aug. 1978.

Dole, Charles. San Francisco, Calif., May 1978, April 1980.

Domke, Paul C. Honolulu, Hi., Dec. 1976, Aug. 1978.

Easterbrook, Maj. Gen. Ernest. Carmel, Calif., June 1977.

Easterbrook, Nancy Stilwell. Carmel, Calif., Jan. 1977.

Emmerson, John K. Stanford, Calif., July 1977.

Epstein, Israel. Beijing, People's Republic of China, June 1991.

Fisher, F. MacCracken. Riva, Md., Aug. 1978.

Harding, Alfred. Washington, D.C., Aug. 1980.

Hitch, S. Herbert. Charlotte, N.C., Oct. 19, 1988.

Jones, Louis. New Orleans, La., 1982, Dec. 1988.

Klein, Jack. San Francisco, Calif., Aug. 1977.

Krause, Gustav. Los Angeles, Calif., Aug. 1979.

Lau, Kenneth. Honolulu, Hi., July 1979.

Ludden, Ray. South Yarmouth, Mass., July 1978.

Ma Haide, Sufei. Beijing, People's Republic of China, May 1991.

McIntosh, Elizabeth P. MacDonald. Leesburg, Va., July-Aug. 1978.

Peers, Lt. Gen. William R. Larkspur, Calif., April 1979.

Peterkin, Wilbur J. Sumner, Wash., Aug. 1976

Pogue, Forrest. Washington, D.C., July-Aug. 1978.

Remenih, Anton. North Hollywood, Calif., Aug. 1977, April 1980.

Romanus, Charles. Washington, D.C., July-Aug. 1978.

Service, John S. Berkeley, Calif., April 1977.

Smith, Wilfred. Washington, D.C., July 1980.

Swift, Carlton. Washington, D.C., Aug. 1978.

Taylor, Gen. Frank. Washington, D.C., Aug. 1978.

Van Natta, Gen. Thomas. Santa Barbara, Calif., July 1979.

Varoff, George. San Antonio, Tex., Feb. 1990.

Wedemeyer, Gen. Albert C. Boyds, Md., Aug. 1978.

Yeaton, Ivan D. Rancho Santa Fe, Calif., Aug. 1979.

Young, Clifford F. Honolulu, Hi., Aug. 1977 and July 1978.

Archival Collections

Hoover Institution on War, Revolution and Peace, Stanford University, Stanford, Calif.

Barrett, David D. Papers.

Davies, John P., Jr. Papers.

Hornbeck, Stanley K. Papers.

Peterkin, Wilbur J. Papers.

Stilwell, Joseph W. Papers.

Wedemeyer, General Albert C. Papers.

Yeaton, Ivan D. Papers.

U.S. Army Military History Institute. Carlisle Barracks, Penn.

Papers of Lt. Gen. Alvan C. Gillem, Department of the Army.

Papers of Lt. Gen. L.J. Lincoln. "Transcript of an Interview of Lincoln by Col. Pappas and Dr. E. Miller," Oct. 28, 1971.

U.S. National Archives, Washington, D.C., and Suitland, Md.

Record Group 59, General Records of the Department of State

Record Group 165, Records of the War Department: General and Special Staffs

Record Group 226, Records of the Office of Strategic Services

Record Group 319, Army Intelligence File

Record Group 407, Records of the Adjutant General's Office, World War II Operations Reports, Asiatic Theater, Peking Headquarters, Sec. III— Operations B, Jan. 5-Feb. 5, 1947

University of Oklahoma Library, Norman, Okla. Western History Collection.

Hurley, Patrick J. Papers.

Government Documents

U.S. Congress. Senate Committee on the Judiciary, Subcommittee to Investigate the Administration of the Internal Security Act and the Other Internal Security Laws. *The Amerasia Papers: A Clue to the Catastrophe of China.* 2 vols. Washington, D.C., 1970.

U.S. Department of State. *U.S. Relations with China, with Special Reference to the Period 1944-1949.* Publication 3573. Washington, D.C., 1949.

————. *Foreign Relations of the United States: Diplomatic Papers, 1942. China.* Washington, D.C., 1956.

————. *1943. China.* Washington, D.C., 1957.

————. *1944.* Vol. 6. *China.* Washington, D.C., 1967.

————. *1945.* Vol. 7. *The Far East: China.* Washington, D.C., 1969.

————. *1946.* Vol. 9. *The Far East: China.* Washington, D.C., 1972.

U.S. Forces. "History of the XX Bomber Command, October 1944-March 1945." Vol. 3, appendix IV; copy in author's possession.

U.S. Forces. China Theater. "History of the Clandestine Branch, G-5 Section, Headquarters." Prepared by Major Martin F. Sullivan. Office, Chief of Military History, Nov. 15, 1945; copy in author's possession.

U.S. Strategic Bombing Survey. *Air Operations in China, Burma, India.* Washington, D.C., 1947.

U.S. War Department, Strategic Services Unit. *Overseas Targets: War Report of the OSS.* Vol. 2. New York, 1976.

Books and Dissertations

Baijia, Zhang. "Chinese Policies towards the United States, 1937-1945." In Harry Harding and Yuan Ming, eds., *Sino-American Relations, 1945-1955: A Joint Reassessment of a Critical Decade.* Wilmington, Del., 1989.

Barrett, David D. *Dixie Mission: The United States Army Observer Group in Yenan, 1944.* Berkeley, 1970.

Bernstein, Barton J., and Allen J. Matusow, eds. *The Truman Administration: A Documentary History.* New York, 1966.

Bianco, Lucien. *Origins of the Chinese Revolution, 1915-1949.* Stanford, Calif., 1967.

Bodde, Derek. *Peking Diary: 1948-1949, a Year of Revolution.* Greenwich, Conn., 1967.

Boyle, John Hunter. *China and Japan at War, 1937-1945: The Politics of Collaboration.* Stanford, Calif., 1972.

Brown, Anthony Cave. *The Secret War Report of the OSS.* New York, 1976.

Buhite, Russell D. *Decisions at Yalta: An Appraisal of Summit Diplomacy.* Wilmington, Del., 1986.

———. *Patrick J. Hurley and American Foreign Policy.* Ithaca, N.Y., 1973.

———. *Soviet-American Relations in Asia, 1945-1954.* Norman, Okla., 1981.

Caldwell, Oliver J. *A Secret War: Americans in China, 1944-1945.* Carbondale, Ill., 1972.

Carlson, Evans F. *Chinese Army.* New York, 1940.

———. *Twin Stars over China.* New York, 1940.

Chennault, Claire. *Way of a Fighter.* New York, 1949.

Clemens, Diane Shaver. *Yalta.* New York, 1970.

Cline, Ray S. *Secrets, Spies, and Scholars.* New York, 1976.

Clubb, O. Edmund. *Twentieth Century China.* New York, 1964.

———. *The Witness and I.* New York, 1974.

Coffey, Thomas M. *Iron Eagle: The Turbulent Life of General Curtis LeMay.* New York, 1986.

Cohen, Warren I. *America's Response to China: An Interpretative History of Sino-American Relations.* Rev. ed. New York: 1980.

Davies, John Paton, Jr. *Dragon by the Tail: American, British, Japanese, and Russian Encounters with China and One Another.* New York, 1972.

Deacon, Richard. *Chinese Secret Service.* New York, 1974.

Denning, Margaret S. *The Sino-American Alliance in World War II.* European Universtiy Studies, Series III. New York, 1986.

Dunlop, Richard. *Donovan: America's Master Spy.* Chicago, 1982.

Emmerson, John K. *A View from Yenan.* Washington, D.C., 1979.

———. *The Japanese Thread: A Life in the Foreign Service.* New York, 1978.

Epstein, Israel. *From Opium War to Liberation.* Peking, 1964.

Etzold, Thomas. *Aspects of Sino-American Relations Since 1784.* New York, 1978.

Fairbank, John King. *Chinabound: A Fifty-Year Memoir.* New York, 1982.

———. *China's Revolution from 1800 to the Present.* New York, 1986.

Feis, Herbert. *China Tangle.* Princeton, 1953.

Ferrell, Robert H. *American Diplomacy: The Twentieth Century.* New York, 1988.

Ford, Corey. *Donovan of OSS.* Boston, 1970.

Forman, Harrison. *Report from Red China.* New York, 1945.

Forrestal, James. *Forrestal Diaries.* Edited by Walter Millis. New York, 1951.

Frillman, Paul, and Graham Peck. *China: The Remembered Life.* Boston, 1968.

Gahn, Mark, and John Caldwell. *American Agent.* New York, 1947.

Garver, John W. *Chinese-Soviet Relations, 1937-1945.* New York, 1988.

Gittings, John. *Survey of the Sino-Soviet Dispute.* London, 1964.

———. *World and China, 1922-1972.* New York, 1974.

Groot, Peter. "Myth and Reality in American Policy Towards China." Ph.D. diss., Kent State University, 1974.

Harding, Harry, and Yuan Ming. *Sino-American Relations, 1945-1955: A Joint Reassessment of a Critical Decade.* Wilmington, Del., 1989.

Head, William P. *Yenan! Colonel Wilbur Peterkin and the American Military Mission to the Chinese Communists, 1944-1945.* Chapel Hill, N.C., 1987.

Hsu, Immanuel C. Y. *The Rise of Modern China.* New York, 1970.

Hull, Cordell. *Memoirs of Cordell Hull.* 2 vols. New York, 1948.

Iriye, Akira. *Across the Pacific.* New York, 1967.

Iriye, Akira, and Warren Cohen. *American, Chinese, and Japanese Perspectives on Wartime Asia, 1931-1949.* Wilmington, Del., 1990.

Kahn, E.J., Jr. *China Hands.* New York, 1975.

Klehr, Harvey, and Ronald Radosh. *The Amerasia Spy Case.* Chapel Hill, N.C., 1996.

Koen, Ross. *China Lobby in American Politics.* New York, 1960.

Kubek, Anthony. *How the Far East Was Lost.* Chicago, 1963.

Laloy, Jean. *Yalta: Yesterday, Today, Tomorrow.* New York, 1988.

Leary, William M., Jr. *Dragon's Wings: The China National Aviation Corporation and the Development of Commercial Aviation in China.* Athens, Ga., 1976.

———. *Perilous Missions: Civil Air Transport and CIA Covert Operations in Asia.* University, Ala., 1984.

Levine, Steven I. "On the Brink of Disaster: China and the U.S. in 1945." In Harry Harding and Yuan Ming, *Sino-American Relations, 1945-1955: A Joint Reassessment of a Critical Decade.* Wilmington, Del., 1989.

Liang, Chin-tung. *General Stilwell in China, 1942-1944: The Full Story.* New York, 1972.

Lindsay, Michael. *Notes on Educational Problems in Communist China, 1941-47.* New York, 1950.

Lohbeck, Don. *Patrick J. Hurley.* Chicago, 1956.

MacDonald, Elizabeth P. *Undercover Girl.* New York, 1947.

MacKinnon, Stephen R. *China Reporting: An Oral History of American Journalism in the 1930s and 1940s.* Berkeley, Calif., 1987.

MacKinnon, Stephen R., and Janice R. MacKinnon. *Agnes Smedley: Life and Times of an American Radical.* Berkeley, 1988.

Marshall, George C. *Marshall's Mission to China.* Introduction by Lyman Van Slyke. Arlington, Va., 1976.

May, Ernest. *The Truman Administration in China, 1945-1949.* New York, 1975.

Melton, H. Keith. *OSS Special Weapons and Equipment: Spy Devices of World War II.* New York, 1991.

Miles, Milton. *A Different Kind of War.* New York, 1967.

Moon, Thomas N., and Carl F. Eifler. *The Deadliest Colonel.* New York, 1975.

Mulch, Barbara E. "A Chinese Puzzle: Patrick Hurley and the Foreign Service Officer Controversy." Ph.D. diss., University of Kansas, 1972.

Neils, Patricia, ed. *United States Attitudes and Policies Toward China: The Impact of American Missionaries.* Armonk, N.Y., 1990.

Payne, Robert. *Chinese Diaries, 1941-1946.* London, 1970.

———. *Journey to Red China.* London, 1947.

Peterkin, Col. Wilbur J. Dixie Mission Memoirs. Stanford, Calif., Peterkin Papers, Hoover Institution.

———. *Inside China, 1943-45: An Eyewitness Account of America's Mission in Yenan.* Baltimore, Md., 1992.

Pogue, Forrest C. *George C. Marshall,* vol. 4, *Statesman.* New York, 1987.

Pye, Lucian W. *China: An Introduction.* Boston, 1978.

Roderick, John. *Covering China.* Chicago, 1993.

Rodzinski, Witold. *The People's Republic of China: A Concise Political History.* New York, 1988.

Romanus, Charles F., and Riley Sunderland. *Stilwell's Command Problems.* Washington, D.C., 1956.

———. *Stilwell's Mission to China.* Washington, D.C., 1953.

———. *Time Runs Out in CBI: The United States Army in World War II: China-Burma-India Theater.* Washington, D.C., 1959.

Rossinger, Lawrence. *China's Wartime Politics.* Princeton, N.J., 1945.

Salisbury, Harrison E. *The New Emperors: China in the Era of Mao and Deng.* New York, 1992.

———. *To Peking and Beyond: A Report on the New Asia.* New York, 1973.

Schaller, Michael. *The United States and China in the Twentieth Century.* New York, 1979.

———. *U.S. Crusade in China, 1938-1945.* 2d ed. New York, 1990.

Schwartz, Harry. *China.* New York, 1965.

Seagrave, Sterling. *The Soong Dynasty.* New York, 1985.

Selden, Mark. *The Yenan Way in Revolutionary China.* Cambridge, Mass., 1971.

Service, John S. *The Amerasia Papers: Some Problems in the History of U.S.-China Relations.* Berkeley, Calif., 1971.

———. *Lost Chance in China: The World War II Despatches of John S. Service.* Edited by Joseph W. Esherick. New York, 1974.

Sherwood, Robert E. *Roosevelt and Hopkins: An Intimate History.* New York, 1948.

Shewmaker, Kenneth. *Americans and Chinese Communists, 1927-1945.* New York, 1971.

———. "Persuading Encounter: American Reporters and Chinese Communists, 1927-1945." Ph.D. diss., Northwestern University, 1966.

Smith, R. Harris. *OSS: The Secret History of America's First Central Intelligence Agency.* Berkeley, Calif., 1972.

Smith, Robert T. "Alone in China: Patrick J. Hurley's Attempt to Unify China, 1944-1945." Ph.D. diss., University of Oklahoma, 1966.

Snow, Edgar. *The Other Side of the River.* New York, 1961.

———. *People on Our Side.* New York, 1944.

———. *Red Star Over China.* New York, 1938.

Spence, Jonathan D. *Gate of Heavenly Peace: The Chinese and Their Revolution, 1895-1980.* New York, 1981.

———. *The Search for Modern China.* New York, 1990.

———. *To Change China: Western Advisors in China, 1620-1960.* Boston, 1960.

Stein, Gunther. *The Challenge of Red China.* New York, 1945.

Stimson, Henry L., and McGeorge Bundy. *On Active Service in Peace and War.* New Yori, 1948.

Stratton, Roy. *SACO: Rice Paddy Navy.* New York, 1950.

Strong, Anna Louise. *Chinese Conquers China.* Garden City, N.Y., 1949.

Sulzberger, C. L. *Coldest War: Russia's Game in China.* New York, 1974.

Tang Tsou. *America's Failure in China.* Chicago, 1963.

Terrill, Ross. *Mao: A Biography.* New York, 1980.

———. *White-Boned Demon: A Biography of Madame Mao Zedong.* New York, 1984.

Tipton, Lawrence. *Chinese Escapade.* London, 1949.

Tong, Hollington K. *China and the World Press.* Author, 1948.

Townsend, James R. *Politics in China.* New York, 1980.

Truman, Harry S. *Memoirs, vol. 2: Year of Decisions.* New York, 1955.

Tuchman, Barbara W. *Stilwell and the American Experience in China, 1911-45.* New York, 1972.

Tucker, Nancy Bernkopf. *Patterns in the Dust: Chinese-American Relations and the Recognition Controversy, 1949-1950.* New York, 1983.

Utley, Freda. *China Story.* Chicago, 1951.

Van Slyke, Lyman P. *The Chinese Communist Movement.* Stanford, Calif., 1968.

Varg, Paul. *Closing of the Door: Sino-American Relations, 1936-46.* East Lansing, Mich., 1973.

Vladimirov, Petr Parfenovich. *Vladimirov Diaries, Yenan China, 1942-1945.* New York, 1975.

Wallace, Henry A. *The Price of Vision: The Diary of Henry A. Wallace, 1942-1946.* Edited by John Morton Blum. Boston, 1973.

Wang, James C. F. *Contemporary Chinese Politics.* Englewood Cliffs, N.J., 1985.

Wedemeyer, Albert C. *Wedemeyer Reports!* New York, 1958.

Welch, Robert W., Jr. *Life of John Birch.* Boston, 1954.

White, Theodore H. *In Search of History.* New York, 1978.

White, Theodore H., and Annalee Jacoby. *Thunder Out of China.* New York, 1946.

Young, Arthur. *China and the Helping Hand, 1937-1945.* Cambridge, Mass., 1963.

Articles and Scholarly Papers

Alsop, Joseph W. "Why We Lost China." *Saturday Evening Post,* Jan. 1950, pp. 14-21.

Ariyoshi, Koji. "Steps to Civil War." *Honolulu Star-Bulletin,* July 3, 1971, p. A-13.

Blum, Robert M. "Secret Cable from Peking." *San Francisco Chronicle,* Sept. 27, 1978, p. F-1.

Bogue, Lt. Col. J. R. "American Liaison Groups." *Military Review* 27 (April 1947: 61-64.

Casberg, Melvin A., M.D. "Go Ahead--Ask Me About My China Trip!" *Medical Economics,* March 4, 1974, 86-92.

Cohen, Warren. "American Observers and the Sino-Soviet Friendship Treaty of August, 1945." *Pacific Historical Review* 35 (Aug. 1966): 347-50.

————. "The Development of Chinese Communist Attitudes Towards the United States, 1934-45." *Orbis* 11 (Spring 1967): 219-37.

Goldstein, Steven M. "Sino-American Relations, 1948-1950: Lost Chance or No Chance?" In Harry Harding and Yuan Ming, eds., *Sino-American Relations, 1945-1955: A Joint Reassessment of a Critical Decade.* Wilmington, Del., 1989.

Gross, Leonard. "John Paton Davies, Jr.: Quiet End to a Shabby Era." *Look,* March 4, 1969, p. 82.

Harrington, Joseph D. "Yankee Samurai." *Pacific Citizen,* April 6, 1979, pp. 9-10.

Hunt, Michael H. "Ideology." *Journal of American History* 87:1 (June 1990): 108-15.

Hunt, Michael H., and Odd Arne Westad. "The Chinese Communist Party and International Affairs: A Field Report on New Historical Sources and Old Research Problems." *China Quarterly* 122 (June 1990): 258-72.

Lindsay, Michael. "Impending Dangers for U.S. China Policy." *Asian Affairs* 5 (Sept./Oct. 1977): 1-7.

MacKinnon, Steven. "On Shooting the Messengers: The Symbiotic Relationship Between U.S. and Chinese Journalism Since the 1930s." Paper presented to the American Historical Association Pacific Coast Branch, Salt Lake City, Utah, Aug. 1990.

McMahon, Robert J. "The Cold War in Asia: Toward a New Synthesis." *Diplomatic History* 12.3 (Summer 1988): 307-27.

Oksenberg, Michael. "China's Confident Nationalism." *Foreign Affairs* 45:3 (1987): 501-23.

Rongqu, Luo. "China and East Asia in America's Global Strategy, 1931-1949." In Akira Iriye and Warren Cohen, eds., *American, Chinese, and Japanese Perspectives on Wartime Asia, 1931-1949.* Wilmington, Del., 1990.

Schaller, Michael. "Command Crisis in China, 1944: A Road Not Taken." *Diplomatic History* 4:3 (Summer 1990): 327-31.

Shanahan, Fr. Cormac. "America's Place in the World." *China Monthly* 6 (Nov. 1945): 30-32.

———. "China's Communist Puzzle." *China Monthly* 6 (June 1945): 9-12.

———. "False Solution in Asia." *China Monthly* 6 (Dec. 1945): 22-24, 26.

Shearer, Lloyd. "Dr. George Hatem--The Most Famous American in China." *Parade,* Aug. 12, 1973, pp. 4-5.

Spengler, Col. Henry M. "American Liaison Groups." *Military Review* 27 (April 1947): 61.

Stone, Barbara F. "The John Birch Society in California: A Profile." *Journal of Politics,* 36.1 (Feb. 1974): 184-97.

Sunderland, Riley. "The Secret Embargo." *Pacific Historical Review* 29 (Feb. 1960): 75-80.

Sutter, Robert G. "Sino-American Relations in Adversity." *Current History* 89.548 (Sept. 1990): 241-44.

Tolstoy, Ilia. "Across Tibet from India to China." *National Geographic,* Aug. 1946, 169-222.

Tozer, Warren W. "The Foreign Correspondents' Visit to Yenan in 1944: A Reassessment." *Pacific Historical Review* 41 (May 1972): 207-24.

Tuchman, Barbara W. "If Mao Had Come to Washington: An Essay in Alternatives." *Foreign Affairs* 51 (Oct. 1972): 44-64.

Wedemeyer, Lt. Gen. Albert C., as told to George Creel. "Don't Count China Out." *Collier's,* July 7, 1945, 24-25, 46.

Wetzel, Nevin. "Chungking Duty in 1942." *Ex-CBI Roundup* 33 (April 1978): 12-17.

Index

AACS. *See* Army Airways Communication System (AACS)

Air and Ground Forces Resources and Technical Staff (AGFRTS), 31, 163-64, 168, 172-73

Air Ground Aid Service (AGAS), 80, 85; effect of Dixie Mission on, 217; favors expansion of Communist radio network, 98; functions of, 34, 75, 77, 80, 81; Peterkin's view of, 44; proposes issuance of arms to guerrillas, 82; relations with Chinese, 81-82

Alsop, Joseph, 24

American fliers: rescues of, 13, 27, 74, 75, 77, 80, 85, 87, 200, 208

American Volunteer Group ("Flying Tigers"), 6

AMMISCA (American Military Mission to China), 172

Anderson, La Donna, 172

Ariyoshi, Koji, 65, 184, 204; interrogates Japanese prisoners, 153; interviews Koreans, 73; and loyalty of Nisei, 72; returns to Yenan, 183; visits Workers and Peasants School, 65-68; Yeaton's view of, 202

Army Airways Communication System (AACS): ordered to leave, 105; Peterkin's view of, 44; relations with Signal Corps, 85-86, 91

Army Military Intelligence (G-2), 12, 25, 155, 156

Army Reorganization Group, 11, 192

Atcheson, George, Jr., 24, 129, 130, 131, 177

Atkinson, Brooks, 20, 39, 136

B-29 Super Fortresses, 1; airfields for, 35; bomb group's need for military intelligence, 23; defects of, 74; effect of raids on Japan, 85

Baglio, lst Lt. J. P.: rescue of, 75-77

Bales, Colonel, 139

Barnett, Bob, 172

Barrett, Col. David D., 13, 14, 37; briefs Marshall, 190, 216; and Casberg, 56-57; Chinese turn against, 216-17; crashes, 28, 30; described, 12; and Eighth Route Army, 210; encourages enlisted personnel to study Chinese, 209; explains Mission's purposes to Chinese, 30; failure to win promotion, 143, 211; and Five Point Plan, 119-24; hints at U.S.